CREATING CONFIDENCE

For my sons Ewan and Jamie Young
and the current generation of young Scots.

CREATING CONFIDENCE

A handbook for professionals
working with young people

Carol Craig

Published by -
The Centre for Confidence and Well-being
45 Union Street, Glasgow G1 3RB
Scotland, UK.
www.centreforconfidence.co.uk

Printed and bound in Scotland by Hay Nisbet, Glasgow
Book design by McKenzie Design, Glasgow
First published in 2007

Contents

Foreword

In this book, Carol Craig reminds us of the well-known Scots saying, 'Better sit still than rise up and fa'. Like many Scots I am aware of the influence such thinking has had on my own life. Not only have I witnessed others who have have been too scared to try to do new things but also I have often felt tempted myself to sit and watch rather than commit to something new and unknown. When Carol asked if I would help support the Centre in producing this book my habitual hesitancy almost triumphed. But the call to stand up and do something different was too strong.

This is an important point in Scotland's history. We have a growing sense of ourselves and what is achievable. In education, the *Curriculum for Excellence* is ushering in new priorities in our schools. One of the four purposes of education is how to create confident individuals. As Carol explains in this book, this is a huge opportunity for Scotland: the new emphasis in education could help us create a more dynamic Scotland by replacing 'canny do' negativity with a much more positive and 'can do' approach. If we could create confidence, not on the basis of wishful thinking or an inflated sense of ourselves, but on the basis of skills, genuine self-belief and realistic optimism then Scotland could perhaps regain its position as a world leader in innovation and ideas.

As a businessman I am very well aware of the importance of confidence in today's workplace. We need young people who are optimistic, enthusiastic and able to work effectively in teams. We need people who are engaged and committed to what they do and prepared to go out of their way to deliver really good services. But we also need people who have good basic skills – who are able to read, write and count. The company I chair, Morris and Spottiswood, believe that at the core of any effective business are two things – people and their ideas. We need people to think differently – to challenge the norm. I truly believe that the only way to grow as an individual is to open your mind and listen to ideas.

Any person who, like me, values ideas will be stimulated by this book. From start to finish it is packed with interesting concepts, challenging facts and useful suggestions. You might not agree with everything Carol says but you are unlikely to find her arguments dull. I am confident that this book will have an enormous impact on the thinking and practices of people not just working in education but beyond.

The Centre for Confidence and Well-being is an extraordinary organisation. It is small, nimble and clearly able to punch well above its weight. Its deliberation on some of the big policy areas of our times is important, not just for Scotland, but also internationally.

All of us at Morris and Spottiswood are delighted to have given the support necessary to produce this book. I am indebted to my sister and my wife for fully supporting this initial commitment to the Centre for Confidence and Well-being.

George Morris

Chairman
Morris and Spottiswood

Using this Handbook

> *Scotland's young people and adult learners live and work in an increasingly complex and uncertain social, political, technological and economic environment. It is clear that the future will require a population with the confidence and skills to meet the challenges posed by fast and far reaching change.*
>
> Graham Donaldson, Chief Inspector of Schools in Scotland

Scotland's *Curriculum for Excellence* now makes 'confident individuals' one of the main drivers of Scottish education. This development is in harmony with other recent Scottish initiatives, such as Schools of Ambition, and Determined to Succeed. As self-confidence matters more in the contemporary world, this emphasis on confidence in the Scottish curriculum may provide a great opportunity to enhance young people's educational experience and leverage their skills.

There are many admirable features about Scottish culture. However, historically, Scotland has had a put-down culture. Scottish egalitarianism tends to level down ('don't think you are different or better than anyone else') and so can easily dampen aspirations. The fear of making mistakes or getting 'it' wrong is still strong, as is the belief that we must prove our worth. These cultural issues may help explain why levels of self-esteem and optimism are low for many youngsters in Scotland.

Learning from America's mistakes

Addressing confidence issues in Scottish schools is a welcome move but it carries a significant risk. To understand this risk we need to look across the Atlantic at the USA. For hundreds of years the country has acted as a magnet for can-do optimists. Historically, American culture nurtured entrepreneurial and dynamic attitudes. However, in the last few decades the 'self-esteem movement' has had a huge impact on parents and teachers throughout America, and teaching young people to feel good about themselves has become the centrepiece in many American schools.

This may seem innocuous but some heavyweight psychologists now warn that this emphasis on self-esteem can end up undermining young people's performances rather than building them. Some also maintain that it is encouraging blame, narcissism and excessive individualism, and setting young people up for depression. The average age for the onset of depression in the US has fallen from the age of 30 a few decades ago, to 15. During the period that self-esteem has held sway in American schools, academic standards have dropped. Employers in the US are also now voicing the view that this generation of young people wants instant success for little effort and is excessively thin-skinned. In short, they do not make good employees.

The need for psychological literacy and evidence

The *Curriculum for Excellence* outlines four purposes for education: the creation of successful learners, effective contributors, responsible citizens and confident individuals. Underlying these four 'capacities' are a number of keywords and many of them refer in some way to psychology or attitudes – motivation, self-respect, mental and emotional well-being, self-awareness and resilience.

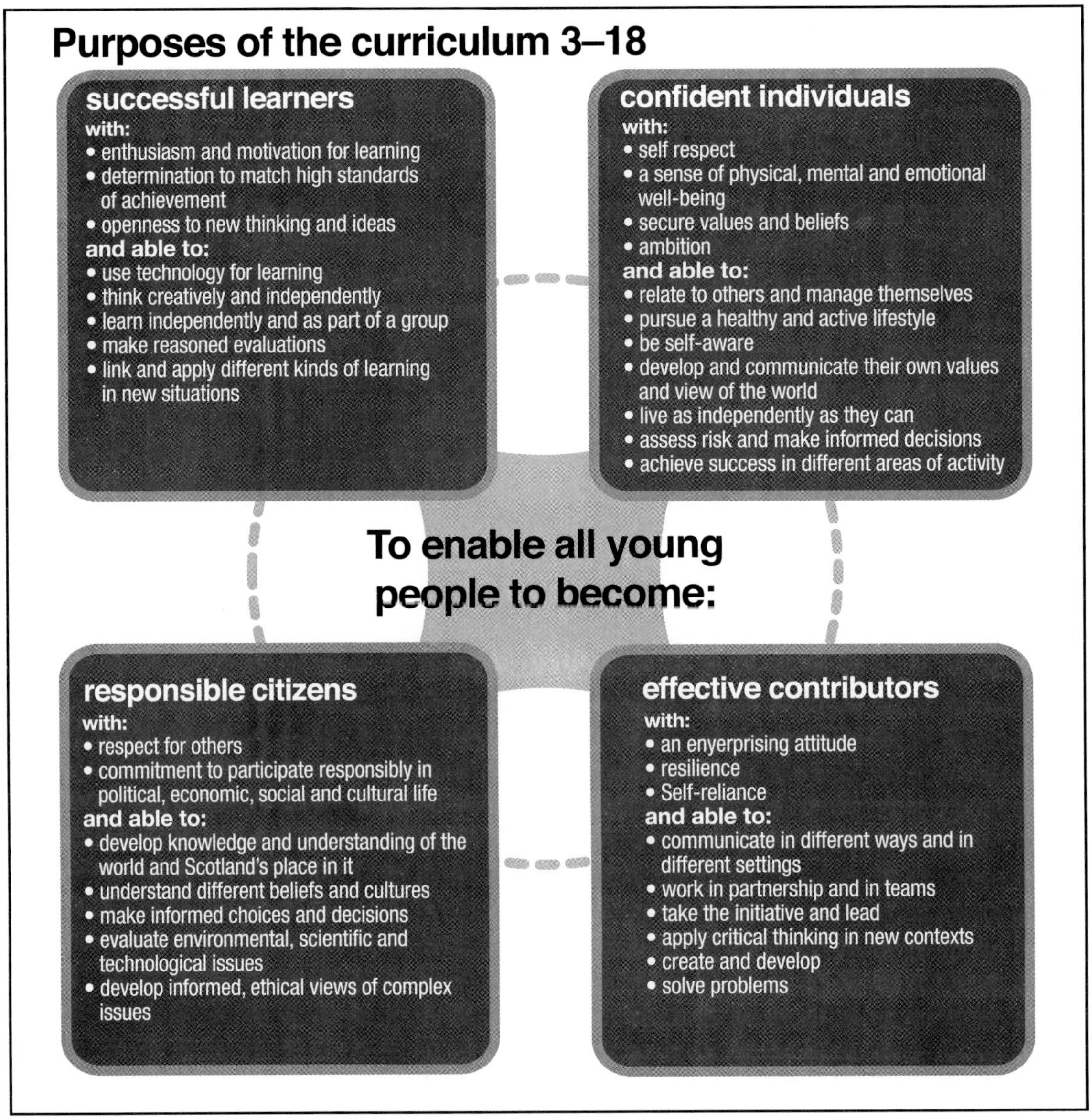

Purposes of the curriculum 3–18

To enable all young people to become:

successful learners

with:
- enthusiasm and motivation for learning
- determination to match high standards of achievement
- openness to new thinking and ideas

and able to:
- use technology for learning
- think creatively and independently
- learn independently and as part of a group
- make reasoned evaluations
- link and apply different kinds of learning in new situations

confident individuals

with:
- self respect
- a sense of physical, mental and emotional well-being
- secure values and beliefs
- ambition

and able to:
- relate to others and manage themselves
- pursue a healthy and active lifestyle
- be self-aware
- develop and communicate their own values and view of the world
- live as independently as they can
- assess risk and make informed decisions
- achieve success in different areas of activity

responsible citizens

with:
- respect for others
- commitment to participate responsibly in political, economic, social and cultural life

and able to:
- develop knowledge and understanding of the world and Scotland's place in it
- understand different beliefs and cultures
- make informed choices and decisions
- evaluate environmental, scientific and technological issues
- develop informed, ethical views of complex issues

effective contributors

with:
- an enyerprising attitude
- resilience
- Self-reliance

and able to:
- communicate in different ways and in different settings
- work in partnership and in teams
- take the initiative and lead
- apply critical thinking in new contexts
- create and develop
- solve problems

The Centre for Confidence and Well-being believes that delivering this new curriculum will be greatly enhanced if teachers and others become more psychologically literate and learn from empirical research. So the Centre's motivation to produce this confidence *Handbook* comes from our desire to present teachers, educationalists and those working with young people with some guidance on building confidence that is supported, where possible, by sound academic research. We believe that if people do not heed this research the situation in Scotland will become worse, not better.

BOX 1: The importance of evidence

A good example of how acting without firm knowledge can backfire comes from Edinburgh in the seventeenth century. Thousands were dying from the plague, and so the town council, desperate to be seen to do something, decided that cats were responsible for carrying the disease. There was no science behind this conclusion but they acted on it anyway, and ordered that all cats be slaughtered. This made the plague worse. Rats were the carriers of the plague, not cats, and without cats as predators the rat population, and hence the plague, skyrocketed.

Not reinventing the wheel

Scottish education has changed substantially, and generally for the better, in the past few decades. Schools are more child-centred and there is more variety in teaching methods. So we do not want to give the impression that no good work is being done to help young people's confidence levels and that we are starting from scratch. Many new practices that have been adopted in some schools are enormously helpful – Assessment for Learning and Co-operative Learning – to name but two. So in Chapter 12 I explain why some of these new methodologies are useful for confidence building.

No exclusive focus on young people

The stimulus for writing this book comes from the *Curriculum for Excellence* and its focus on creating confident individuals. However, we need confident teachers to help pass on these skills. It is for this reason that I do not exclusively dwell on young people's confidence issues and often talk about confidence issues in ways that are relevant to teachers and others working with young people. Creating and encouraging confident teachers, and more confident schools, is an important part of the process of building confidence in young people. This is more likely to happen if teachers understand what confidence means for them and how they can develop and model it.

Teachers and other professionals

Given the new *Curriculum for Excellence* the time is ripe for a book specifically aimed at classroom teachers and educational policy makers. However, the broad issues addressed, as well as many of the specific techniques, are of great relevance to other professionals who work with young people. I am thinking here of youth workers, college lecturers, social workers, adult educators, community development workers and so forth. For the sake of simplicity I have made teachers the focus of my advice and geared much of the content towards working with young people in a school environment.

Diversity

In this *Handbook* I make few references to gender or other equality issues. There are certainly some gender differences, in levels of self-esteem for example, and this is pointed out in Chapter 6. However, the emphasis throughout this book is on creating the conditions for confidence to flourish and these conditions are relevant to all young people, irrespective of whether they are male or female, black or white, or have special needs.

Using this *Handbook*

This *Handbook* brings together a wide variety of research. People are convinced in different ways, and so in compiling the *Handbook* I have separated it into several parts based on different reasoning and evidence. This allows busy teachers and other professionals to concentrate attention on what they find most important or useful. At the end of each main chapter there is a 'key points summary' to help readers navigate their way more easily through the material.

Well-being

I have not restricted the content of this *Handbook* exclusively to confidence. Certainly this is the main focus but I have also added material that is more pertinent to well-being – such as Positive Psychology. I have done this because we need to think much more about the well-being of young people in Scotland. At the beginning of 2007 UNICEF produced a report on young people's well-being across 21 developed nations. The UK was bottom of the list. This is a worrying state of affairs. For reasons set out in Part 2, Learning from America's Mistakes, I am particularly concerned that in pursuing a confidence agenda we may undermine young people's well-being even further. Positive Psychology helps us to understand why this might be the case and what we need to do to promote well-being – hence its inclusion in this *Handbook*. These various strands are woven together in the penultimate chapter where I set out the Centre's Model of Confidence within a Compass of Well-being. This compass helps us to direct confidence towards flourishing, well-being and happiness.

Overview of contents

In Part 1 I look at various ways to define confidence and why it matters more in today's world. In Part 2 I examine what has happened, particularly in the US, with the promotion of self-esteem and how this has caused problems for young people. In Part 3 I look at what the particular barriers to confidence may be in Scotland and present some supporting evidence. In Part 4 I begin to put forward better alternatives to self-esteem for building confidence – for example, optimism, self-efficacy, resilience, Carol Dweck's work on 'mindsets', and other theories and ideas. Part 5 looks at well-being. The first chapter here outlines Positive Psychology and what it has to offer. The second chapter warns of the potential dangers of teaching emotional literacy in schools. In Part 6 I outline the model of confidence the Centre is now developing and how we may integrate confidence and well-being. The last chapter looks at the issue of confidence in Scottish schools.

Tools, Tips and Techniques

The aim of this *Handbook* is not simply to give people background information on some big ideas on confidence and related topics. It is also to increase teachers' ability to create the conditions for confidence to rise. So throughout the book there are text boxes which outline a confidence building tool, tip or technique. These are different from the other text boxes which are often used for stories or examples. To make the Tools, Tips and Techniques stand out we have tinted the boxes and titled them TTT. There are 24 TTTs throughout the book.

My background

Finally, I want to make clear that I am not a psychologist. My own academic background is political science. I then became involved in training and personal/team development and ran courses for over fifteen years – many of them in schools. During this time I became interested in psychology, and since setting up the Centre for Confidence and Well-being in 2005 I have read widely on the topic. I am particularly interested in Positive Psychology. Since this is about moving away from a disease focus and looking at how individuals, families and organisations can flourish there is much more of a role for an interested lay person like myself. I see this book as bridging two distinct worlds. One world is the academic world of psychology, which talks a strange language and which often does not communicate well outside narrow silos of particular research interests. The other world is inhabited by teachers and other professionals working with young people. They are often disconnected from the academic world but are nonetheless interested in how their work can be guided by some of the more relevant, and empirical, psychological research.

Further information and support

Notes and references related to this *Handbook* can be found on the Centre's website. Please go to www.centreforconfidence.co.uk where you will also find a detailed booklist. A list of additional resources that readers can access on line is included at the back of the book.

There is also a discussion forum related to this *Handbook* on the Centre's website, where you can post questions or points relating to the topics covered here. The Centre will also use the site to post any additional material that may be useful to readers.

PART I

confidence: definitions and importance

1

Confidence Matters

Confidence is that feeling by which the mind embarks in great and honourable courses with a sure hope and trust in itself.

Marcus T. Cicero

The self-help sections of bookshops are packed these days with volumes on confidence and so it is easy to believe that this is a newfangled idea – the product of our self-obsessed age. However, as the quote from the great Roman politician and philosopher shows, the idea of confidence, and its importance, has a long pedigree. As confidence is so central to what we achieve in life, inevitably it has been a key term used by people involved in outward or action-oriented activities such as sport, enterprise, business and public speaking. Indeed, mental preparation to enhance an athlete's confidence is at the heart of the growing discipline of sports psychology. If you Google 'confidence and coaching' you will be deluged with almost seven million hits.

What is confidence?

Confidence is a word which we frequently use in everyday language yet rarely do we stop and think what it means. Most dictionary definitions of confidence focus on two related ideas:

- confidence is about being certain of your own abilities
- confidence is about having trust in people, plans or the future.

Confidence is thus not simply a feeling that things will go well but also a judgement on our own or others' abilities. When the abilities in question are our own, having confidence suggests a high level of self-assurance. Since confidence involves the belief that things will turn out well, confidence may sometimes be used interchangeably with optimism.

As confidence is a multidimensional concept it is not a term much used by psychologists. Indeed, the academics who are most likely to use the term are economists. Confidence is a key concept in economics as confidence is necessary both to investment and to the operation of markets.

Instead of confidence, psychologists are more likely to use terms which may still be difficult to define but which are more focused and so more amenable to measurement. The most commonly used terms by psychologists are: self-esteem, self-efficacy and optimism.

Self-esteem

Millions of words have been written about self-esteem and many critics believe it is a slippery concept. However, there is general agreement that there are two broad ways to define and measure self-esteem. One is to see it as the evaluation a person makes of their capabilities; the other is to see it as the essentially emotional feeling an individual has about their self-worth. The latter is the more common definition and is the one used in the most popular tool to measure self-esteem – the Rosenberg Self-Esteem Scale.

I put self-esteem under the spotlight in the next section. However, it is worth saying here that self-esteem has some importance in life but that the claims made for it have been exaggerated. More importantly, what practitioners have done in the name of self-esteem, particularly in the USA, appears to be undermining young people's well-being, and we must be careful not to repeat these mistakes.

I shall also argue more fully below that since confidence is about belief in one's abilities, taking action and being optimistic, we can effectively ignore self-esteem and concentrate on these more important, dynamic ingredients of confidence.

Psychologists use other related concepts to describe the emotional judgement a person makes about themselves such as self-acceptance, self-worth or self-respect and have huge and heated debates about the precise meaning of the terms. One vital difference in the underlying ideas, no matter what nomenclature psychologists use, is whether the positive feeling about the self is linked to abilities or simply to a sense that at heart you are a worthwhile person.

Self-efficacy

Self-efficacy is the term that psychologists use to describe the belief a person has that they can reach their goals. Unlike self-esteem, which is more of a global judgement on the self and its worth, self-efficacy specifically isolates the way an individual assesses their competence in relation to achievements, goals and life events. Self-efficacy expert, Professor Albert Bandura from Stanford University, argues that 'ordinary realities are strewn with impediments, adversities, setbacks, frustrations and inequities'. He therefore claims that people need 'a robust sense of efficacy' to keep trying. Research on self-esteem suggests that parents (through genes and parenting style) have the biggest influence on a young person's self-esteem. However, Bandura and others argue that schools have a huge part to play in developing young people's feelings of self-efficacy and this is why a whole chapter in Part 4 is devoted to the topic.

Optimism

In everyday life we usually use the word optimism to reflect positive feelings about life. Often we refer to someone who is optimistic as seeing 'the glass as half-full, rather than half-empty'.

In psychology, there are two main ways to define optimism. Scheier and Carver, for example, authors of the popular optimism measure, the Life Orientation Test, define optimism as 'the global generalized tendency to believe that one will generally experience good versus bad outcomes in life'. In everyday language this means 'looking on the bright side of life'. In such a definition, pessimism is the tendency to believe that 'if something will go wrong for me, it will'. The other main way to define optimism is to use the concept of 'explanatory style'. This is the approach taken by Professor Martin Seligman, author of *Learned Optimism* and co-author of *The Optimistic Child*. He argues that each of us has our own 'explanatory style', a way of thinking about the causes of things that happen in our lives. Optimists are those who see adversities as temporary and restricted to one domain of life while pessimists often see problems as permanent and pervasive.

In Part 4, we devote one whole chapter to optimism and its relevance to young people's confidence. Here all that matters is realising that no matter how optimism is defined, it is an important ingredient in confidence.

The confidence formula

In this *Handbook* I use the following formula for confidence:

Confidence = self-efficacy + optimism.

In other words, confidence is an individual's belief that he/she can reach specific goals plus the general belief that the future is bright.

If an individual's confidence increases it may well be accompanied by a rise in self-esteem. However, for reasons I shall explore more fully in the next chapter, I do not think it useful to pursue increases in self-esteem more directly, as this can interfere with well-being. The Centre for Confidence and Well-being has now evolved a model of confidence which I set out in the penultimate chapter: a model which brings together many of the approaches covered in the book and acts as a useful résumé and reinforcement of what has gone before.

Confidence is not about public speaking

One of the biggest mistakes teachers and parents can make about confidence is to equate it with speaking in groups. Recently I attended a meeting on the *Curriculum for Excellence* and one well-meaning teacher said in passing: 'I'll know I'm doing my best to create confident individuals when each one of the children in my class can get up in front of their classmates, give a talk and enjoy it'. As the other teachers in the group nodded in agreement, my heart sank. Not only is this teacher unlikely to achieve her goal, she is also likely to undermine some of her pupils' feelings of self-worth in the process. To explain this assertion I want to say something about my son, Jamie.

Jamie's story

Jamie has always been a quiet, reflective boy. He was able to concentrate and amuse himself if he needed to. In class he never presented a problem for the teacher and with his peer group he was popular but happy to fit in with others and had no need to be in the limelight. As an assertiveness trainer it would have been very easy for me to look at my quiet son and believe he was lacking something – confidence. What Jamie needed, I could have concluded, was to be more confident and outgoing with others – particularly in class or in social events. I could then have tried to get him to be more talkative, outwardly confident or assertive. In other words, I could have communicated to my son that he wasn't all right the way he was and he needed to develop into a different person. Fortunately I did not do this. I could see that Jamie's quietness in class was not about being generally under-confident. He was simply by nature quiet and reserved. He likes spending time with people but has little need to communicate much of what is going on in his head to others. Jamie is also the type of person who likes living in harmony with people and with his environment – he likes to accept what is and adapt to it rather than try to shape or determine the world round about him. These are huge strengths. Strengths which mean he has strong relationships with others, resilience and a capacity for real happiness.

So rather than communicating to him that he wasn't all right the way he was, I valued and supported the person he was. One of Jamie's real strengths, and his type of confidence, became very apparent when he left school. He wanted to travel and arranged a four month trip which involved flying to Chile and joining a group of people to travel around Latin America in a truck. His father and I were anxious. I am not sure that I could have done this when I was 30, let alone 18. But Jamie looked at both of us and said with great conviction 'I'm totally confident that I can do this'. Another of Jamie's strengths is that he is self-contained – all these years of mulling things over in his head and being quiet means he has developed enormous inner resources. He was confident that he was able to travel to the other side of the world, and even if he hardly spoke to another person and things were tough, he would cope. And he did. So Jamie may not be confident about talking in front of a group or giving a presentation but he is confident about other types of activities. An overzealous teacher determined to build Jamie's confidence and equating this with speaking in public could have undermined his sense of himself rather than encouraged his confidence to rise.

Quietly confident

I am aware that there are some children who do not mix well with others. They are often loners and can be picked on by others. As this can create long-term social and psychological problems, it may be helpful for teachers to try to integrate this type of child into social groups. But there are many children, like my son Jamie, who are just quiet – they are not anti-social – yet teachers often see their quietness as a problem. I often tell the story about Jamie when I speak and I regularly find a small queue of people eager to tell me a similar story about their child.

One mother who was also a teacher told me that her eight-year-old daughter was also very quiet and reflective. She was a very conscientious, meticulous young girl who worked hard and excelled at written work. The girl earned lots of praise for this at school but her current teacher regularly communicated to her that this was not enough and set goals for her to interact and talk much more in class. 'Rather than understanding my daughter's strengths and respecting who she is' this mother told me, 'the teacher is focusing on what she is not and is really telling her she is not ok as she is. If she were seventeen and about to enter higher education or work, then it would be fair enough to encourage her to make an effort to develop oral communication skills but I just don't think it is appropriate to do this to a young girl of eight'.

The emphasis in current attainment targets on group work, talking and interacting can be beneficial, as this focus can help to validate difference, and caters for differing strengths, but we must be careful not to equate the desire to communicate in groups with confidence. Confidence is not a type of activity; it is an individual's belief that they can reach their self-determined goal and that the future is bright.

Why confidence matters

Given the confidence formula I outlined above – self-efficacy plus optimism – it is easy to see why confidence matters to young people. Those who are confident will find it easier to:

- try new things and be more open to learning
- relish challenging tasks
- risk making mistakes
- express themselves as individuals
- say they don't understand and ask for help
- concentrate and not be side-tracked by fear of failure.

But it is also true that confidence is becoming more important in society at large.

Why confidence is more important in modern societies

In the past there was little space for people to make decisions as individuals. Much of life was dictated by survival – either finding and cooking food or maintaining a roof over one's head. There was some scope for innovation and resourcefulness, particularly when things were scarce, but much of what people did in life was dictated by tradition. So fish were gutted, corn sown or socks knitted in a time-honoured fashion. When rural life began to break down and many people migrated to towns they were often employed in factories, warehouses, shops and offices. And of course society was much more hierarchical than it is today. Employees called managers 'sir' and accepted that they should carry out orders without question.

So in the past people's lives were mapped out for them and they acquired attitudes, rather like old clothes, from elders and betters. In such an environment, self-confidence hardly mattered, as people's lives were fairly predictable and there was little space for personal manoeuvre. Of course, there were times when self-confidence would have helped an individual to face up to life's challenges but most people had to do things whether they felt confident or not. A young bride left her community for another even if she felt under-confident and ill-equipped for the ordeal because it was her duty. A young soldier went to war even though he felt fearful – again because this was what duty dictated.

In earlier societies governed by duty and tradition, there was some element of choice for individuals but it was limited. A minority bucked the system and refused the life that was on offer and no doubt self-confidence was a personal characteristic that served them well. In Scotland a significant number became a 'lad o' pairts' seeking a new life through education. Some became self-made men forging their destinies through business, science or exploration. Many emigrated. So people used to live their lives on pre-determined tracks. They steamed ahead, not because they felt confident or courageous but because their ancestors had helped to set them on the course they were now travelling. Indeed, when a person's life is set in such a way, self-confidence is not only unimportant, it is irrelevant: those who conformed in this traditional world were accepted because they knew their place and they expected to be effective if they performed things in time-honoured ways.

Few believe they can live any longer in that world. They may hanker after its authority, certainty and predictability but it has gone forever. Human societies have always had to evolve and adapt to changing circumstances. Industry and technology have changed dramatically through the ages. This is why we talk about an 'Industrial Revolution' in the eighteenth century. Society has never been completely predictable – wars, famine, plague and changes in technology saw to that. *But there was still an expectation that life should be predictable* – that a son could follow in his father's footsteps; a daughter could benefit from her mother's, even her grandmother's, experience. That expectation has gone. It is as if we are now living in a change machine that has slipped into fast forward. Everything has speeded up. Rightly or wrongly, generations now feel they grew up in different worlds with different attitudes, behaviours and expectations. The tracks laid by previous generations to help guide us through life have become obsolete – indeed, they are barely discernible. And in this world where we must all find our own way, and become self-energising and self-steering entities, confidence is no longer 'a nice to have' option – it is essential.

In the past decade there has been a rash of books on how change – global, technological, spiritual and political – is affecting not just society and organisations, but the individuals within them. It is impossible to outline the various ways human society and individuals themselves are being transformed through technological and other developments and to link this to the increased importance of confidence. All we can do here is point out some of the big landmark changes which mean that self-confidence and related characteristics now have something of a survival value.

i. Increase in choice and opportunities

Nowadays, people have many more choices to make in life. These might be what course to study at university from the thousands which are now on offer; whether to get married; how to spend free time, as well as the literally millions of consumer choices most people face every day. Of course, many people are excluded from such choices because they have little money, but even the unemployed living on benefits have more choice in their daily lives than had previous generations. A certain amount of choice is beneficial for individuals and allows people to express themselves but research carried out by Professor Barry Schwartz and others shows that most people are drowning in a sea of choices. Paradoxically, more choice does not add to well-being but undermines it. The more conscious we are of the goals that are meaningful to us, the more we are able to resist being undermined by the proliferation of choice.

ii. The mass media and social comparisons

In his book *Britain on the Couch* clinical psychologist Oliver James presents evidence to show that many people in modern society do not feel good about themselves and that depression is one of the leading illnesses of our age affecting one in four of the UK population. James sees the 1950s as a watershed and the advent of mass media as the catalyst. He argues that it is quite natural for human beings to compare themselves with others; before the advent of television most people compared themselves with others in their immediate world – neighbours, siblings, colleagues. In other words, they measured themselves against people who were not that different so the comparison was at least realistic and attainable. The mass media have changed all that. Now we sit in the intimacy of our own living rooms and compare ourselves with the rich, famous and glamorous. Women compare themselves with beautiful, thin women who are not typical and who would not look like that if they lived more ordinary lives. Men are not immune to the damaging effects of the comparison game. They too feel oppressed and diminished by fit, attractive, males who are rich and successful. James argues that such social comparisons not only damage our sense of self and our mental health but also our relationships as they can lead us to feel dissatisfied with our partners. Yet again, the more we can do to focus on the personal goals we have in life, the less likely we are to be distracted and undermined by the mass media.

iii. From hard graft to 'soft skills'

Just as our personal lives have been transformed in recent years so too has the world of work. Much has been written about the decline of old smokestack industries such as coal, engineering and shipbuilding and the rise of high-tech and communications industries such as call centres. Scotland has seen more than its fair share of such changes. Glasgow was once one of the great workshops of the world. Now it has transformed itself into a shopping mecca. Not only is Glasgow rated to be the UK's second retail centre, it has acquired the reputation as Scotland's 'style' capital. Now the service sector provides 83 per cent of Glasgow's employment. Even if we focus on Scotland's production jobs, we can see with our own eyes how, within a couple of decades, activity has shifted from the Clyde and the coal and steel towns of Lanarkshire, to the high-tech companies in new towns such as Livingston and Glenrothes. As some of these new employers, for example, Motorola, go through their own economic difficulties as a result of even newer developments in technology, we must also register just how unpredictable working life now is for many people. It was not always so. In the past, many followed in their father's, or even their grandfather's, footsteps.

Nonetheless it is easy to make too much of the disappearance of a 'job for life'. It has certainly disappeared from our expectations and nowadays there are very few school-leavers who could walk into a job confident that it would see them through to retirement. But in reality many people still continue to work for long periods of time, if not their whole working lives, in the same industry or profession – teachers, social workers, civil servants and lawyers. But that does not mean to say they do not have to contend with a great deal of change. Much of this change is challenging as it is about the acquisition of additional skills such as computer technology or customer care. Most managers, including head teachers, are no longer expected just to tell people what to do in a top down fashion: they are encouraged to be leaders who inspire and motivate their staff. It is no longer enough for professionals, such as lawyers and accountants, to be good technical employees in a highly competitive sector: they are now expected to market and sell their services to clients. Most organisations, struggling to become better in a highly complex world, now realise the benefit of real team working and expect employees to work productively with others rather than to be independent agents. It may sound easy but team working requires good interpersonal skills.

It is claimed that we now live, not in the Industrial Age, but in the Information Age. Ours is 'the knowledge economy'. This means that there is a shift in value away from raw materials, land or other tangible assets towards 'knowledge' and 'information'. One telling example of this shift is how much it now costs to produce a car. Twenty years ago 70 per cent of the cost of producing an individual car was attributable to labour and raw materials. Now it is design, software and marketing that account for 70 per cent of its cost.

But all this emphasis on knowledge, information and technology can easily lead us to imagine that the skills that are increasingly in demand are technical or computing skills and that jobs will become more and more high-tech. But many thriving employment areas, as the example above shows, are in specialisms such as marketing, which require more understanding of human beings than knowledge of computers. Adair Turner, a former director-general of the CBI, is one analyst who believes that the revolution in computer technology will not generate an endless supply of new jobs. Indeed, he argues that the future growth in UK jobs will be what he calls 'high touch' rather than high-tech. Ironically, even in the knowledge industry itself, managers are not as interested as you might think in hiring people with good technical skills and are often intent on recruiting people who are self-confident, who have good social skills and the 'right' personality to fit into their company culture. The Scottish manager of a Japanese computer company recently stated they were increasingly aware that they could teach new employees the technical skills they needed to work there; what they could not easily instil in employees were new attitudes or self-confidence.

For a variety of reasons, the business world is much more competitive than it was decades ago. The public sector too is now under increasing pressure to perform and meet targets. This means that employers in both sectors are convinced that to keep ahead they must recruit the best possible staff.

BOX 2: Generally, employers are looking for staff who are –

- self-motivated and do not need to be told what to do
- open, rather than resistant, to change and learning
- problem-solvers with good 'can-do' attitudes
- good at getting on with people and so good at customer relations
- good team players.

Conclusion

Given the importance of confidence, particularly in the world we now inhabit, those drawing up the *Curriculum for Excellence* were right to make one of the main purposes of education the creation of 'confident individuals'. This could be a huge opportunity for Scotland provided that the actions we take to develop confidence are sophisticated, genuinely empower young people and are based on strong empirical evidence.

Key points

1. The importance of confidence has been recognised by thinkers for centuries.
2. Confidence is a multifaceted term used more often in business, sport and economics than in psychology.
3. Psychologists prefer terms such as self-esteem, self-efficacy and optimism as these are more easy to define and thus to measure.
4. Confidence can be defined as self-efficacy (belief that you can reach your goals) plus optimism.
5. Confidence is not about being able to speak in groups.
6. Confidence is of prime importance for pupils in the classroom.
7. In modern fast-moving times, those who will survive and thrive are those who feel confident they can adapt to change and learn new skills.
8. In the modern world of work, self-confidence, positive attitudes and good interpersonal skills matter and are now highly prized by employers.
9. The *Curriculum for Excellence* is right to establish the development of confidence as one of the four main purposes of education.

learning from america's mistakes

2 The Concept of Self-Esteem

> *There is now an almost automatic assumption that if you scratch the surface of a social or individual problem, a state of low self-esteem will be revealed. … it is the forces of culture and not of scientific investigation that has led to the universalisation of the problem of self-esteem. As a result, the problem of self-esteem has acquired a free-floating character that can attach itself to any issue. Its ability to jump from one problem to the next suggests that the self-esteem deficit has become something of a folk myth that is transmitted through the conduit of our cultural imagination.*
>
> Frank Furedi

The problem with self-esteem

The idea of self-esteem has a positive, democratic, egalitarian ring about it: it urges us to see that everyone, irrespective of status in life, should be able to feel good about themselves. Indeed, does it not echo Robert Burns and his famous line 'the rank is but the guinea's stamp/ the man's the gowd for a' that'? In other words, if we see self-esteem as part of our birthright as individuals, who could possibly disagree with the attempt to increase these good feelings, particularly for young people?

The problem with self-esteem, however, is that it has become such a popular concept. It has, in the words of Nathanial Branden, the intellectual father of the movement in the USA, become 'trivialized' – emptied of all meaning. Almost all ills in society are now attributed to low self-esteem. It has become such a widespread concern across society at large that we see hugely different characters joining hands in a concerted effort to do something about it. In the US arch right-wingers like Nathanial Branden stand alongside liberal figures like Oprah Winfrey or Gloria Steinem – united in the belief that low self-esteem is the scourge of modern society. In the UK too there is a convergence of supporters from left and right of the political spectrum – for example, leaders of the employers' organisation, the CBI, alongside the Socialist Teachers Alliance, agreeing on the need to raise young people's self-esteem.

But this widespread support should not deflect attention from the fact that the evidence does not uphold the idea that self-esteem is a silver bullet. What's more, attempts to boost self-esteem artificially may backfire, leading, ironically, to feelings of powerlessness and depression.

In this chapter I present information on the rise of self-esteem as a concept and what the research says about its importance. In the next chapter I shall explain why seeing self-esteem as a silver bullet, and then taking aim to increase it deliberately in young people, can result in making matters worse, not better.

A short history of self-esteem

> *Though an overweening conceit of our own merit be vicious and disagreeable, nothing can be more laudable than to have a value for ourselves, where we really have qualities that are valuable. ... it is certain that nothing is more useful to us, in the conduct of life, than a due degree of pride, which makes us sensible of our own merit, and gives us a confidence and assurance in all our projects and enterprises.*
>
> David Hume

As the quote from the great eighteenth century Scottish Enlightenment thinker, David Hume, shows, the idea that it is important to value and think well of yourself has been around for a long time. The first pure psychological use of the term self-esteem can be traced back to 1890 and the work of William James, who is generally seen as the father of modern psychology. James had a very simple definition of self-esteem: success divided by pretension. According to James, the more success we have and the lower our expectations or pretensions, then the higher our self-esteem. To raise self-esteem, therefore, we have two options: lower our expectations of ourselves or increase our achievements.

In *The Optimistic Child* Professor Martin Seligman gives a brief history of self-esteem starting with William James. Seligman believes the beauty of this definition is that it stresses two ingredients of self-esteem which have been present in debates about the concept ever since: namely, self-esteem includes the idea of 'feeling good' and 'doing well'.

In his subsequent summary Seligman maintains that James's work was then largely ignored for 75 years as a result of academic and socio-economic factors. World wars and economic depression did not create fertile territory for a focus on how people felt about themselves and psychology itself was dominated during this period by various schools of thought (Freudianism and behaviourism, for example) which had in common the belief that individuals' lives were determined largely by forces outwith their control.

Seligman argues that the 1960s changed all this. First the rise of wealth and consumerism meant that it was easier to conceptualise the individual at the centre of his/her destiny. And psychology, partly as a result of Seligman's own 'learned helplessness' experiments, created theories which put the 'self-directed' individual at the centre of his or her own life.

The rise of the self-esteem movement

From the late 1960s onwards, self-esteem became a fashionable and influential idea. One of the first exponents was a young psychology professor called Stanley Coopersmith from California who introduced a way to measure self-esteem. A more influential figure was Nathaniel Branden – a psychotherapist and devotee of the philosopher Ayn Rand. His writings on self-esteem are philosophical and intellectual, and for most Europeans extremely right-wing. Self-esteem may simply have remained a largely philosophical concept, debated by academics, if it had not been taken up by politicians in California in the late 1980s. John Vasconcellos was a state assemblyman who believed that low self-esteem was the cause of crime, teenage pregnancy, drug abuse and school underachievement. He believed that boosting young people's self-esteem could be seen as a 'social vaccine'. Money spent on this, he argued, would dramatically reduce the problems plaguing modern society. John Vasconcellos even believed that improving self-esteem would help the state balance the budget since those with high self-esteem earned more money and so paid more in tax.

Vasconcellos persuaded the California State Governor, George Deukmejian, to set up a task-force on self-esteem and personal and social responsibility. Following a three-year study of the literature it produced a report which did not completely corroborate Vasconcellos's views. Indeed, in the introduction to the report one of its authors writes: 'one of the disappointing aspects of every chapter in this volume ... is how low the associations between self-esteem and its [presumed] consequences are in research to date'. The response of those involved in the movement was not to question the importance they were attaching to self-esteem but to try to find more evidence. The task-force was disbanded in 1995 and replaced by a not-for-profit organisation called the National Association for Self-Esteem (NASE).

The challenge to the claims for self-esteem

Roy Baumeister is a psychology professor in the US. Although he was a supporter of the self-esteem movement he was concerned about the paucity of hard evidence to support the claims being made for self-esteem. He was also concerned about some of the approaches and underlying assumptions of the research that had been undertaken. Many of the studies that are repeatedly quoted used only subjective assessments of self-esteem and, since self-esteem is a socially desirable characteristic in western societies, such self reports had to be viewed sceptically. Moreover, although there appeared to be some link between self-esteem and academic performance, for example, it was difficult to discern if the academic performance caused the self-esteem or vice versa.

As a result of his research carried out in the 1990s, Baumeister concluded that the premise that low self-esteem was a problem, and that curing it could eradicate many social ills, was 'completely false'. The link between self-esteem and academic achievement, he concluded, was weak or non-existent. It just was not true that bullies always lacked self-esteem or that high self-esteem was important for good relationships. On the plus side, he did find that people with high self-esteem tended to be happier, show more initiative and were less prone to eating disorders. But he no longer believed that it was simply possible to artificially boost self-esteem. Later, Baumeister said that coming to these conclusions was 'one of the biggest disappointments of his career'.

The demise of the notion that raising self-esteem is some kind of panacea was further hastened in 2001 with the publication of Professor Nicholas Emler's work. Emler was at that time a professor of psychology at the London School of Economics. His research, including longitudinal studies of children, supported Baumeister's findings that low self-esteem was not a risk factor for educational problems or problems such as violence, bullying, delinquency, racism, drug-taking or alcohol abuse. Other trenchant critiques of self-esteem have come from other psychologists such as Professor Martin Seligman and will be summarised in detail in the next chapter.

Why the US bandwagon rolls on

It is now over ten years since in-depth research completely demolished the notion that self-esteem building is a panacea. Yet in the US the self-esteem bandwagon rolls on, almost unabated.

Lauren Slater, a psychologist, therapist and writer, has advanced the most likely explanation why, despite the damning evidence and critiques of the idea that self-esteem is a cure-all, interest in the subject continues, at least in the US. She argues that the pursuit of self-worth has become the dominant 'paradigm' and it has inveigled its way into education programmes, rehabilitation and therapy. She also believes it fits with how Americans see the world:

> *Self-esteem, as a construct, as a quasi religion, is woven into a tradition that both defines and confines us as Americans. If we were to deconstruct self-esteem, to question its value, we would be, in a sense, questioning who we are, nationally and individually. We would be threatening our self-esteem. This is probably why we cannot really assimilate research like Baumeister's or Emler's.*

Slater also believes that challenging self-esteem flies in the face of 'inexorable market forces' and how many people make a living. While she does not argue that therapists have any desire to 'perpetuate a perhaps simplistic view of self-esteem' they are, she argues, 'the cultural retailers' of the self-esteem concept.

Self-esteem in the UK

The UK, with its inclination to a 'put down' rather than a self-worth culture, may seem less fertile territory for the importance of self-esteem but this is not the case. There is a thriving 'self-help' book market in the UK and many of these titles focus on self-esteem and how to build it. A search on Google using 'self-esteem' and 'UK' as keywords came up with three million hits. While many of them did not refer to UK material, many did, including, for example, an uncritical story on the BBC's website in 2002 about how new tests had been developed to assess 'children as young as three' to see how high or low their self-esteem was. The story continues 'self-esteem can be one of the key factors in determining how successful a child will be at school and later in life'.

Across education in the UK many teachers are consciously aiming to improve pupils' self-esteem, either through increased praise and awards, or through specific programmes. A retired head teacher member of the Professional Association of Teachers put forward a motion at the 2005 annual conference proposing that the word 'fail' be deleted from school vocabulary and replaced with the term 'deferred success' as a way to protect young people with fragile self-esteem. The motion was defeated but some argued it was unnecessary as schools no longer use the word 'fail' anyway.

In 2004, two prestigious and influential think tank bodies published reports on self-esteem. One was for Demos and called *The Self-Esteem Society.* In it the author acknowledges the research by Baumeister and Emler but still proposes widespread action to create a self-esteem society. Her argument is that we need to boost self-esteem to protect and develop democracy. She argues that individuals with high self-esteem make 'good citizens' and 'good choices'. However, as we will see below, research on young people in the US – a high self-esteem culture – shows that this is not the case. Young people there feel powerless, have poor academic skills, and compromised well-being. What is also odd about the Demos research is that they conducted their own poll and asked people to rate their own self-esteem. Only six per cent of the sample rated their self-esteem as low or very low – so hardly something that needs widespread action.

The Work Foundation produced a similar paper in 2004, called *Me, Myself and Work*. It makes passing reference to Emler's work but largely ignores his conclusions and those of Professor Roy Baumeister. Referring to the California task-force's original research the author erroneously claims that their research supported the idea of self-esteem as a panacea. It did not. Oblivious to this point, the author then goes on to exhort the Labour Government to do more to ensure that self-esteem is increased in 'early years, general education ... welfare to work' and so forth, without one question of the merit and empirical justification for such an approach.

In his book *Therapy Culture*, the Kent-based sociologist Professor Frank Furedi illustrates how the concept of self-esteem lies at the heart of many government backed initiatives in the UK not just in education but also in Welfare to Work, family policy and health. Furedi's unsettling critique of this development will be presented in the next chapter.

A conundrum

Perhaps one of the reasons why self-esteem has become such an important concept in modern society is that we all understand it and know its relevance to our own life. David Hume was right: it feels great when we are proud of ourselves. Even Martin Seligman, an arch critic of the self-esteem movement, acknowledges that self-esteem is a 'delicious feeling'. Baumeister and colleagues explained eloquently, in an important 2003 paper for the American Psychological Society, why people are routinely drawn to the notion that self-esteem is of vital importance in all our lives:

> *Most people feel that self-esteem is important. It is difficult, if not impossible, for people to remain indifferent to information that bears on their own self-esteem, such as being told that they are incompetent, attractive, untrustworthy, or loveable. Increases and decreases in self-esteem generally bring strong emotional reactions. Moreover, these fluctuations are often coincident with major successes and failures in life. Subjective experience creates the impression that self-esteem rises when one wins a contest, garners an award, solves a problem, or gains acceptance to a social group, and that it falls with corresponding failures. This pervasive correlation may well strengthen the impression that one's level of self-esteem is not just the outcome, but indeed the cause, of life's major successes and failures.*

The issue then is not whether self-esteem exists or even if it is important in people's lives – it is, according to the research, a salient characteristic of happy people. The issues are whether it is something which can be artificially boosted by professionals, and the techniques we might employ to do this. It is also about how relevant self-esteem issues are across different domains such as education and work. A further issue concerns whether, by focusing on self-esteem and how people feel about themselves, we are simply creating a generation who are obsessed by themselves and their own lives. These questions are explored in later sections.

The evidence on self-esteem

In this section we shall look at how self-esteem is measured and what research says about the importance of self-esteem to a variety of outcomes. As we shall see, high self-esteem can have important beneficial outcomes – happiness, for example – yet in other respects it is unimportant or may even be undesirable.

Measuring self-esteem

As there are many different ways to define self-esteem, there are a number of ways to measure it. One of the most widely used measurement tools is Rosenberg's Self-Esteem Scale which has been in use since the 1960s. This self-report questionnaire includes statements such as 'I take a positive attitude towards myself' and 'I wish I could have more respect for myself'. (*See supporting resources for more information*). Rosenberg's scale is widely used in research and has been shown to be one of the most reliable measures.

While Professor Baumeister accepts the validity and reliability of such measures in his research into the importance of self-esteem, he thought it vital to make a distinction between self-reported self-esteem, which he thinks may be inflated because of social pressures, and self-esteem which is measured, or corroborated, more objectively. By deciding to focus on analysing self-esteem studies that had more robust, objective measures, the number of studies for him to examine dropped dramatically. Baumeister was also intent on being rigorous about causality. Being able to point to a correlation meant nothing since it was impossible to tell what caused what. For example, if drug users had low self-esteem, was this a cause of the drug use, or was it how they felt about themselves because they used drugs? Or was there another factor which caused both the drug taking, and the low self-esteem, such as poverty?

Professor Nicholas Emler is also relaxed about the measurement of self-esteem but concerned about the issue of causality. His research mainly involved looking at longitudinal studies, which tracked children over time.

Levels of self-esteem

Baumeister *et al* have shown that few people report low self-esteem. The norm, for the American population at least, is on the high side. This leads Professor Emler in his book on self-esteem to point out that when researchers refer to people who have high self-esteem, such people have a very positive view of themselves, and those with low self-esteem a 'slightly' positive view of themselves.

Self-esteem research

The following are some of the most important findings, particularly for young people, that have emanated from research undertaken mainly by Baumeister and colleagues and set out in their 2003 paper and Professor Emler's research which he published in 2001.

i. Academic performance

Baumeister's early research indicated a very weak link between academic performance and self-esteem. This conclusion is amply demonstrated in unpublished research into the 1970 British Cohort Study reported by Nicholas Emler. This showed that self-esteem levels at age ten were only 'trivially related to later educational attainments'. It also has to be borne in mind that any link between self-esteem and performance may be due to the fact that good results enhance self-esteem rather than vice versa.

More recently, the argument on self-esteem and academic performance is that there is little relationship. For example, the highest achieving students in American schools – white girls – often get the lowest self-esteem scores. This is also true of Asian students. Asian culture does not encourage self-esteem yet young Asians often excel academically. In the US the group who consistently score high on self-esteem are black boys and they often achieve the least academically at school.

The factors which have consistently been shown in research to have an influence on academic achievement are: ability, IQ, and family background (socio-economic status). Baumeister also argues that any attempt to artificially boost self-esteem for young people may backfire. He explains why in his 2003 paper:

> *...students may ordinarily work hard in order to be permitted to feel good about themselves, and an intervention that encourages them to feel good about themselves regardless of work may remove the reason to work hard – resulting in poor performance.*

As psychologists, Professor Baumeister and his colleagues are interested in psychological studies and do not make reference to educational trends on academic achievement. We shall examine these trends more fully in Chapter 3 but it is worth pointing out here that recent commentators, such as Professor Jean Twenge in *Generation Me*, highlight the worrying drop in educational attainment figures in the US over the past few decades. Twenge is not arguing that the decline in academic standards in American schools is attributable exclusively to the emphasis on building self-esteem in schools but, like a number of critics, she argues it is a contributing factor.

ii. Relationships

It is often argued that you have to be able to 'love yourself' before you can love others or have good relationships but self-esteem is not as important for relationships as was previously thought. People who record high self-esteem often say they have better social and interpersonal skills than people with low self-esteem but this is not actually the case. Studies have shown that people who have high self-esteem often have an inflated sense of their social skills, a view often contradicted by others. One study did find, however, that people with high self-esteem were more likely to initiate new relationships and interactions and this was supported by others. It is not difficult to see why good self-esteem would be helpful in this respect. On the other hand, having an inflated sense of yourself is not a characteristic which other people find endearing.

Low self-esteem may affect a person's love life in that they do not think they are worthy of love but their relationships may be more stable and enduring. People with high self-esteem report that they are more likely to terminate relationships if they are dissatisfied. This could lead to more unstable family life for children.

iii. Anti-social behaviour

In this category we can list anti-social behaviour such as delinquency (eg stealing and vandalism) as well as cheating. As far as delinquency is concerned studies are contradictory but there is, on balance, some evidence of a weak link between low self-esteem and this type of behaviour. Little correlation has been found between disciplinary problems in school and self-esteem. When it comes to cheating, children who report high self-esteem are over-represented in groups that are most, or least, likely to cheat. Baumeister *et al* explain this finding in the following way:

> *The results were consistent with the view that self-esteem is a heterogeneous construct, in that children who cheated the most and who cheated the least both had high self-esteem. More precisely, those who were high in both self-esteem and need for approval cheated the most, whereas those who were high in self-esteem but had a low need for approval cheated least. The authors proposed that a distinction between true and defensive high self-esteem could account for their results.*

iv. Performance at work or on specific tasks

The Work Foundation publication *Me, Myself, Work*, mentioned in the previous section, asserts that self-esteem is very important for performance at work. In fact much of the pamphlet is predicated on this assumption. But the 2003 paper by Baumeister and colleagues argues that while this is a common assumption it is not necessarily true. They refer to one 2001 study of the relationship between work performance and self-esteem where the researchers surveyed the results of 5,000 participants across 40 studies and found that 'most of them showed weak positive relationships'. However, unlike school where across the board it was difficult to see any strong relationship between self-esteem and academic achievement, 'the reported link between self-esteem and job performance is highly variable'. They make the point that this may be because jobs vary considerably and some may require more self-esteem for good performance than others. However, they also cautioned not to assume causality. Self-esteem might in some cases improve job performance. On the other hand being good at your job may lead to an increase in self-esteem.

A number of laboratory studies have tried to ascertain a link between self-esteem and performance but again Baumeister reports 'self-esteem seems to have little or no direct relationship to task performance'. The tasks studied were arithmetic problems and video games requiring non-verbal intelligence.

One area relevant for work where self-esteem does seem significant is 'persisting longer in the face of failure' and also knowing when to quit. Another 2002 study also shows that students with high self-esteem were more likely to achieve their goals and were more likely to get satisfaction from achieving them than those with low self-esteem. These types of studies lead Baumeister *et al* to assert that 'in performance contexts, high self-esteem people appear to use better self-regulation strategies than low self-esteem people'.

While I am generally persuaded by the research presented by Baumeister and colleagues on the relevance of self-esteem to various aspects of people's lives, I do not find the evidence presented on 'job and task performance' entirely convincing. As well as the 'self-regulation' strategies initiating conversation and speaking out in large groups mentioned above, we shall see below that those with high self-esteem have better coping skills. What's more, since they are more likely to be happy, they may well have a slightly more positive approach to life. Certainly for some jobs these skills/attitudes are unimportant but if you examine the type of employees/skills employers say they want in the UK, high, or at least moderate, self-esteem may be a more important factor in the modern workplace than Baumeister and colleagues acknowledge.

v. Happiness

Baumeister *et al* conclude from examining a large variety of studies of various age groups that there is a close correlation between reported self-esteem and happiness levels. This is particularly true in individualistic cultures like the US (and much of Western Europe) and less true in collectivist cultures, which urge people to pay more attention to the group and relationships than to internal feelings or 'attributes'. As a result of these wide-ranging studies, Baumeister *et al* write:

> *Taken together these findings uniformly indicate that self-esteem and happiness are strongly interrelated. They suggest that high self-esteem may pay off handsomely for the individual in terms of subjective happiness.*

They go on, however, to point out that since happiness is a subjective state of mind it cannot easily be corroborated objectively. Given that people with high self-esteem tend to say positive things about themselves (such as having good social skills) even when this is not always the case, it is possible that they overrate how happy they feel about their lives as well. The authors caution us to be aware that it is still not possible to say that high self-esteem causes happiness. It may be that having success in life causes happiness to rise. Or it could be that some kind of dispositional tendency to feel good tends to lead to high self-esteem.

vi. Coping and depression

A number of writers on self-esteem have advanced the idea that high self-esteem may act as a 'buffer', which protects the individual when times are tough. In other words, when life is going well self-esteem may not matter very much but it helps individuals weather the storm when things go wrong.

Various studies have tried to substantiate, or undermine, the buffer hypothesis and the results are very mixed. Some confirmed the idea that high self-esteem had a protective effect when life was hard or stressful. Others indicated that the advantage of self-esteem was when life was good, not when it was bad. Some studies also concluded that low self-esteem 'poisoned the good times' and that everyone suffered when times were hard. However, Baumeister and colleagues were still prepared to conclude that while more research is needed 'the findings consistently suggest that low self-esteem leads to poorer outcomes, including depression and possibly physical illness, under some circumstances'. Low self-esteem, 'self-blame' and stressful or hard times seemed to increase a person's vulnerability to depression.

As we shall see however in a later section, Professor Martin Seligman argues that parents' and teachers' attempts to bolster their children's self-esteem is contributing to the escalating numbers of young people suffering from depression. This analysis is supported by the empirical research conducted by Professor Jean Twenge. A number of studies internationally suggest that those with low self-esteem are more likely to commit suicide or have suicidal thoughts.

BOX 3: Summary of evidence on self-esteem

High self-esteem is positively correlated with:

- initiating relationships with others (moderate correlation)
- sexual experimentation in young people
- racist attitudes
- violence (bullies, sociopaths, etc, report high self-esteem)
- speaking out in large groups
- achieving goals through self-regulation
- happiness
- better management of stress so some positive health outcomes.

Low self-esteem is positively correlated with:

- teenage pregnancy (only one of a number of factors)
- eating disorders (again only one of a number of factors)
- teenage smoking in girls (but could lower self-esteem then be the cause?)
- unemployment/low income in males
- vulnerability to depression
- suicide and suicidal thoughts
- victims of bullying.

Self-esteem is irrelevant for:

- academic performance
- many job or performance tasks
- alcohol or drug abuse.

Preliminary conclusions

Given their research, critics like Baumeister and Emler believe that those with high self-esteem can be a menace to society while those with low self-esteem are more likely to damage themselves. However, while there is some merit in these conclusions they also overlook the strong relationship between happiness and self-esteem and the fact that low self-esteem appears to be a risk factor for depression. Research shows that happy people tend to be healthier and contribute more to society. While it is true that it might not be the self-esteem that causes happiness (it might be a third variable) it cannot be ruled out as totally irrelevant. Nonetheless, those of us working at the Centre agree with some of the conclusions these critics draw.

BOX 4: Some preliminary conclusions on self-esteem

1. While there are many positives associated with high self-esteem the evidence suggests that raising self-esteem is certainly not a panacea or magic bullet to cure all social ills.
2. Deliberately trying to raise the self-esteem of young people may be counterproductive.
3. There may be some significant social costs to a society focused on boosting self-esteem.
4. Some of the positives for self-esteem may be related to other factors, and identifying and building these may be more beneficial for society than attempting to boost self-esteem.

Differences in self-esteem

Any study of self-esteem has to ask why it varies from individual to individual. Professor Nicholas Emler in his book *Self-Esteem: The Costs and Causes of Low Self-Worth* surveys and presents the evidence on the roots of self-esteem under three headings:

- factors that have weak effects or none
- factors that have moderate effects
- factors that have a substantial effect.

i. Weak/irrelevant factors: race, class, gender

As Professor Emler points out, it is commonly assumed that an individual's self-esteem will be affected by ethnicity or race. For example, it is often argued that black people, or those from ethnic minorities, will have lower self-esteem than white people, given the supremacy of the latter in western culture. However, the evidence does not support this view. In the US, black people consistently report higher self-esteem than white people. A variety of reasons have been advanced for this finding including the idea that most people care about the approval of friends and family more than the views of others in the wider society. Social class is also commonly thought to be closely correlated to self-esteem but it is only 'modestly' so according to Professor Emler.

Gender is often seen as an important variable in self-esteem and here there is some evidence to support this view. Women, on average, have lower self-esteem than men but as Emler points out: 'The difference is highly consistent but it is also small. One factor influencing the size of the difference is age. The largest differences are apparent in late adolescence; they are smaller both before and after.'

ii. Modest factors: success and failures, appearance

It is also commonly assumed that people who are successful in life will have high self-esteem and that those who suffer frequent failure will have low self-esteem. There is, according to Professor Emler, some evidence to support this but it is not as strong a factor as people think. Emler argues that people who have high self-esteem are better at discounting or ignoring failure (eg they attribute it to bad luck or poor teaching) and so their self-esteem is less damaged by the failure. On the other hand, those with low self-esteem also tend to 'discount' success. 'Those blessed with high self-esteem', Professor Emler writes, 'ignore all the evidence of inadequacies. Those who lack self-esteem equally consistently deny that there is any positive evidence, using many of the same tactics in reverse.'

Appearance is routinely advanced as a major factor in the level of a person's self-esteem. However, as we shall see in another section, what matters is not whether a person is objectively attractive but whether they think they are.

iii. Substantial factors: parents, genes

Professor Nicholas Emler is unequivocal in his view about the source of an individual's self-esteem. 'To the question "what are the most important influences on self-esteem?" the simple answer is "parents"', he writes. Emler agrees with Stanley Coopersmith, one of the early thinkers on self-esteem, on the reasons for this parental influence. Summarising Coopersmith, Emler argues that parents' behaviour is of crucial significance in the development of children's self-esteem (see Box 5).

BOX 5: Parents' behaviour that has most impact on children's self-esteem

- the amount of acceptance, approval and affection parents show their children
- the degree to which the discipline parents give to children is based on explanation rather than punishment or coercion
- the extent to which parents involve children in family decisions and value their contributions.

The importance of parents

Coopersmith's pioneering work on self-esteem has subsequently been supported by research. Approval and acceptance seem to be particularly important in the development of self-esteem. What is also surprising is that research suggests that the importance of parents to a person's self-esteem does not end with childhood but continues not just into adolescence but into adulthood.

Given the importance of self-esteem it is hardly surprising that a variety of studies has shown how physical and sexual abuse by parents has what Emler refers to as a 'devastating effect on self-esteem'. One study suggests that victims of child abuse were four times more likely than other people to be the lowest scorers on measures of self-esteem. Family breakdown is also another contributing factor in low self-esteem, according to research. Emler also argues that parents make another substantial contribution to children's self-esteem through their genetic inheritance. Quoting the famous 1998 study into almost 4,000 twin pairs, Emler argues that 'about a third of the variation in self-esteem scores could be attributed to inherited differences in the sample'.

Some psychologists have argued that a person's self-esteem will in part be a reflection of how they are seen by others. But Emler disputes this. He writes: 'It seems that the actual reactions of others may have little influence on what we think of ourselves. It is almost as if, after our parents have had their say – and their genetic influence – we become increasingly deaf to other, especially dissenting voices.'

Can self-esteem be overdone?

Confidence is a sweet spot between arrogance and despair.

Rosabeth Moss Kanter

Advocates of self-esteem generally argue that genuine self-esteem is such a fantastic quality that you cannot have too much of it. Robert Reasoner, for example, writing on the NASE website asserts that 'having high self-esteem is equivalent to having good health'. However, if having exceptionally good health is the outcome of a life dedicated to one's own health (aerobic exercise, diet, meditation, etc) you could be overly obsessed with yourself (self-centred) or overly pleased with how good your health is (smug). In other words, working on your self-esteem may backfire, particularly if it interferes, as it could easily do, with relationships.

The golden mean

A common mistake people make is to think that because something is good, more of it must be better. But this is not always the case. The Greek philosopher Aristotle talked about 'the golden mean'. This is the idea that qualities can be overdone or underdone. An excessive pursuit of self-esteem will not only lead to self-centredness and smugness but could weaken relationships, a major source of happiness and well-being, and thus be counterproductive. There appears to be an *optimal* level of self-esteem beyond which more does not mean better. Too much emphasis on self-esteem can fuel a culture of narcissism, which would be detrimental to individuals and society as a whole.

Finally, Judaeo-Christian culture is founded on the notion that excessive self-love, and pride, are sinful. Those who were thought highly of in the past were those who wore plain clothes and were humble, not full of pride or vanity. Modern democratic societies have also been heavily influenced by notions of egalitarianism. This is probably the reason why everyday vocabulary has dozens of words to describe people who think too highly of themselves: arrogant, conceited, big-headed, smug, know-it-all, vain, proud, smart-aleck, etc. Scottish culture, in particular, is full of contemptuous phrases to puncture the ego of folk who think too much of themselves. So we should be very cautious about trying to completely overturn the thinking and values on which our societies are based. Thinking well of yourself and feeling worthy of happiness are important and, we think, attractive qualities, but like everything else in life they can be taken too far.

Difficulties with the concept of self-esteem

> *One does not need to be a trained psychologist to know that some people with low self-esteem strive to compensate for their deficit by boasting, arrogance and conceited behaviour. What educated person does not know about compensatory mechanisms?*
>
> Nathaniel Branden

Definitional problems

One of Professor Roy Baumeister's criticisms of self-esteem is that it is too broad a concept so that the people who can be classified as having 'high self-esteem' are a very heterogeneous group. It is very difficult to discuss difficulties with defining self-esteem for the simple reason that so much has been written about it – approximately 2,000 books and then countless articles and programmes all claiming they have techniques to boost self-esteem. For the sake of simplicity let us take the definition which is used by the National Association for Self-Esteem (NASE). Their definition is closely linked to Nathaniel Branden's work and they define self-esteem as 'the experience of being capable of meetings life's challenges and being worthy of happiness'.

Like Branden, NASE make a distinction between 'authentic' and 'inauthentic' self-esteem. Those with authentic self-esteem have an accurate perception of themselves and take responsibility for their own shortcomings and life choices. Their sense of themselves and self-confidence does not require that they look good in other people's eyes. This means that they have no reason to belittle others and so their self-esteem does not lead to arrogance.

Those with 'inauthentic' self-esteem have a strong need to look good in other people's eyes. This group is intent on impressing others to feel worthy. They can be very competitive, blame others for any of their own failings, and can puff themselves up and put others down to feel good about themselves. So their version of feeling worthy is not about how they evaluate themselves but how they are seen by others. It is external and 'defensive'. Psychologists, including Baumeister, broadly accept there is a distinction to be made between genuine self-esteem and 'inauthentic', defensive or unstable self-esteem.

The problem for the exponents of the benefits of self-esteem is that as self-esteem is socially desirable, people with defensive, externally based (low) self-esteem will also report 'high' self-esteem when asked. As these people appear to have a high opinion of themselves, others may sometimes think they have high self-esteem. However, Nathaniel Branden may well be right, in the quote given above, that non-psychologists often understand that a person who acts as if he or she is superior may have a chip on their shoulder. But that still does not take away from the fact that unless researchers control for other variables, such as the importance of other people's opinions, no distinction will be made between those with authentic and inauthentic self-esteem.

This is why Baumeister argues that one of the fundamental difficulties with the concept of self-esteem is that it ends up referring to a mixed bag of people, some of whom have realistic and genuine self-belief and feel worthy, as well as others who do not feel worthy and are intent on proving their worth in the eyes of others – an intention that can lead to all sorts of negative behaviour, such as cheating.

Narcissism

The mixed bag idea is complicated further when we realise that people who can be classed as 'narcissists' will also end up in the high self-esteem group. We shall explore narcissism more fully in another section but broadly it is a word used to describe people who love themselves too much. Some theorists argue that in western individualistic society some degree of narcissism is essential for the healthy personality. Others argue that as babies we are all narcissistic. People with a narcissistic personality disorder are those who exhibit a number of the following characteristics: grandiose sense of self; fantasies of unlimited success; lack of empathy; craving attention, adulation, etc, from others; manipulative behaviour (using others as pawns in their egotistical quest); arrogance and the belief they are better than others; obsessed with themselves. It is estimated that about 75 per cent of narcissists are male. Narcissism may be the result of an abusive childhood but some research suggests it is genetic. The paradox of narcissism is that narcissists belittle others in the quest to elevate themselves but also need to see themselves reflected well in those that they do not rate. Current measures of self-esteem are likely to describe narcissists as people with 'high self-esteem'.

Teachers' and parents' natural inclinations to praise

As Professor Martin Seligman outlines in *The Optimistic Child*, there are usually two elements to self-esteem: doing well and feeling good. Most individuals are aware that there is (albeit a temporary) boost to self-esteem from praise, success and being treated well by others. They are also aware that failure and criticism lead (again perhaps temporarily) to loss of self-esteem. Both of the elements that contribute to this innate knowledge of self-esteem are on the 'feeling good' side. So, unless I have some notions of psychology, if you ask me to help a child build his/her self-esteem, the most natural thing for me to do is hand out praise, restrict criticism and reduce the bad feelings which come from failure. If you tell me that self-esteem is really important – so important that just about every modern social problem is attributable to self-esteem – then I am likely to give out even bigger dollops of praise and even excise the word 'criticism' from my vocabulary. This tendency may be stronger in women as they often pay more attention to feelings than do men and often have more invested in being 'caring'. As women play a dominant role in child-rearing both at home and school then it is even more likely that 'the feeling good' side of self-esteem will be overplayed.

What has been described above are exactly the conditions that have been ripe for the rise of self-esteem in homes and schools throughout the US and increasingly in the UK. And, as we shall see in the next chapter, the consequences are deeply worrying.

Key Points

1. Self-esteem is seen as a panacea in modern society.
2. Definitions of self-esteem usually include two ingredients: doing well and feeling good.
3. The self-esteem movement claims that all social ills are attributable to low self-esteem and that nurturing young people's self-esteem is like a 'social vaccine'.
4. Empirical research has not supported the claims of the self-esteem movement yet it continues to exert huge influence on American parenting and teaching practices.
5. Even critics of self-esteem accept it can be measured. Rosenberg's Self-Esteem scale is still the most widely used, and accepted, instrument.
6. High self-esteem does correlate with happiness but self-esteem cannot be seen as a panacea. Indeed research shows that some people who are violent (bullies and sociopaths, for example) are more likely to have high, not low self-esteem. Racists too are more likely to have high self-esteem.
7. Low self-esteem is one of the factors involved in teenage pregnancy, eating disorders, suicide and depression.
8. Differing levels of self-esteem are largely accounted for by genes and parenting style.
9. The parenting style most likely to encourage the development of a child's self-esteem is loving and accepting while providing discipline and clear rules.
10. Self-esteem can be overdone. People who think too highly of themselves can appear arrogant and feel entitled – these are not qualities we admire in others.
11. Self-esteem is too broad a term to be meaningful. It presents difficulties in distinguishing narcissists from those with an accurate sense of their own worth and who are good at relating to others.
12. If you tell parents and teachers that children's self-esteem, or even confidence, is really important, they are instinctively likely to pile on the praise, cut back on criticism and protect the child from mistakes and failure. This approach may be well-meaning but it has a negative effect on young people. The reasons why are outlined in the next chapter.

Self-Esteem and Well-Being

3

> *Baby-boomer child-rearing and the self-esteem movement in schools . . . (are) not alleviating the on-going epidemic of depression and might even be creating it.*
>
> Martin Seligman

It is over ten years since Professor Martin Seligman set out his critique of the self-esteem movement in *The Optimistic Child*. As he points out, the problem is not simply that much of what it says is 'gaseous' and does not make sense, it could be doing harm by setting children up for depression. This is also the viewpoint taken by other psychologists. In this chapter we set out the basis of Martin Seligman's critique of the self-esteem movement, together with the critique advanced by Dr Jean Twenge in *Generation Me*, Professor Jennifer Crocker's arguments about 'the costly pursuit of self-esteem' and Professor Frank Furedi's warnings of how the fixation with self-esteem ironically disempowers individuals.

The dangers of promoting 'feeling good'

As we've already seen, Seligman points out that most definitions of self-esteem include the notion of 'doing well' and 'feeling good'. He is convinced that high self-esteem can be a 'delicious feeling' but he knows 'no effective technology' for teaching children to feel good about themselves which does not first teach them how to do well.

There is little doubt that Seligman's view that encouraging children to feel good about themselves is the mainstay of the self-esteem movement in schools and in many homes in the US (see Box 6). In the last section we gave an explanation for why the feeling good side of self-esteem has been most promoted.

BOX 6: Under the banner of boosting self-esteem the following have become common currency in American schools.

- Children are repeatedly told that they are 'special'; they may have to repeat this on numerous occasions or colour in 'I'm special' worksheets.
- Children are told that they must 'love' themselves and are given various exercises to help this to sink in.
- Children are given lots of talking exercises where they have to talk about themselves and their special qualities. Usually they are only allowed to use positive adjectives.
- Children are constantly praised, or even rewarded, when they achieve very little.
- Children are protected from criticism and failure as it might make them feel bad.
- Competition or other activities which might allow some children to shine and others to feel bad are avoided.

Professor Jean Twenge's research for *Generation Me* illustrates that these types of activities are not confined to liberal states but are widespread throughout the US and this approach is taught in teacher training colleges.

This whole approach is a far cry not just from Nathaniel Branden's exacting, philosophical work on self-esteem but even from the views of NASE. If you were to follow Branden's recommendations you would follow a fairly harsh regimen to encourage children to be critical, independent thinkers who take complete responsibility for themselves and their lives. There would also be a great emphasis on skills development to boost self-efficacy. Instead, the approach of those promoting self-esteem in American schools is likely to develop 'inauthentic' self-esteem in that it is not trying to encourage the development of the child's inner resources or thinking. As Seligman points out, this approach also deliberately tries to disconnect how the child feels about him or herself from any talent, success or achievement. Self-esteem has not to be contingent on performance or even how the child behaves to others or on their ethics.

It has become commonplace in American schools to:

- encourage self-esteem based on nothing tangible
- encourage 'pseudo' self-esteem simply based on praise and how you are subjectively viewed by others
- ignore the child's own value system or preferred approach. These self-esteem exercises do not recognise or validate differences. All children have to fit into this approach even if they are naturally modest or feel patronised by routine praise.

The Seligman approach

> *Self-esteem is like the speedometer of a car. It tells you how well you are doing. But if you want the car to go faster you don't do anything to the speedometer, you turn your attention to the engine.*
>
> Martin Seligman

As the above quote suggests, Seligman's argument is that high self-esteem may be a great feeling but by itself it does not produce, or 'cause' anything. Feeling good about yourself is a by-product of 'doing well' and doing well, according to Seligman, is about 'good commerce' with the world. This is similar, he argues, to what Aristotle says about happiness. It is not a feeling which can be separated from what we do. Just as happiness arises from 'right action', so self-esteem rises because of the way we engage productively with the world. This is why Seligman writes: 'What California (and every state) needs is not children who are encouraged to feel good, but children who are taught the skills of doing well – how to study, how to avoid pregnancy, drugs, and gangs, and how to get off welfare'.

Seligman's sharp critique of self-esteem came about as a result of visits to schools when he was piloting his optimism and resilience programme for young people. His critique was also informed by 25 years of research into child and adult depression. He says all depressed people have four kinds of problems:

1. behavioural (eg passive, helpless and indecisive)
2. emotional (eg sad)
3. somatic (eg disturbed sleep and appetite)
4. cognitive (eg may think life not worth living and feel worthless).

He points out that only the last 'half-symptom' amounts to the feeling side of self-esteem and is 'the least important' problem facing people who are depressed. To get someone out of depression, Seligman claims, you need to get them active and hopeful again and you do not do this with empty praise or other techniques promoted by the self-esteem movement. He writes: 'If your child suffers from feelings of worthlessness, hates herself, or feels no confidence, it is a reflection that she believes her commerce with the world is going badly. Once her commerce with the world improves and she realizes it, she will feel good.'

So we can see why Seligman believes that boosting self-esteem will do nothing to stop the epidemic of depression. But why does he believe that it might actually cause it?

The rise and causes of depression

Depression is one of the biggest disorders of the modern age yet it was virtually unknown at the turn of the twentieth century. Only three per cent of women born around 1910 in the US had a severe depression by the time they were 30, but for those born in the 1950s this figure exceeded 60 per cent - a twenty fold increase. While men are not quite as susceptible to depression as women, the rise in figures for men follows a similar trend. Seligman presents arguments and evidence to show that this rise is not about definitions. Nor is it the result of any biological changes. He believes it has to do with societal changes during the twentieth century, particularly the rise of individualism and the 'feeling good' society and its emphasis on the self. The victims of this epidemic are becoming younger and younger. A few decades ago in the US the average rate for the on-set of depression was 30. Nowadays it is fifteen. The figures for depression are particularly high in the US but a similar pattern in the rise and age profile of those vulnerable to depression can be seen throughout the western world.

Seligman outlines a number of more specific reasons why changes in culture are making people, particularly the young, vulnerable to depression.

i. Meaning

Seligman argues that one of the inevitable casualties of the rise of individualism is 'meaning': 'The individual, the consuming self, isolated from larger entities, is a very poor site for a meaningful life. However, the bloated self is fertile soil for the growth of depression'. But why should this be? In his most recent work, *Authentic Happiness*, Seligman argues that meaning and happiness are inextricably linked and that we need to serve goals larger than ourselves. Here he expresses this idea but makes more of the fact that if people are isolated from larger concerns they will believe that all that matters in life is what happens to them. This means that the set-backs, failures and problems which are an inevitable part of life can become overwhelming and so they often feel unable to cope. Previous generations were consoled during difficult times by patriotism, the belief in the importance of the family or the wider community and their faith in God. This not only provided solace and consolation it also buffered people from depression.

ii. The importance of bad feelings

This tendency to overemphasise the negativity of events going wrong in your life has also, according to Seligman, been exaggerated and encouraged by the self-esteem movement. As a psychologist he is very aware that 'strong emotions such as anxiety, depression, and anger, exist for a purpose: they galvanize you into action to change yourself or your world, and by doing so to terminate the negative emotion'. Feeling bad can help us learn to become more optimistic and to overcome feelings of helplessness. Inevitably, such feelings carry pain but they are an effective 'alarm system' which warns us of 'danger, loss, and trespass'. Artificially trying to protect children from bad feelings will undermine their development, rather than aid it.

iii. Flow

Professor Mihaly Csikszentmihalyi's concept of flow (ie, becoming totally engaged in an absorbing activity) will be described in more detail in later chapters. Seligman uses it in *The Optimistic Child* to point out that flow, an important ingredient in a full and satisfying life, only occurs when we are involved in activities that stretch and challenge us. This is why he writes: 'the cushioning of frustration, the premature alleviation of anxiety, and learning to avoid the highest challenges all impede flow'. Again, trying to protect children from bad feelings, such as frustration, will undermine their quality of life, and development, not enhance it.

iv. Persistence

Seligman explains another way bad feelings can be put to good use under the heading 'persistence'. He points out that any complex task involves a series of steps that can lead to failure. If the child gives up too early then they will learn to become 'helpless' and not experience 'mastery':

> *In order for your child to experience mastery, it is necessary for him to fail, to feel bad, and try again repeatedly until success occurs. None of these steps can be circumvented. Failure and feeling bad are necessary building blocks for ultimate success and feeling good.*

Quite simply, 'children need to fail'. This is why he argues that if we try to protect them from this we shall reduce their mastery and hence their authentic self-esteem.

Seligman's conclusions

Seligman argues convincingly that a much better way forward is to abandon the feeling good injunctions of the self-esteem movement and to concentrate instead on explanatory style, and teaching children the skills involved in optimism and enhancing resilience. (*We shall return to these topics in later chapters.*)

Writing in 1995 Seligman also predicts that what is happening in schools and the 'feel good ethic' in general will lead to the production of low self-esteem 'on a massive scale'. However, this is not the conclusion of Professor Jean Twenge. She agrees fundamentally with the analysis Seligman outlines in *The Optimistic Child*. She provides further evidence of the rise of anxiety and depression in young people, and like him thinks that this is an outcome of the self-esteem movement. But she also shows that the self-esteem movement has encouraged the rise of self-esteem in young people, as well as an obsession with self and narcissism.

'Generation Me'

Dr Jean Twenge is currently an associate professor of psychology at San Diego State University. Her book *Generation Me*, published in 2006, is the result of thirteen years of unique research into generational differences. When she was a young psychology researcher, Twenge realised that from the 1950s onwards psychology students and more serious researchers had undertaken a myriad of research projects into the attitudes and personality traits of school children and college students. Many of them had used exactly the same questionnaires as measurement tools. What Twenge did was to locate all these thousands of studies and put them together into a meta-analysis, with data from 1.3m young Americans. Her goal was to assess shifts over time. The book is the outcome of twelve different research projects in which she has been involved along the way.

Generational shifts

Self-esteem and other characteristics may have a genetic component but they are also affected by the prevailing environment. Twenge argues that her book corroborates an ancient Arab proverb which says: 'Men resemble their times more than they resemble their fathers'. In other words, her research shows that there have been huge shifts in the attitudes and personalities of young people in the US over the last few decades.

Twenge is not the first researcher to talk about generational shifts in attitudes. Ideas of this type are the mainstay of market research. But her work is unique because it is based on detailed psychological data from the 1950s onwards. From her research Twenge describes two generations. The first comprises the baby boomers who were born between 1946, at the close of the Second World War, and the late 1960s. This older generation has been the subject of much prior analysis. The second generation she describes includes the people born in the 1970s, 1980s and 1990s. This later generation therefore includes those currently at school, right up to those in their mid 30s. She calls this group Generation Me.

One of the big differences between the generations is the importance of the self. As part of her research, she examined almost 70,000 college students' responses to the Rosenberg Self-Esteem Scale. What she discovered was that by the mid 1990s, 'the average GenMe college man' had higher self-esteem than 86 per cent of college men in 1968. The figure for women was 71 per cent. Similar trends have been shown in children's attitudes to themselves. Twenge argues that what is mysterious about their high self-esteem figures is that the late 1980s and 1990s were not very child-friendly and divorce rates were high – something that often affects how children feel about themselves.

Twenge argues that the self-esteem figures rose over this period not just because of baby boomers' parenting style but because they were systematically subjected to self-esteem building exercises in school. The various techniques and approaches used have been outlined elsewhere in this section. Twenge argues that this has had profound implications for the personalities, attitudes and skills of Generation Me.

The rise in narcissism and entitlement

As Twenge points out, psychologists agree that narcissism is not a positive personality trait. Narcissists are overly focused on themselves, find it difficult to empathise with others, often manipulate others to achieve their goals and can be very hostile, if not downright aggressive, if they do not get the respect they think they are due. As a result of these traits, narcissists often find it difficult to sustain relationships with others. Lillian G. Katz, who works at the University of Illinois Early Childhood and Parenting Collaborative, believes that some school self-esteem programmes encourage an excessive focus on the self and may have unwanted effects. 'As commendable as it is for children to have high self-esteem, many of the practices advocated in pursuit of this goal may instead inadvertently develop narcissism in the form of excessive preoccupation with oneself', writes Katz.

Twenge has indeed found in her research that narcissism is much more common now than in past generations. Only 12 per cent of teenagers in the early 1950s agreed with the statement 'I am an important person' but by the late 1980s this had risen to 80 per cent. Other psychologists have also found a rise in narcissistic personality traits. Twenge links the rise of narcissism with the growing sense of 'entitlement' among Generation Me. She says this can take the form of students 'demanding' better grades, irrespective of the effort they have put in, or speeding drivers and road rage which have become increasingly a feature of contemporary society.

Twenge points out that the everyday culture which surrounds 'GenMe' also supports a narcissistic focus on the self. This can be seen in the lyrics of songs like Whitney Houston's classic 'The Greatest Love of All', which turns out to be for yourself. It can also be seen in the countless magazine articles and pop psychology books on relationships that often promote the idea that loving yourself and being your own best friend is more important than forming relationships. In fact if you feel too attached to others it will be labelled 'co-dependency'. All of this turns on its head the psychological research which repeatedly shows that the most important thing for happiness is not self-love but good stable relationships.

Unrealistic ambitions

Twenge presents evidence to show that 'GenMe' have much higher ambitions for themselves than previous generations and that it is not difficult to understand why: they grew up repeatedly being told they could become whatever they wanted to and to believe in themselves and to 'follow their dream'. These expectations are often to earn some kind of advanced academic award and to make a lot of money. No doubt as a result of the mass media, many now want to have careers in acting, sport, music, media, etc, even though they often do not put in the effort necessary to really excel at such pursuits. Twenge repeatedly points out that the problem for these young people is that they have big dreams of success and money for themselves at a time when competition for jobs and access to higher education has never been tougher.

Depression, anxiety and loneliness

Twenge, like Seligman, presents evidence on the rise of depression in the US, particularly in young people. But she goes further than this and looks at the incidence of anxiety. She analysed data on over 40,000 college students and 12,000 children who completed anxiety measures between the 1950s and 1990s. As she says herself, the results are stunning: anxiety increased so much that the average college student in the 1990s was more anxious than 85 per cent of students in the 1950s and 71 per cent of students in the 1970s. The trend for children was even more striking: children as young as nine years old were markedly more anxious than kids had been in the 1950s. The change was so large that 'normal' schoolchildren in the 1980s reported higher levels of anxiety than child psychiatric patients in the 1950s. This may help to explain why the suicide rate for children under fourteen has doubled in the past 25 years.

Another startling finding from Twenge's research is that 'when' you are born now has more influence on your anxiety levels than your family background. In other words, young people from stable, loving families are more vulnerable and more at risk from anxiety because of the times in which they live.

Like Seligman, Twenge argues that one of the reasons why depression and mental health problems have increased is that the pre-occupation with 'the self' means that when life is challenging or disappointing young people cannot put it in perspective. But she believes that it is also because young people are much more lonely and isolated than before. Research indicates that four times more Americans nowadays describe themselves as 'lonely' as compared with those in 1957. Twenge believes that for young people this loneliness often results from the collapse of dating, later marriage and a high divorce rate. The frequent moves demanded by modern business can compound the problem. Echoing the famous line from Janis Joplin's song, 'freedom is just another word for nothing left to lose', Twenge argues that young people pay dearly for their values of independence, freedom and putting themselves first. She writes: 'I often feel that many of us are one breakup, or one move away from depression – our roots are not deep enough, our support system too shallow.'

In one of the most perceptive passages in the book, Twenge writes:

> *One of the strangest things about modern life is the expectation that we will stand alone, negotiating break-ups, moves, divorces, and all manner of heartbreak that previous generations were careful to avoid. This may be the key to the low rate of depression among older generations: despite all the deprivation and war they experienced, they could always count on each other.*

Cynicism and feelings of control

One of the most significant findings of Twenge's research is that young people increasingly believe that they are not masters of their own fate. An important concept in psychology is 'locus of control'. A significant difference between people is whether they believe they are in control of their own lives and have an 'internal' locus of control or whether they think their lives are determined by others or by fate – an 'external' locus of control. Research repeatedly illustrates that people who believe in the power of external forces are more likely to suffer from depression and anxiety and to get stressed easily. They are less likely to work hard (what's the point?) and so do less well educationally. They are also more likely to blame others for problems and to claim to be victims. Feeling powerless they are also more likely to be cynical about politics and see little point in becoming involved in collective action.

Twenge believes that one of the most significant features of her research is that it shows an extremely large shift from internal to external locus of control in young people in the US. Indeed her research shows that 'external control beliefs increased about 50 per cent between the 1960s and the 2000s'.

The links between feelings of powerlessness and self-esteem

Twenge argues that the emphasis on the self, and self-esteem in particular, is mainly responsible for the increase in external locus of control. This is how she explains this apparent paradox:

> *Suppose that you're a student and you fail a test. If you acknowledge that you were lazy about studying – or just plain stupid – your self-esteem will suffer. If you can blame the teacher's unfair test, however, you can slide through the experience still feeling good about yourself. We say that bad things aren't our fault.*

In other words, if you continually tell young people that they can achieve anything in life if they just believe in themselves and want it badly enough, then failure can be so difficult to bear, and so much a poor reflection on the self, that it is often better for them to believe life has treated them unfairly than to accept the truth of their own shortcomings.

Applicability of Twenge's research

Jean Twenge's research is on changes in young people's attitudes in the US. However, given the influence of the mass media and the rise of individualism and materialism round the globe, much of what she describes is also relevant outside America, albeit in a somewhat diluted form.

Twenge's research warns us of the dangers of stumbling into this territory, unarmed by a sound knowledge of research to guide and encourage good practice in the classroom. It must become essential reading for educators in Scotland interested in how they can encourage the development of 'confident individuals'.

'The Costly Pursuit of Self-Esteem'

> *The person who is not concerned with feeling worthy, and valuable, or with avoiding feelings of worthlessness, is a rarity in American culture.*
>
> Jennifer Crocker and Lora E Park

Jennifer Crocker is a professor of psychology at the University of Michigan and she has conducted extensive empirical research into self-esteem. Like Baumeister and Emler she is critical of the claims of the self-esteem movement and, like Twenge and Seligman, critical of some of their practices. However, Crocker takes a different tack. Understanding her research and theories helps us to understand further why self-esteem building may undermine well-being and be counterproductive.

Crocker's research

Crocker argues that those studying self-esteem are usually only interested in the level of an individual's self-esteem and whether it correlates with certain outcomes such as academic performance or aggression. Since recent studies suggest that self-esteem is not as important as previously thought, the whole topic of self-esteem is now being dismissed as irrelevant by many psychologists. However, Crocker argues that self-esteem does play an important part in people's lives in a way that often goes unrecognised. She argues that, in American culture at least, individuals take steps to prove their worth and that this 'pursuit of self-esteem' has high costs as it can undermine individuals' well-being and their relationships.

The pursuit of self-esteem

Crocker argues that individuals have two different levels of self-esteem. The first is 'trait' self-esteem, which includes the general sense of self-worth that an individual has about him/herself and which seems to be determined, in part, genetically. This means that some individuals are born with high, or low, self-esteem. However, individuals' self-esteem also varies on a day-by-day basis depending on external circumstances such as successes, failures, mistakes, and so on. This means that individuals who have high trait self-esteem will still suffer from fluctuations in their self-esteem, as will people who have low self-esteem. She argues that these variations can feel unpleasant and motivate the individual to avoid situations where their self-esteem might be compromised. She writes:

> *People are not merely passive victims, their self-esteem tossed around by events over which they have no control. Instead, they actively pursue self-esteem by attempting to validate or prove their abilities or qualities in the domains in which their self-worth is invested.*

In a paper co-authored with Lora Park, Crocker argues that the pursuit of self-esteem goals is widespread in the US because of deeply held beliefs within the culture. She particularly cites 'the Protestant ethic' which links a person's worth with their accomplishments. This is further heightened, she argues, with the American emphasis on 'self-reliance' and individualism. What is more, the Protestant ethic and self-reliance have led to the 'belief in a meritocracy' and this too has fuelled the idea that some individuals are 'worthier' than others. Crocker and Park write:

> *Taken together these ideas lead Americans to conclude that their worth or value as individuals is not a given, but must be demonstrated, proven, or earned; consequently they pursue self-esteem. The goal is to be superior to other people ... and the corresponding fear is to be worthless – to fail as an individual, lacking personal qualities that make one worthy and valuable.*

This belief system is also prevalent in parts of Europe, particularly Scotland which has also been greatly influenced by Calvinism and the Protestant ethic. Crocker and Park are, however, at pains to point out that such a belief system is alien to eastern cultures, such as Japan where ideas of interdependence and belonging are strong. It is also alien in many native cultures where individuals are an integral part of kinship and social groups. In other words, they do not have to prove their worth to gain respect or feel they belong to the group.

Like Seligman, Crocker admits that boosts to self-esteem that arise from success or praise, for example, can feel fantastic. However, she also argues that while these may temporarily feel good, unless an individual can guarantee that they only ever succeed and do not fail, this boosted self-esteem level will inevitably drop. Even if it only drops back to its normal level, the individual often experiences a feeling of deflation and the desire for another additional boost of feeling good from success. Indeed Crocker maintains that the pursuit of self-esteem can become 'addictive' but ultimately counterproductive since it undermines rather than contributes to individuals' long-term well-being. Why?

The 'costs' of pursuing self-esteem

Like many contemporary psychologists, Crocker subscribes to the Self-Determination theory of Professors Edward Deci and Richard Ryan. This theory, which is supported by international empirical research, asserts that for individuals to thrive and experience well-being they need the opportunity for 'competence', 'relatedness' and 'autonomy'. Like Deci and Ryan, Crocker argues that the pursuit of self-esteem can distract individuals from fulfilling these basic needs and may actually conflict with them, thus undermining well-being.

i. Costs to 'autonomy'

The notion of autonomy is not about being an independent individual but about feeling that we can choose our own actions and be motivated by intrinsic goals. According to Crocker when an individual pursues self-esteem this is about being 'worthy' in the eyes of others and so autonomy is compromised. For example, this pursuit could mean studying certain subjects to get good grades or impress others rather than being motivated by interest and personal satisfaction.

ii. Costs to learning and competence

The basic need of competence is about being able to learn and grow as an individual. Crocker argues that when individuals are driven by self-esteem, learning and growth take a back seat and it is egotistical goals that are in control. Thus failure which may present an individual with opportunities for learning and growth may not be faced up to by a person intent on building, or protecting self-esteem, and he or she is much more likely to find excuses for the failure. Crocker writes:

> *When people discount, dismiss, or excuse their mistakes and failures, they are unable to appraise their flaws and shortcomings realistically to identify what they need to learn. Even if the test is unfair, the evaluation is biased, or there is a good excuse for failure, there is often some important information or lesson to be learned from these negative experiences. Yet, when people have the goal of validating their worth, they do not seem open to these lessons.*

There is an expression which sums up some of Crocker and Park's reservations about the pursuit of self-esteem – 'anything that is worth doing is worth doing badly'. There are all sorts of activities such as dancing, music, singing, art, for example, which hold huge growth potential and fulfilment for individuals but they are often avoided because people fear they will not prove their worth through participation in such activities.

iii. Costs to relationships

For Crocker the biggest downside of the pursuit of self-esteem is relatedness. She maintains that by focusing on one's own needs (eg to win or appear worthy) an individual ignores others' needs and feelings and this undermines relationships. Quoting her own empirical research,

Crocker argues that when people pursue their own ego needs they are not 'present' to support others. The fact that not everyone can be a winner and that competition is a zero sum game compounds this problem. The temptation to blame others also injures relationships with other people.

The pursuit of self-esteem affects relationships irrespective of whether the individual has high or low trait self-esteem. Crocker claims that research shows that people with high self-esteem often sacrifice their relationships (eg others' needs and feelings) for their achievements. Those with low self-esteem often indulge in reassurance, seeking from others, which can be annoying and undermine their relationships. Those with low self-esteem can also be overly sensitive to rejection. Research shows that 'rejection sensitivity' can lead to hostility and jealousy, both of which undermine relationships.

iv. Health costs

Crocker argues that as well as undermining the fulfilment of our need for autonomy, competence and relatedness, pursuing egotistical goals undermines an individual's health. Although she argues that more research is needed to substantiate this claim, she asserts it is reasonable to conclude that the anxiety individuals have about failures and mistakes leads to stress and therefore undermines their physical health. She also argues that when self-esteem plummets as a result of failure it is not uncommon for individuals to turn to alcohol or to go on eating binges that further compromise their health.

Finally Crocker argues that there are mental health costs to pursuing self-esteem. She acknowledges that some research shows that those who are low in self-esteem are more vulnerable to depression but still maintains that the pursuit of self-esteem goals can lead to depression no matter what the individual's level. The longitudinal research carried out by Twenge, and summarised above, certainly supports Crocker's conclusion, since Twenge shows that while self-esteem has risen in the US over the past few decades (as a result of the self-esteem movement) so has narcissism, depression and anxiety.

Criticism of Crocker's work

Followers of Ayn Rand and Nathaniel Branden are critical of Crocker's work. They point out that she is a social psychologist and so sees self-esteem as contingent on others' opinions. As extreme individualists they believe that humans are able to base self-esteem on their own, rather than others', judgements. Crocker accepts that if it were possible to have self-esteem which was not dependent on others' views then some of the costs she identifies would disappear. However, she argues that research indicates that, in the US at least, people with 'non-contingent' self-esteem are a 'rarity'.

At the Centre we firmly accept the view that the individual self is more of a social being than a separate individual, and so we accept Crocker's view that non-contingent self-esteem is very difficult to achieve. We believe that it is possible to train yourself to stop evaluating yourself using others' views, but the thinking and methodology we accept for doing this is more in tune with the ideas and practices promoted by theorists such as Albert Ellis, a staunch critic of self-esteem theorists such as Nathaniel Branden.

'The Diminished Self'

> *The therapeutic imperative is not so much towards the realisation of self-fulfilment as the promotion of self-limitation.*
>
> Frank Furedi

Seligman's argument, that attempts to build young people's self-esteem undermine mastery, was outlined at the beginning of the chapter. However, it is Professor Frank Furedi in the UK who has done most to show how the elevation of ideas about self-esteem, and related psychological concepts such as emotional intelligence, undermine and disempower individuals. Furedi sets out his ideas in a book entitled *Therapy Culture*. Personally, I find aspects of the book off-putting, such as his unspoken desire just to turn the clock back to the

1950s and his complete lack of answers to any of the problems he adumbrates. I also find aspects of Furedi's analysis myopic – such as his failure to acknowledge the damaging effects of advertising or the mass media. However, it is impossible to read Furedi's book and not feel uneasy. It certainly had this affect on Alan McLean who read it and promptly wrote one of his most interesting pieces for *The Times Educational Supplement.*

At the beginning of *Therapy Culture* Furedi makes clear that he is not disputing the value of a genuinely therapeutic relationship between a practitioner and client. What he is critiquing is how ideas from psychology, psychotherapy and counselling have insinuated their way into everyday culture. In contemplating the ideas behind 'therapy culture' Furedi rightly traces back their origins to earlier, humanistic psychologists such as Carl Rogers and Abraham Maslow. Maslow's 'hierarchy of needs' is still much quoted and it is widely known that Maslow saw the pinnacle of human need to be'self-actualization'. However, Furedi argues that paradoxically the movement which Rogers and Maslow spawned has not led to a strong, actualized self, focused on self-improvement and transcendence, but a self which is 'fragile' and 'diminished'.

In the course of the book Furedi sets out a number of different arguments in support of the idea of a 'diminished self'. The following is a summary of the most relevant to our look at self-esteem.

Fragile self-esteem

The fixation with self-esteem easily leads to the idea that people's feelings and emotions are fragile and easily affected by their environment. This view is extended not just to individuals but to groups. Furedi writes:

> *The proposition that certain groups suffer from a collective state of low self-esteem is grounded in the so-called damage theory of personality. According to this theory, the experience of racism and oppression permanently damage the psyches of the victim, consigning them to a permanent state of low self-esteem.*

Furedi argues that this sense of collective, damaged self-esteem is extended beyond race and oppression to whole communities or even generations. This view of the world suggests people to be vulnerable – easy prey to forces that undermine their strengths and leave them weakened and disempowered.

Help-seeking

In the past, people in the UK and some other western cultures valued stoicism and containment of emotional expression – hence the British notion of 'the stiff upper lip' or British reserve. According to Furedi, in the new climate of emotionalism this is frowned on and seen as a sign of weakness. People are now expected to talk about their problems openly. This can be seen in the endless confessionals of celebrities and in how ordinary people too are prepared to air their feelings in the media. However, it is not so much friends and family that we are encouraged to open up to but professionals. There is now a widespread assumption that individuals need help from countless experts such as counsellors or other professionals.

The vulnerable self

In the past people were seen as being able to cope on their own or with the help of their family or community. The factors mentioned above, when combined with other forces Furedi outlines, lead to a view of people based on implicit notions of weakness, vulnerability and risk, rather than strength and agency. Nowadays people do not have distressing experiences – they are 'traumatised' or 'victimised'. Either way it undermines the notion of resilience – of being able to triumph over adversity.

Positive Psychology

Furedi is undiscriminating in his book – everything associated with psychology's impact on the culture is roundly criticised. Like many critics of self-esteem he is still on occasion positive about the concept of 'confidence' since this is more about taking action than simply about how people feel about themselves.

In his book Furedi gives very little inkling of how he thinks the weakening effect of 'therapy culture' can be overcome and how we can move towards a culture which is more conducive to a notion of human strength and positive action and development. But this is exactly what Professor Martin Seligman and others are trying to do with Positive Psychology. These ideas, and what they have to offer schools, will be outlined in Chapter 14. It is worth pointing out here that this is the framework which the Centre for Confidence and Well-being has adopted since its inception in 2005.

We share Furedi's concern that what has been lost in recent years is a sense of agency and transformative action. However, unlike him we think that there are actions we can take. Here, and elsewhere, the Centre advises against underpinning confidence with notions of self-esteem, and how the individual feels about the self. We think it is much better to use more dynamic notions of confidence: namely our ability to act in the world and to think optimistically.

Key Points

1. Most of the self-esteem building practices in America have been about encouraging 'unwarranted self-esteem' – ie where it is not tied to performance or virtuous behaviour. Teaching children the 'skills of doing well' is a much better way to build self-esteem.
2. The excessive focus on the importance of feeling good, encouraged by the self-esteem movement, leads people to get life's natural ups and downs out of perspective. This then makes them vulnerable to depression.
3. Depression in the US, and elsewhere in the west, has increased twenty fold. Psychologists, like Seligman, attribute much of this rise to individualism and the decline of meaning and purpose in people's lives.
4. We are not doing children a service by trying to protect them from bad feelings. Such feelings have a purpose – eg they galvanise people to take action.
5. Frustration, and negative emotion, are inevitable parts of the learning process. Children need to be taught to persist.
6. Since self-esteem became a central part of the curriculum in American schools, narcissism has started to rise, as have young people's depression and anxiety.
7. Loneliness has quadrupled since the 1950s. Some critics like Jean Twenge argue this is because of the excessive focus on the self which is a part of the ethos of the self-esteem movement.
8. An unexpected result of the rise of self-esteem in the US is the increase in the number of young people who do not feel responsible for their lives and have a tendency to blame others for their problems. This has led to feelings of powerlessness and cynicism.
9. One of the main problems with self-esteem may not be its level or what it correlates with, but the pursuit of self-esteem.
10. Individuals pursue self-esteem goals as they think they must prove their worth: this is part of the legacy of the Protestant work ethic.
11. Pursuing self-esteem goals undermines an individual's well-being as it interferes with relationships, learning, a sense of control and personal satisfaction.
12. If we are keen to create 'confident individuals' in Scotland, and pay attention to well-being, we need to pay heed to what psychologists in the US are saying about the dangers of trying to boost self-esteem or encourage self-esteem goals.
13. Paradoxically, much of the current emphasis on psychology and counselling in the culture is undermining the idea of self-realisation and leading instead to people feeling vulnerable and in need of constant help from professionals.

America's Shame, Scotland's Gain?

> *Today begins a new era, a new time in public education in our country. As of this hour, America's schools will be on a new path of reform, and a new path of results. Our schools will have higher expectations. We believe every child can learn. Our schools will have greater resources to help meet those goals. Parents will have more information about the schools, and more say in how their children are educated. From this day forward, all students will have a better chance to learn, to excel, and to live out their dreams.*
>
> President George W. Bush, January 8, 2002

For decades now Scotland has been a magnet for inward investment from the US. Often the companies cite the skills of the workforce as one of their reasons for locating here. When they are in operation, leaders of American companies often say how impressed they are by the skills and work ethic of their Scottish employees. However, they are usually aware too of the Scots' proclivity to pessimism, negativity and 'cannae dae' attitudes.

If we look at America's academic record we can see why Scotland, despite its negativity bias, is an attractive location. For decades now America's record on educational achievement has become a national scandal. Here are a few statistics that show the extent of the problem.

1. American high school students are continually at the bottom of the league for developed nations in maths and science, outranking only Cyprus and South Africa.
2. 73 per cent of public school eighth graders taking the National Assessment of Education Progress (NAEP)'s mathematics exam in 2003 performed below the 'proficiency' level. 32 per cent performed below the 'basic' level.
3. 70 per cent of public school eighth graders taking the NAEP's reading exam in 2003 performed below the 'proficiency' level.
4. About half of college students need to attend remedial classes in maths or English. It is estimated that $16.6 billion a year are spent trying to improve the basic academic skills of students in the US.
5. *Education Week* concluded in 1999 that 'most fourth graders who live in US cities can't read and understand a simple children's book, and most eighth graders can't use arithmetic to solve a practical problem'.

As this data shows, academic achievement is not only a problem for students but there are also millions of children, particularly from poor backgrounds, who never master basic skills.

Interestingly, during a period that witnessed an acute drop in academic standards, America suffered from grade inflation. In 2004, 48 per cent of first year college students reported getting an A average in high school. The equivalent figure in 1968 was 18 per cent.

The Nation's response

There has been considerable activity in the US in recent years to remedy the problem. Much of this has been at state level. But since 2002, as the above quote from President Bush shows, there has been a big push at federal level to improve academic standards. Part of President Bush's initiative is called 'No Child Left Behind' and it is an attempt to improve educational standards at the bottom end. At the same time there has been a great deal of effort to improve America's world-wide competitiveness by improving educational standards, particularly in maths and science. This has led to various initiatives designed to target potential high achievers. Commentators point out that there is a great deal of tension between these two agendas. What is interesting from our point of view is what they have done to make these improvements and the benefits which have been won.

i. Money, money, money

As educational attainment figures have dropped more and more states have thrown money at the problem. Between 1960 and 1990 class sizes decreased by a third and teachers' salaries tripled. Since 2001, federal spending on education has increased by $15 billion – an increase of almost 40 per cent. Spending on programmes designed to improve teacher quality has reached almost $3 billion under the Bush administration. This allows local school districts to use federal funds to hire new teachers, increase teacher pay, and improve teacher training and development.

ii. Tougher standards

Twenty years ago a physican called John Jacob Cannell undertook some private research which he published as the 'Lake Woebegone reports'. He named them after the mythical Minnesota town created by Garrison Keillor where 'all the women are strong, all the men are good-looking, and all the children above average'. The first of Cannell's reports documented that all 50 states 'were testing above the national average in elementary achievement and concluded the testing infrastructure in America's public schools was corrupt'. The second of his reports outlined what he called 'the systematic and pervasive ways that American educators cheat on standardized achievement tests'.

Cannell's two reports received a huge amount of publicity and spawned what is now referred to as the movement for 'tougher standards'. During the 1990s this movement led to increased testing in many states. Schools that did not perform well were sanctioned or put on probation, while the high performing ones were rewarded. Individual pupils who failed were held back a grade. This 'high stakes' testing, as it is called, is now mandated by law as part of President Bush's No Child Left Behind initiative.

A battle royal now rages in America between 'the tough standards' lobby who see rote learning, homework and testing as the way to drive up standards, and more liberal educators who decry such a crude approach to education.

iii. America's report card

The National Association for Educational Progress produces an annual Report Card on the state of American education. In their latest report (2005) they are quite candid that all the pump priming (and presumably introduction of more tests) is hardly making a difference. They write: 'When will public policy makers finally understand that simply focusing on reducing classroom size, pumping more and more money into public schools, raising expenditures per pupil, hiring more school staff, and raising teacher salaries will not improve learning?'

The link between low standards and self-esteem

One of the great ironies about standards in America is that while their young people do not score well academically, they are very positive about their own achievements. For example, one survey showed that American pupils were likely to rate themselves as good at maths even though their competency was low on tests. The opposite was true for Korean students.

In the past decade two books have been published which link the crisis in standards with the ethos and practices of the self-esteem movement: *Dumbing Down our Kids: why American Children Feel Good about Themselves but Can't Read, Write,* or *Add* by Charles J. Sykes and *The Feel-Good Curriculum: The Dumbing Down of American Kids in the Name of Self-esteem* by an educational psychologist called Maureen Stout. However, these arguments are not ones routinely discussed in the debate on how to raise standards in American schools. (Testimony perhaps to Lauren Slater's argument outlined in Chapter 2 that the belief in the importance of self-esteem is so much part of the American psyche that the nation cannot bear to examine the facts.)

A whole range of reasons have been advanced to explain why American standards have dropped, including that of dumbing down textbooks after the war, types of reading schemes adopted, the lack of standardized tests and so forth. No doubt there is something in these arguments. But it is also very likely that the ethos and practices driven by the self-esteem movement have played an important contributory part. It doesn't take much imagination or analysis to see that the following could easily lead to grade inflation, demotivation and lowered standards:

- unwarranted praise
- protecting children from criticism, failure and mistakes
- not encouraging children to persevere in case it makes them feel bad
- outlawing competition or opportunities for some children to be seen to achieve
- taking time in the school day for children to focus excessively on themselves and their feelings.

American employers

The decline in academic standards and basic literacy and numeracy is a major problem for American employers. Even a decade ago it was estimated that American employers spend in excess of $30 billion a year training their employees in basic skills. What is more it is estimated that a similar sum is lost to employers every year as a result of employees' poor skills. Economists like John Kendrick of George Washington University and John H. Bishop from Cornell University argue that the decline in American productivity is partly attributable to the decline in academic achievement in the US.

Jean Twenge in *Generation Me* argues that employers these days also complain that young employees want to get on quickly and make lots of money but they do not want to work their way up through an organisation or put in real effort. What is more, they are very thin-skinned and do not like being corrected.

In conclusion

There's little doubt that the aims and intentions of many people involved in trying to boost young people's self-esteem have been well-meaning. However, if we combine lowered standards, poor employee skills and the depression and anxiety which psychology critics, such as Professor Martin Seligman, lay at the door of the self-esteem movement we can see that their legacy has been toxic.

Scotland

Scotland was once the most literate country in the world. Even when other countries caught up, Scotland still retained a good reputation for its education system. Although this has declined somewhat, Scotland still performs well academically. However, about twenty per cent of the population have literacy or numeracy problems and a similar number of young people perform badly in Scottish schools. This is why some people talk about Scottish education having a large 'underperforming tail'.

Scotland has a new *Curriculum for Excellence.* This emerged from the National Debate on Education, which started shortly after the new Scottish Parliament was set up. The new *CfE* has widespread support not just in Scottish education but right across Scottish life. Its vision for a balanced curriculum that maintains a focus on learning and academic skills while highlighting the importance of workplace and interpersonal skills could become the much needed focal point for real and deep-seated change. However, as this section shows, emphasising the importance of confidence carries considerable risks if it means that we follow in the footsteps of many teachers and educationalists in the US. But if we could attend to confidence issues in Scotland, while not making these same mistakes, huge benefits could accrue.

In the remaining section of the *Handbook,* I examine the better courses of action open to us in building confidence in Scottish schools. First, I want to look at confidence issues and Scottish culture.

Key Points

1. In the past few decades American academic standards have dropped and American pupils perform badly when compared to other developed countries.
2. American politicians, at both state and federal level, have spent considerable amounts of money trying to improve the problem.
3. There is now a movement in America called 'tougher standards' which is trying to improve academic performance, and standardised testing is now compulsory.
4. Despite increased expenditure and various activities, academic standards have hardly improved.
5. American critics hardly factor in self-esteem building as one of the reasons for academic decline, but it is not difficult to see why unwarranted praise and protecting children from failure and competition would lead to grade inflation and reduce motivation and learning.
6. American employers are having to spend huge sums of money on training as a result of poor school standards. This is also why countries like Scotland, where the population has good skills, act like magnets for inward investment.
7. American employers are also beginning to complain that young people have high expectations but do not want to work hard.
8. Scotland has always had a good reputation for education.
9. The broad support behind *Curriculum for Excellence* and its balanced view is a welcome opportunity for Scotland.
10. The emphasis on confidence could bring Scotland various benefits so long as we do not repeat America's mistakes in trying to boost self-esteem artificially.

confidence in Scotland

The Scottish Picture

> *The curse of Scotland is these wee hard men. I used to blame the English for our mediocrity. I thought they had colonised us by sheer cunning. They aren't very cunning. They've got more confidence and money than we have, so they can afford to lean back and smile while our own wee hard men hammer Scotland down to the same dull level as themselves.*
>
> Alasdair Gray

The Scots' Crisis of Confidence

At the beginning of the new millennium I started the research for a book which was ultimately published in 2003 called *The Scots' Crisis of Confidence*. It was the result of my experience of running courses in Scotland for more than fifteen years and reflected my abiding interest in cultural and political issues. In it I draw on Scottish history and culture to present what I hope is a plausible account for how Scottish values may unwittingly undermine individual and collective confidence. My book is unashamedly eclectic, drawing on everything from the Bible to *The Broons.*

In this chapter I summarise some of the main points of the book, particularly those that are of most relevance to young people and schools. I do this by telescoping my argument and focusing in on what I consider to be the most important barriers to confidence in the culture. I have also included some new material and perspectives. In the next chapter I present some empirical evidence to support my case.

Confidence Barrier 1: Confused Messages

When I give talks in Scotland about confidence issues I often begin by asserting that even in modern Scotland there is still the strong belief that you are 'worthless til you prove you are worthwhile'. Even though I have argued this in the presence of more than 7,000 Scots I have never been challenged on this assumption – even privately after the event. I am aware that modern culture with its emphasis on material values, good looks, celebrity status and so forth generally encourages people to feel dissatisfied with themselves. However, my contention is that for centuries Scots have been brought up with, and live with, the sense that they must prove they are worthwhile, valuable people and that if they cannot they are worthless.

But there is also a catch: unlike in the US, where people are given a simple message – go forth and use the opportunities available to prove your worth through material success – the Scots are given confused messages in the form of two competing injunctions. I often liken this tension in the culture to the sense that we are being pushed forward and held back at the same time. The push comes from our strong need to prove our worth or what we are made of as well as the hope of showing that we may be one of God's chosen people. However, as we move forward it is as if there is someone at our backs, pulling on our jackets, whispering in our ears: 'don't think you are anybody special or better than anyone else'. This can easily impede our progress by introducing the fear that trying to succeed, or being successful, carries significant risks.

The difficulties of Scottish egalitarianism can be seen if we compare our values with those of America. Their egalitarianism is founded on the idea that everyone is of equal worth and so anyone is able to get on. In other words, it is an aspirational form of egalitarianism. Of course, it is a myth to say that everyone has equal chances in life in the US, but it is a myth most of the population buy into, including poor black Americans.

Scottish egalitarian values, by contrast, are based on the notion that if everyone is equal then no-one is better than anyone else. The poet Alexander Scott summed this up pithily in his two-line poem:

> *Scotch Equality*
>
> *Kaa the feet*
> *Frae thon big bastard.*

This belief system may impede individualism and promote collective values, and so has some benefit within the culture, but it exacts a hefty price – our form of egalitarianism levels down and can easily encourage mediocrity. This may be why many Scots have achieved more when they left the country and freed themselves from these levelling down impulses.

In Scotland there has always been one area of life where it has been acceptable to get on – education. In the eighteenth and nineteenth centuries there was also a respect for business. But in the twentieth century, particularly as a result of Thatcherism and the Scots' desire to affirm their traditional values, the 'don't you think you are better…' notion was given a vital shot in the arm.

So in Scotland there is a great pressure to achieve and show that you are not worthless but, at the same time, another set of values weakens the pursuit of that achievement for fear that you might be getting above yourself. Neither set of values is great for our well-being or confidence. The fact that they conflict with one another simply makes matters worse. Being pushed forward and held back at the same time leads to inertia, frustration and feelings of powerlessness. In other words, they do not create the conditions which encourage us to feel like confident individuals or to maximise our sense of well-being.

Confidence Barrier 2: Fear of Attention

There is another broad strand in Scottish culture that also undermines confidence. What I am thinking of here is the Scots' dislike of drawing attention to themselves by speaking up in class or other public arenas. This too leads to conformity as it means people do not want to be different or put their heads above the parapet. Australians (whose culture has been influenced by Scots) call this 'the tall poppy syndrome'. Young people's fear of speaking in class may have lessened a lot in recent years but nonetheless university tutors say that Scottish students still speak less than students from other parts of the world. Teachers from England also often recount that pupils in Scottish schools are less expressive than they are in many English schools.

Confidence Barrier 3: The Fixed Mindset

When I wrote my book I devoted some time to describing what I called the perfect/worthless seesaw. This was how I tried to describe the deep Scots' desire to do everything right so that they were not criticised or blamed by others. However, in the past few years I have discovered the work of an empirical psychologist from the US, Professor Carol Dweck, and I think that her 'self theories' help us to understand much better what is going on in Scotland than does my earlier attempt. I devote the whole of Chapter 7 to Carol Dweck's work on 'mindsets'. All I intend to do here is summarise enough of her theory so that I can use these ideas to create an understanding of Scottish culture.

Dweck argues from her empirical research that there are two basic mindsets about achievement. The 'fixed mindset' upholds the idea that people's ability is fairly fixed and not open to change. According to such a view, people are either intelligent, sporty, arty, good at maths, etc, or they are not. This mindset also labels people according to personal characteristics. So people are either good or bad, caring or selfish, etc. The 'growth mindset' has a different starting point. It sees people as essentially malleable. In other words, people are not fixed but have huge potential for growth and development and that with enough motivation, effort and good teaching they can become better at almost anything. They can also change many aspects of themselves and their behaviour.

BOX 7: Comparison of fixed and growth mindsets

Effect of fixed mindset

- Ability and many personal characteristics are fixed by nature.
- Failure, mistakes and criticism must be avoided at all costs as they reveal bad things about you.
- It is riskier to try and fail than not try at all.
- If you have to work hard it shows that you are not a 'natural'.
- We must compete with others to prove that we are intelligent and have good qualities.
- Confidence is fragile and so has to be protected.

Effect of growth mindset

- Ability and many personal characteristics are malleable.
- Failure, mistakes and criticism can be helpful as they help you learn and improve.
- People improve through effort and hard work.
- It is not competition with others which is the most important thing – it is self-improvement.

In a nutshell, much of my argument about Scotland in *The Scots' Crisis of Confidence* is that we are the land of the 'fixed mindset'. Why should it be particularly strong in Scotland?

The Scots have a tendency to see everything in black or white. This tendency to polarise is characteristic of all Judaeo-Christian cultures and derives its power from the Christian belief that God is a single being who is all that is good and pure while the Devil incarnates all that is evil. (This is not the view of eastern or native religions.) In Scotland, the influence of Calvinism may have increased the tendency to polarise even further. Whatever the reason, the Scots tend to see people in very simplistic terms. They are either good or bad; clever or stupid; generous or selfish; talented or hopeless. The old Scottish proverb 'Ye're either aa dirt or aa butter' sums up such a view of people.

In 2004 Bill Duncan, a Scottish teacher and novelist, published his entertaining, though poignant, book *The Wee Book of Calvin*. The most striking feature of Duncan's distillation of the Scottish Calvinist mentality is the way that individuals – often children – are judged and labelled. Needless to say the labels are mainly damning and suggest worthlessness. One telling example from Duncan's books reads: 'Ye can tell the criminal from the face in the crib'. The philosophy Duncan darkly outlines is also predicated on the view that people do not change. This is pithily expressed in Duncan's line: 'Yer sins go doon beside yer name in the Book o no rubbin oot'.

Confidence Barrier 4: The Fear of Getting 'it' Wrong

I've been asking Scottish audiences for the past few years if they understand what 'getting it wrong' means and only about two people have said they did not. People from other cultures, including that of England, may or may not understand what this phrase means depending on their specific personality or upbringing. Again I think this idea that there is a right way to do everything and 'woe betide you if you get it wrong' acts as another check on the culture of Scottish confidence: a fear summed up admirably in the old Scots proverb: 'Better sit still than rise up an fa'.

The fear of getting 'it' wrong has at its core another assumption – that we are all the same and should be thinking and acting in the same ways. A decade or so ago I did some work with the management team of a small, international company in Dumfries. The CEO was American and had worked right round the world. In fact he was something of an expert on how countries' business cultures varied. His observations on Scotland were at one with what I am presenting here. However, for him the most remarkable factor about Scotland, which he said he had never encountered anywhere in the world, is that Scots have no concept that 'there is more than one way to skin a cat'. 'Everyone thinks there is one right way to do something and judges and criticises others for not doing it the right way', he remarked. In such an environment those with the most power or who are the most bullying or critical intimidate and undermine quieter, or less confident types. Generally, people are at their most confident when they are working on their goals and carrying out tasks in their preferred way. Trying to do something by someone else's formula will generally be more stressful and undermine confidence.

'It wisnae me'

Accompanying the fear of getting 'it' wrong is also the fear of being blamed for making mistakes. Nowadays, management consultants talk about a 'blame culture' existing in some organisations and such a culture certainly flourishes throughout Scottish life. This was admirably summed up by the journalist Douglas Fraser in his contribution to *Being Scottish*:

> *Something or somebody else must be to blame. The boss. The rich. The poor. The central belt. Lairds. Edinburgh lawyers. Subsidy junkies. Catholics. Protestants. The poll tax. The current Scotland football manager. Men. Wummin. Lanarkshire politicians. People who blame other people.*

If anything goes wrong the Scots are not likely to analyse the problem, learn from it and ensure that it does not happen again. No – in true 'fixed mindset' mentality, the hunt is on to find the 'eejit' who has made the mistake and rub his or her nose in it. In such an environment people are not likely to admit their mistakes (as this will damn them as people) and will often try to deflect the blame by saying 'it wisnae me'. In Scotland an unedifying stand-off inevitably follows when someone somewhere has messed up. Such punitive views of people's misdemeanours may even account for the fact that the Scots lock up a higher percentage of criminals, or young people who have gone off the rails, than do most European countries.

Confidence Barrier 5: Scottish Pessimism

> ***Scotch Optimism***
>
> *Through a gless*
> *Darkly.*
>
> ***Scotch Pessimism***
>
> *Nae*
> *Gless.*
>
> Alexander Scott

A fifth barrier to confidence (and well-being) in Scotland is the prevalence of pessimism. A later chapter is devoted to optimism and pessimism and in it I set out detailed definitions of these terms. All I intend to do here is give a brief description and present a plausible argument for why pessimism is an issue in Scotland.

Optimism and pessimism can be defined in two broad ways. The first way is to see it as an attitude, or disposition, where an individual either focuses on problems and what is wrong or on opportunities and what is good. Seeing the glass as half full or half empty is a good way to think about this way of defining optimism and pessimism. Another way of defining optimism and pessimism, advanced by Professor Martin Seligman and others, is based on what they call 'explanatory style'. What this means is how we interpret good and bad events.

For example, when things go wrong do we see the problem as –

- permanent or temporary
- pervasive or restricted to this one thing
- personal (ie my fault) or the result of a number of other factors.

Using either definition it is easy to notice the prevalence of pessimistic thinking in Scotland when you listen to people's conversations, read newspapers, listen to what is said on TV or radio or pay attention to what politicians and people involved in sport say. Scottish pessimism is particularly noticeable in the face of good events: we don't expect them to last and tend to see them as a 'fluke'. An additional feature is that Scots commonly see good fortune not simply as something that is temporary but as something which they will need 'to pay for'.

It is not too difficult to work out why the Scots may have a particular proclivity to pessimistic thinking. The first reason is the influence which Calvinism historically had on Scottish culture. If you are brought up to believe that life should be hard and that human beings are worthless then you are being schooled to think pessimistically. The second reason is emigration. In *The Optimistic Child* Professor Martin Seligman writes about the people who left Europe and Asia and emigrated to the USA:

> *What kind of mentality does it take to feel oppressed by caste and class, to leave family and possessions behind, and to journey in the hope of a better life? Optimism. These men and women had it in abundance and they became a nation of optimists.*

If the USA is the land of migrants and optimism then is Scotland the land of emigrants and pessimism? Here are a few facts which support the idea that this might be the case. Historians argue that examining international data shows that for almost a hundred years Scotland 'emerges clearly as the emigration capital of Europe for most of the period'. There are many reasons why emigrants choose to leave their homeland. Experts refer to them as the 'push/pull' factors. The Scots were, as we know from the clearances, often pushed by landlords who wanted to do something else with their estates. They were also pushed to leave Scotland by unemployment, poverty and atrocious living conditions. But often it was not those suffering the poorest conditions who left. Many emigrated because they were pulled by the opportunities and the possibilities of life in a new country. Emigration attracted Scots who had reasonable lives in Scotland but who believed that they could have even better lives and opportunities if they went to other lands. In other words, emigration siphoned off many of the Scots who were the most optimistic. This is very likely to have intensified pessimism within Scottish culture. Of course, Scotland was also a destination for immigrants from Ireland and other countries but until recent times out-migration was always larger than in-migration.

Confidence Barrier 6: Social Class

The centrepiece of the opening of the Scottish Parliament was undoubtedly Sheena Wellington's beautiful rendition of Robert Burns's 'A Man's a Man for a' that'. In the speech that followed, First Minister Donald Dewar reminded us that 'at the heart of the song is a very Scottish conviction: that honesty and simple dignity are priceless virtues not imparted by rank or birth but part of the very soul'.

But while we believe class should not matter – that human beings are equal – Scottish statistics tell us a different story. It may be painful for modern Scots to accept, but Scotland is a society deeply divided by social class. Educational attainment, life expectancy, physical health, mental health and crime – all are affected by wealth and postcode. This is a real, physical divide. Stand at the railway line which separates the affluent Glasgow suburb of Bearsden from Drumchapel, one of Scotland's poorest housing estates, or go to countless other points around Scotland and you will see this divide with your own eyes. The life expectancy rate for men in areas of Glasgow is 54 – that is twenty years less than in affluent areas.

As elsewhere in the United Kingdom, as Scotland becomes wealthier, the class divide widens. Poverty is getting worse in Scottish society and it is often accompanied by the great scourges of modern life – unemployment, alcoholism and drugs, which then exacerbate the problem of poor housing or lack of resources.

Nowadays we often refer to poverty as 'social exclusion'. We understand that the problem is not just about money but it is about a group of people being excluded from modern society. What I think we have failed to do is recognise that the problem has psychological components. Recently, I spoke to a woman from China who is living in Scotland, as she has married a Scot, and her view of Scotland is illuminating:

> *What is tragic about Scotland and which makes me so sad is your poor people. They feel worthless and they have no hope. Our poor people are simply poor. They don't feel bad about themselves and they hope that one day they will have better lives.*

Could it be that the particular characteristics I have outlined above for Scottish culture – feelings of worthlessness, the lack of a growth mindset and feelings of pessimism – are particularly strong for the poorest members of society? Is this why Glasgow has more than 90,000 people of economically active age out of work – often on disability benefit – rather than in the jobs which exist in the city and which are increasingly filled by migrants? Is this why Scotland as a whole has a much bigger problem with the Not in Education, Employment or Training (NEET) group? Scottish figures for the NEET group are higher than for other UK and European countries.

Relevance of these barriers to the present day

People reading this in the new millennium may think that citing facts about Scotland's Reformation or quoting literary types on nineteenth century Scotland is irrelevant. What affects young people today is celebrity culture, advertising and the mass media. Of course, this is true but they are also socialised by parents and teachers who pass on a value and belief system to them. This is what makes us Scottish as opposed to English, American or French. And this belief system, though diluted over the centuries, is still urging us to be careful about drawing attention to ourselves, that it is a terrible thing to make a mistake and that if we do anything wrong we will be harshly criticised, blamed and punished. Looking at Scottish history also helps us understand why there are still, in contemporary Scotland, the vestiges of the idea that there are 'right' answers and ways to do things and woe betide you if you get 'it' wrong.

None of this mentality supports the development of confidence to do things differently. Scots who stand out from the crowd and behave differently are in a sense going against the grain of Scottish culture.

What needs to be done

I have outlined above a number of real barriers in Scottish culture which we need to address and dismantle if we want to realise the *Curriculum for Excellence's* desire for more 'confident individuals'. In embracing this new agenda it may be tempting for us to be glib about some of the shifts we need to make. What I am thinking about here is teachers or head teachers who casually talk about how it is all right to make mistakes and learn from failure and how we must all have positive attitudes. In the process they ignore the fact that in people's heads they have software programmes running which make it difficult for them to move into this new way of thinking. I believe we can move forward and make changes if we examine some of these old beliefs and challenge them, rather than pretend they are not there.

To address the barriers I outlined earlier in the chapter we need to:

- give young people clear messages that making something of yourself and your life is acceptable and laudable
- encourage individuality rather than fear it
- adopt more of a growth mindset and see people not in terms of their limitations but their potential
- appreciate difference more and break down the outmoded notion that there is only one right way to do things
- become more conscious of the prevalence of pessimistic thinking and challenge it, not with unrealistic positive thinking, but with facts
- tackle social inequality and the feelings of worthlessness that often accompany deprivation.

One of my fears is that we try to move forward, not recognising the beliefs that many of us have from centuries of conditioning, and then try to superimpose some of the worst American practices – unwarranted praise, an overemphasis on how the child feels in the moment and a continual effort to boost the feel-good factor by videoing award ceremonies.

My best-case scenario, which I think is very likely, is that we move forward to new types of thinking and acting and that we do this by building on our strengths.

Strengths and traditions Scotland can build on

Along with the barriers outlined above there are aspects of Scottish society and values that are advantageous to us in building young people's confidence.

i. A resilient people

Even a cursory look at Scottish history shows that the Scots have had to endure many distressing events: the loss of political sovereignty; poverty and famine; rapid industrialisation and urbanisation; chronic economic uncertainty; the migration of loved ones; and huge war fatalities. Even in recent times many families in Scotland have been affected adversely by economic restructuring. Despite this, or perhaps because of it, the Scots have a reputation for being a people who are particularly hardy and resilient.

When I undertook research for my book I was struck by how many commentators on Scotland over the past few centuries had pessimistically predicted either the demise of Scotland or of Scottishness. In the 1920s, for example, George Scott Moncrieff described Scotland as 'an abortive carcass rotting somewhere to the North of England'. In true pessimistic style such commentators took the problems of the day, made them worse than they were and then projected this intensified problem into the future. But the prophets of doom have been proved wrong: not only has Scotland failed to dissolve into 'North Britain' but also a Scottish Parliament sits once again in Edinburgh and many more Scots give priority to their Scottish rather than their British identity.

Nowadays the resilience of modern Scots is not what it once was. Asylum seekers, and immigrants into Scotland, are often aware that they are much more resilient than some of the people in the communities where they settle. We have a growing level of mental health problems and people suffering from stress. However, this is not just a Scottish phenomenon, but a change in western culture to which I shall return later.

ii. An emphasis on society

The Scots have always had a strong notion of society and social obligation. In everyday life it has been expressed in the idea of us all being 'Jock Tamson's bairns'. Scottish intellectuals emphasise the importance of society and the collective, and social science as we know it was founded in Scotland in the eighteenth century.

iii. Scepticism

Traditionally the Scots have been a logical, sceptical and intellectual people. This can be overplayed and make us resistant to new ideas and to the importance of emotional life. However, it could protect us from embracing some new-fangled, but ill thought out ideas.

iv. Mission and purpose

The Calvinist legacy to Scotland has been positive as well as negative. We owe our commitment to education to this aspect of our history. Historically it also encouraged many Scots to have a strong sense of mission and purpose and to want to make a contribution to the wider society. This can be evidenced in the level of volunteering and charitable giving in Scotland. Our level of giving to charities is the highest in the UK. We also have a strong tradition of wealthy individuals who want to devote this wealth to schemes for general social improvement. We have also a strong belief in the importance of authenticity, honesty and personal integrity and these principles are seen internationally as something which the Scots have traditionally upheld.

Personally, I believe there should be much more emphasis on teaching Scottish history in schools and that this could be useful in the development of confidence. More importantly, I think we can tap into these strong Scottish values when trying to nurture confident individuals in Scottish schools. This is a theme I shall return to in the last two chapters of this *Handbook*.

Key Points

1. An important barrier to confidence in Scotland is that Scots are not brought up to feel that they are worthwhile human beings – they have to prove this through their actions and achievements.
2. Scottish egalitarianism is of a type that says that everyone is of equal worth therefore no one should think they are better than others. In other words, Scottish egalitarian values level down. (American egalitarianism, by contrast, is aspirational.)
3. Professor Carol Dweck's concept of 'the fixed mindset' is very relevant to Scotland as there is a pronounced belief in the culture that people's potential and characteristics are fixed and not amenable to change.
4. It is very common for Scots to fear making mistakes or getting 'it' wrong. This fear is partly due to the fact that Scottish culture does not promote an understanding, or a valuing, of difference.
5. Scottish culture has a strong tendency to be pessimistic. This in part means that Scots have a tendency to see problems as intractable and worse than they actually are.
6. Despite the Scottish commitment to equality, Scotland is a country deeply divided by wealth and class. The confidence barriers in Scotland are particularly strong for people living in more deprived areas.
7. Scottish culture encouraged people to have undoubted strengths. Traditionally these have been resilience, a sense of social connection, scepticism and a strong desire for social improvement.
8. Scottish strengths could be harnessed to create the conditions for nurturing 'confident individuals'.

Supporting Evidence

Facts are chiels that winna ding.

Robert Burns

In the previous chapter I made various assertions about barriers to confidence in Scotland and I simply justified these claims with reference to aspects of Scottish culture. In this chapter I set out some of the empirical evidence.

One of the immediate difficulties I faced when writing *The Scots' Crisis of Confidence* is that there has been very little data collection in Scotland that could either prove or disprove my case. There was one piece of evidence I could cite – A World Health Organisation study from the mid 1990s on the self-confidence of fifteen year olds in 25 countries. It found that Scottish teenagers were third bottom of the list – only higher than Estonia and Slovakia – for feelings of self-confidence. Admittedly they only asked one question – do you always feel confident? – and a rather strange question at that. Does anyone ever feel confident all the time? I doubt it. So it is possible our teenagers were being more honest rather than lacking in self-confidence.

Determined to Succeed research

In 2005 the Scottish Executive published research related to the development of Determined to Succeed (DtS) – the school enterprise initiative. The research was carried out by a company called The Research Business International and aimed 'to benchmark young people and children's attitudinal values, perceptions and opinions about "enterprise", including confidence, self-expression, notions of success and career success'.

The research was undertaken with a good cross-section of P7 and S4 students in Scottish schools. Just over six hundred took part in the survey. The researchers ultimately divided the sample of S4 students in to four segments, depending on their responses to various questions (see Table 1).

The researchers undertook a similar exercise for the P7 cohort. The researchers gave them different labels but essentially they fall into very similar segments (see Table 2).

If we focus on confidence and self-belief we can see that the researchers indicate that 42 per cent of S4 students appear deficient in these positive attitudes to themselves and that 'the quietly optimistic' (29 per cent) would also benefit from more nurturing of self-belief, presumably to help them become more dynamic and ambitious.

A similar segmentation exercise was carried out on the P7 cohort (see Table 2). Of the P7 students, 71 per cent of the group are seen to be lacking in self-belief or confidence. What is interesting is that the group the researchers class as 'potential entrepreneurs' (25 per cent) apparently lack self-belief and are put in this category mainly because they are competitive and interested in making money and being their own boss.

The researchers also ask the S4 students how they are seen by others in three different contexts – at home, at school and with friends (see table 3). Their responses suggest that they think they appear most confident with friends (72 per cent); then at home (69 per cent) and then at school (51 per cent). It is interesting to note that this means that almost half of these pupils do not think they appear confident at school.

What I find fascinating about this data, which the researchers hardly mention, is how these young people often report more positive views of themselves at *school* than at home. For example, only 51 per cent said they would be seen as 'clever' at home whereas 73 per cent said they would be seen in this way at school. The responses are set out in full in Table 3 but we have regrouped them to show more clearly the differences between home and school (see Tables 4a and 4b).

Table 1: Segmentation of S4 responses to various questions about themselves and the future.

Quietly Optimistic	Determined Individuals
29% *High in self-belief but not outwardly ambitious* • Team players rather than individuals. • Positive outlook on education and the local environment. • Want a job that they will enjoy. Needs from DtS: More nurturing of 'their already high interest in education as well as their self-belief'.	28% *Competitive, high in self-belief* • Leaders rather than team players. • Want to be their own boss and to make money. • Negative about their local environment and may move away to achieve success. Needs from DtS: To channel their drive and enterprising spirit.
Under-confident Aspirers	**Just Want a Job**
31% *Fairly ambitious but have 'lower than average self-confidence'* • Not clear about their future. • Would settle for an undemanding job. • Their low self-confidence may result from parental control. Needs from DtS: To increase their self-confidence and self-sufficiency.	12% *'Very low self belief'* • Neither ambitious nor competitive. • Not positive about education. • More likely to say they will settle for any job. Needs from DtS: To engage them more fully either in education or in whatever interests them outside of school.

Table 2: Segmentation of P7 responses to various questions about themselves and the future.

Confidently Optimistic	Potential Entrepreneurs
33% Positive about themselves and education.	25% Competitive, adventurous and curious but 'lower on average on self-belief' and tend to worry.
Shy and Intelligent	**Drifters**
33% Positive about education but lack confidence and are prone to worry.	13% Low in self-belief and negative about education.

Note: The figures here add up to 104 per cent but these are the precise figures given in the report.

Table 3: How S4 students believe they are perceived in different situations

	At home	At school	Out with friends
Confident	69%	51%	72%
Loud	64%	37%	77%
Responsible	59%	63%	53%
Lazy	58%	16%	14%
Easy going	56%	43%	68%
Clever	51%	73%	39%
Optimistic	42%	50%	44%
Ambitious	40%	63%	37%
Creative	38%	51%	35%
Hard-working	35%	76%	21%
A leader	33%	27%	40%
Adventurous	32%	25%	68%
Popular	30%	44%	62%
Successful	26%	63%	28%
Negative	19%	21%	9%
Stupid	19%	13%	27%
Quiet	17%	45%	8%
A follower	12%	22%	19%
Shy	14%	32%	8%
None of these	3%	2%	2%
Percentages add up to more than 100 due to multiple responses			

Table 4a : How S4 students report they are perceived at home in comparison to school, where the home response is higher

	At home	At school	% higher at home
Confident	69%	51%	18%
Loud	64%	37%	27%
Lazy	58%	16%	42%
Easy going	56%	43%	13%
A leader	33%	27%	6%
Adventurous	32%	25%	7%
Stupid	19%	13%	6%

Table 4b : How S4 students report they are perceived at home in comparison to school, where the school response is higher

	At home	At school	% higher at school
Hard-working	35%	76%	41%
Clever	51%	73%	22%
Successful	26%	63%	37%
Ambitious	40%	63%	23%
Responsible	59%	63%	4%
Creative	38%	51%	13%
Optimistic	42%	50%	8%
Quiet	17%	45%	28%
Popular	30%	44%	14%
Shy	4%	32%	28%
A follower	12%	22%	10%
Negative	19%	21%	2%

At no point in the report do the researchers define confidence, and the young people were not primed to think about confidence in any particular way. What appears to emanate from this research is that young people feel confident to be themselves when they are with other young people or at home, and less confident when at school. So if we examine what young people say about how they appear at home it seems to fit in with this type of basic self-expression. In other words, they can be easy going, adventurous and loud at home, which fits in with being confident to be themselves. This is obviously much more difficult within the classroom setting, which may be why almost a third of young people say they are 'shy' in school and almost half say they are 'quiet'. However, if we define confidence as doing something in the world – agency, self-efficacy and ambition – then a completely different picture emerges. It is in school, rather than at home, that students are more likely to experience themselves as hard-working, clever, successful, ambitious, creative and optimistic.

The importance of school for fostering the type of attitudes and sense of self that are important for confidence also emerges when we compare how these young people report how they think they are seen when 'out with friends'. Slightly more than a quarter (27 per cent) say they are perceived as 'stupid' with friends and clearly it is not that cool either to be seen as clever, hardworking, creative or ambitious (see Table 3).

The researchers are right to see their research as mainly positive. The overwhelming numbers of young people in their sample are positive about themselves and about their educational experience. The number of S4s who report that their parents encourage them to do well at school is 76 per cent and the equivalent figure for P7s is 73 per cent. Few report that they think education is a waste of time. However, this still means that almost a quarter of students in the two cohorts studied here have parents who, they say, do not encourage them to do well at school.

The importance of parents

When I give talks in Scotland on confidence it is usual for people to say that we can achieve little if the education system does not support confidence. However, the research from Professor Emler on self-esteem, reported in Chapter 2, suggests that parents have a much larger part to play, at least in building self-esteem, than people often recognise. This research on DtS, quoted above, indicates that schools may be better at nurturing and encouraging self-efficacy and attitudes to ambition and achievement than some parents. As I argued in the last chapter, Scottish culture can be very judgemental and prone to label and dismiss people. I am certain this happens still within schools but, since looking at this research, I am more concerned that such unhelpful, negative judging happens more in homes in Scotland than in the classroom.

The Centre's research

The research studies conducted for Determined to Succeed (both the report quoted above and others) are useful in some respects but limited in others. The main limitation is that they do not adequately define the terminology employed nor are they able to give any international comparisons. The report examined above simply cannot tell us whether there is more of a problem of confidence in Scottish schools than in other countries.

As soon as the Centre was set up we were keen to encourage people across a variety of organisations to collect data that would be helpful in understanding confidence levels in Scotland and internationally. With support from the Scottish Executive the Centre ran a number of action research training courses to help people acquire the insights, skills and tools to measure the impact of their action research projects and to help the Centre gather data. We also commissioned Dr Elaine Duncan, a psychologist from Glasgow Caledonian University, to undertake research and then advise us on potential measurement tools that we could encourage action research participants to use.

Ultimately Dr Duncan concluded that while confidence is a term used widely in sport, business, economics and everyday life, there was no one widely accepted way to define confidence and no one instrument that measures it adequately. Instead, Dr Duncan recommended to the Centre a practical and pragmatic alternative: that we take four, short questionnaires, all measuring different constructs, which together make up what we often think of as 'confidence'. The four constructs she suggested were: self-esteem, optimism, life-satisfaction and happiness. These questionnaires are mainly suitable for adults but can be used by young people and teenagers.

The Centre's Confidence Research System

To make these usable by a variety of groups, the Centre, with the support of the Scottish Executive, has now put these four questionnaires on line so that they can be completed and analysed quickly. We are calling this project the Confidence Research System.

Why we are measuring self-esteem

Those who read the first part of this *Handbook* will know that the Centre is not encouraging an emphasis on self-esteem as a way to build confidence; we disagree with the idea that self-esteem is a panacea and we are fairly critical of what has been done in the name of self-esteem. Nonetheless, as we made clear in these earlier chapters, we still think that self-esteem exists and that it can be measured. However, we endorse Professor Martin Seligman's view that a person's level of self-esteem is simply an indication of how well that person thinks they are doing in life – the speedometer rather than the engine, to repeat Seligman's useful metaphor.

The Centre is now using a definition of confidence which includes self-efficacy and we have added a measure of this construct to our Research System. We have also added a questionnaire which measures resilience. The questionnaires, and scoring instructions, are included in the Resources section at the end of this *Handbook*.

The Centre's results

The Centre now has data from research undertaken on the initial four questionnaires from students in secondary schools in Scotland. We have also found a number of other Scottish studies. All I plan to do here is give some of the most interesting findings. This is a work-in-progress and anyone interested in this data should check the Centre's website for updates. For the sake of brevity I only report findings for two of the scales we are using: Rosenberg's Self-Esteem Scale and the Life Orientation Test (Revised) (LOT-R), which measures optimism.

At the time of writing the Centre has results from more than 2,787 students across 22 secondary schools in Scotland. Most of these students are in first, second or third year. There is a good split between male and female. The schools are drawn from different geographical areas. We do not think that our results are exactly representative of the Scottish school population and may over-represent schools which achieve lower academic results and have more pupils from poorer socio-economic groups. On top of this group of 22 schools we also have results for every student (728) attending one large secondary school in a declining, industrial area in Scotland's central belt. Fewer students in this school go on to university than the Scottish average and it also has a higher number of students receiving free school meals. Given Professor Emler's research, which suggests that academic performance and social class do not usually have a large bearing on self-esteem levels, this information on types of school may be irrelevant and I am reporting it here to be clear that we are not saying that these results are necessarily representative. The mean results from the 22 schools are very similar to the whole school that has been involved in our measurement project, but we shall report them separately.

So that we are able to compare across questionnaires, the Centre has translated all the results into a percentage scale. Below, we report our results alongside data we have been collecting from a variety of international studies.

Self-esteem

International data suggests that self-esteem varies according to culture. Eastern cultures, such as Japanese, where collectivist values predominate, generally report lower self-esteem than western nations. In the west, self-esteem figures are generally much higher. Indeed, it is common for mean figures to be over 65 per cent. As we saw in Chapter 2, when reporting on research carried out by Professor Nicholas Emler, males tend to score slightly higher than females. Self-esteem varies to some extent over the life course. Children's self-esteem tends to drop as they enter adolescence and remains lower until their late teens/early twenties when it rises slightly and stays at this level until past mid life.

The Centre is in the midst of locating international research studies of school students for comparison purposes. Table 5 lists what we have managed to locate at present, alongside our own two research studies.

Table 5: Self-esteem results for young people of secondary school age

Studies	Mean for self-esteem	Standard deviation
US school students	74%	N/A
Australian teenagers	64%	6.1
22 Scottish secondary schools	63%	16.3
Large Scottish secondary school	62%	17.1
Irish secondary school students	58%	4.5

It is easier to locate international information on levels of self-esteem for university students. We have listed this in Table 6 and included a recent sample of university students from the University of Glasgow. The mean results for Scottish school students do not look too low in comparison to Ireland and Australia but the picture is certainly made more complex when we look at university students, where the Scottish figures do appear to be low. It is also relevant that the Scottish research quoted here involved students at Glasgow University, one of the Scottish universities with high entrance requirements.

Table 6: Self-esteem results for university students

Studies	Mean for self-esteem	Standard deviation
US black students	79%	4.8
Serbian students	79%	5.0
Chilean students	77%	4.3
Israeli students	77%	5.5
Peruvian students	77%	4.6
US white students	75%	4.7
Turkish students	74%	5.0
English (Lancaster) university students	69%	5.0
Fijian students	63%	4.2
Glasgow University students	**62%**	**5.4**
US Asian university students	62%	5.0
Czech Republic students	62%	4.1
Bangladeshi students	59%	5.2
Hong Kong students	58%	3.7
Japanese students	52%	4.4

In our research study of 22 schools, 79 per cent of students scored higher than 50 per cent on Rosenberg's Self-Esteem Scale. This leaves 21 per cent who scored below – that is more than one in five. An even higher percentage of pupils in our single school scored lower than 50 per cent – 24 per cent. However, these figures may not be representative of the overall school population, as we know there is variation between postcodes and we do not claim to have a representative sample. But it is worth pointing out that for a western culture, taking 50 per cent as the mid point below which we can talk about low self-esteem may be inaccurate. Self-esteem tends to be high in western nations. So if we take the figure of 60 per cent as the critical figure, what we find is that 45 per cent of young people in Scotland in our study scored below this figure.

i. Variation between schools

There is also a large variation across our schools. The range of school means is 58 to 71 per cent (13 per cent difference). In our study of 22 schools, four schools had means below 60 and three had means above 70. The probability of these differences occurring by chance is one in a thousand. What is more, the differences between schools cannot be explained in terms of gender composition or age.

ii. Postcode

Some of this variation between schools can be explained by postcode. If we only look at postcodes where we have more than 100 respondents we find that the self-esteem mean for schools varies by postcode by around 7 per cent. For example, the mean for a postcode in a peripheral housing estate is 60 per cent in contrast to a mean of 67 per cent in a more affluent suburb.

iii. Ethnicity and gender

Most of the school students who completed these questionnaires recorded that they were white and there are not sufficient numbers of students from other ethnic groups to say anything meaningful about ethnicity at this stage. The data did yield some differences in gender. The mean for boys was around 4 per cent higher than for girls – this is consistent with international data. The boys' self-esteem increased slightly with age in the schools we examined, whereas the figure for girls showed no change with age; again this is consistent with international studies.

iv. Do these self-esteem scores matter?

As I mentioned earlier, these students also completed questionnaires on optimism, life satisfaction and happiness. The optimism figures will be examined below but it is worth pointing out here that there was a strong, positive correlation between self-esteem and happiness, life-satisfaction and optimism. In other words, those students who scored high on self-esteem were also likely to score higher than average on happiness, life-satisfaction and optimism. This is consistent with the international research findings reported in Chapter 3.

What does the self-esteem data mean for Scotland?

At this stage all we can do is raise a few preliminary questions and observations:

- Our data, and the other data reported for Scotland, seems to suggest that self-esteem levels for young people and students are lower, on average, than for many other western nations.
- The data that we have collected on Scottish secondary school students reveals variation in results both within and across schools.
- Some of this variation may be accounted for by social class but there still appears to be a variation which is about schools, rather than postcodes.
- Is the variation between schools about the school itself or is it more of a reflection of the community in which the school is located?
- If parents have the biggest impact on the formation of young people's self-esteem does the variation in self-esteem in Scotland reflect large differences in parenting styles?
- Why is it that a country such as Scotland which emphasises equality and 'a man's a man' should produce such variation in feelings of worth?

Optimism

Now let us turn attention to the optimism results. This was the lowest of the four questionnaire responses in all of the 22 schools studied. We are still tracking down international studies using this optimism test but can report some data for comparison purposes (see Table 7).

Table 7: Comparison of international studies of optimism using LOT-R

Studies	Mean for optimism	Standard deviation
Small Scottish-based university sample of students	50%	5.2
22 Scottish secondary schools	56%	6.6
1 large Scottish secondary school	57%	6.6
45-60 year olds in large Scottish town	56%	N/A
Chinese students	58%	3.4
US college students	60%	4.3
American heart by-pass patients	63%	4.1
Italian university students	70%	N/A

This shows that on a standard optimism test the Scots appear to gain quite low scores. It is also worth pointing out here that this is a standard optimism questionnaire, which does try to gauge feelings of pessimism in the face of good events (ie, the belief that good times will last). The questionnaire is not designed in any case to measure whether an individual thinks that they may have to pay for good fortune – a feeling which I have found to be fairly widespread, even in modern Scotland.

The Centre's optimism data on schools

Again, there was a large variation in optimism across the schools we studied. The mean varied from 47 per cent to 63 per cent, a variation of 16 per cent. The data also varied according to age. The mean in our 22 schools started at 57 per cent in S1. This fell slightly in S2 and S3. It then rose to 60 per cent in S4 but dropped to 56 per cent in S5 and then to 51 per cent in S6 – that is a drop of 9 per cent between S4 and S6. The variation between postcodes for self-esteem was 7 per cent, the same as it is for optimism. There was little gender difference in optimism and as yet we do not have enough data to discuss differences in ethnic groups.

Conclusions

The data which the Centre has collected, when taken alongside the research undertaken by DtS, suggests that there is a sizeable number of students in Scottish schools (and universities) who feel fairly negative about themselves or the future. The self-esteem and optimism figures for some students in deprived areas are particularly low. The empirical data does appear to support the existence of the various barriers to confidence which I outlined in the last chapter.

However, those of us working at the Centre for Confidence and Well-being do not think that we should try to rectify these trends with the type of simplistic self-esteem interventions (outlined in the previous chapters) which have been tried in the US. Approaches such as these have led to a serious decline in academic standards and appear to have encouraged narcissism and depression. Instead, we urge a range of different approaches and activities. And it is to these that we now turn.

Key Points

1. Research undertaken for Determined to Succeed, the enterprise in schools initiative in Scotland, reveals that confidence may be a problem for 40 per cent of S4 students and over 70 per cent at P7.
2. This research also shows that young people seem to have a more favourable sense of themselves at school rather than at home or out with friends.
3. Schools may be better than parents in Scotland for fostering confidence.
4. The level of self-esteem of young people in Scotland at university level is low by international standards.
5. Research undertaken by the Centre on the self-esteem of secondary school students suggests that there is considerable variation across schools and by postcode.
6. Research undertaken by the Centre also suggests that the level of optimism for young people in Scotland is fairly low.

Cartoons by Graham Ogilvie

How different mindsets work after a 'setback'
What's the point in putting good effort after bad?
I'll do less on this
I'll spend more time on this subject
I'll work harder
helpless
resilience
Exam results
graham@ogilviedesign.co.uk

It's one thing having 'brains and talent' . . . .
I don't need to put out effort, things will come to me
But it won't 'give' you success
Brains! Talent.
graham@ogilviedesign.co.uk

The great way of thinking about 'learning something new'
This thing just keeps growing and growing
OFF-SHOOTS
graham@ogilviedesign.co.uk

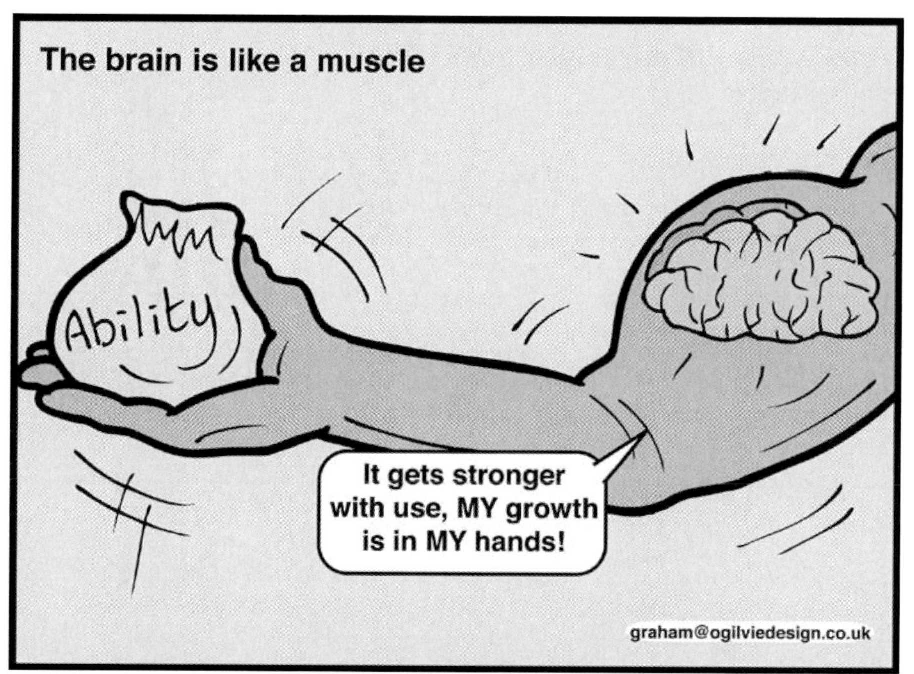
The brain is like a muscle
Ability
It gets stronger with use, MY growth is in MY hands!
graham@ogilviedesign.co.uk

The 'Eureka' moment can be life changing
School
So let's talk about the growth mindset
Mind Sets
Fixed
Growth
You mean I don't have to be dumb!!!
graham@ogilviedesign.co.uk

Praising children's intelligence puts them in a fixed mindset
Praise gives confidence and helps achievement
Fabulous! - You are going to be the next Monet!
I'll ALWAYS need praise
graham@ogilviedesign.co.uk

The adult result of too much childhood praise
employee awards
Best of Year
Bloggs
Bloggs
Best of Month
Best of Day
I don't have an award - I feel terrible
Bloggs
graham@ogilviedesign.co.uk

Praise the effort that leads to success
It's not about the big bang at the end
strategy
critique
effort
Well done for constructing this
It's up to ME to light the touch paper
graham@ogilviedesign.co.uk

Praise is NOT a villain
As long as it's the 'right' praise
It's good to feel appreciated and encouraged
Tell me about the colours you chose
graham@ogilviedesign.co.uk

Criticism is a gift
Oh no - bad feedback, what a disaster
you are 86% OK
things you can alter are
Hang on - feedback is how we learn to grow!
graham@ogilviedesign.co.uk

What's best . . pessimism or optimism!?
I was shot in the arm, I'm SO unlucky, always in the wrong place at the wrong time!
I've been shot in the arm - that was lucky, it could have killed me!
graham@ogilviedesign.co.uk

We seem to have a constant need to 'prove ourselves'
Scotland the best small country in the World!
The best at WHAT?
Record
Survey Scotland is worst performing small country
Who's right and who's wrong?
graham@ogilviedesign.co.uk

Let's challenge the Scottish fixed mindset
Aye - this one's going to be trouble
You can see it in his face - what's afore ye will no go past ye
graham@ogilviedesign.co.uk

Being 'positive' gives us new ideas
It's great to have the buzz
But you also need ME to make things happen
graham@ogilviedesign.co.uk

When we target an intervention at a belief
Fixed
Growth
We can switch it on
graham@ogilviedesign.co.uk

PART IV

good ways to create confidence

Mindsets: How We View Success and Failure

> *In my research, I have been amazed over and over again at how quickly students of all ages pick up on messages about themselves – at how sensitive they are to suggestions about their personal qualities or about the meaning of their actions and experiences. The kinds of praise (and criticism) students receive from their teachers and parents tell them how to think about what they do – and what they are.*
>
> Carol Dweck

Carol Dweck is a professor of psychology at Stanford University and has been conducting research on motivation and personality for over twenty years. Her work has enormous practical implications for teachers and parents as well as those working in sports or business settings. Dweck's ideas often go under the name of 'self-theories' and the World Education Fellowship named her book of that name 'book of the year' in 2000. Despite this acclaim, Dweck's ideas have not received much attention in the UK. However, the Scottish educational psychologist Alan McLean has disseminated and built on her theories in his book *The Motivated School.*

One reason why Dweck's work has not received the attention it deserves is that her scholarly style and heavy use of empirical research makes it unattractive for the lay reader. Fortunately this has now changed for in 2006 she published a book called *Mindset: The New Psychology of Success*. In this volume she popularises her ideas and tries to engage non-psychologists. She does this mainly by using terminology that is more meaningful to the lay reader. It is this version of Dweck's work which we mainly use here.

Two mindsets

Based on her empirical research, primarily with young children, Dweck argues that people throughout the world can be divided into two basic 'mindsets'.

The fixed mindset

The first she calls 'the fixed mindset'. This mindset upholds the idea that people's ability is fairly fixed and not open to change. According to such a view, people are either intelligent, sporty, arty, good at maths, etc, or they are not. This mindset also labels people according to personal characteristics. So people are either good or bad, caring or selfish and so on. In Dweck's original work she referred to this as an 'entity theory' in that it treats human capabilities and characteristics as if they were 'carved in stone' and individuals as if they are 'finished products'. In other words, it views human abilities and behaviours as innate, unchangeable things, like inanimate objects such as tables and chairs.

The growth mindset

The growth mindset has a different starting point. It sees people as essentially malleable. In other words, they are not fixed but have huge potential for growth and development. This mindset accepts that a small minority of people are born with unusual levels of talent or ability (the geniuses). At the other end of the spectrum are people who have such severe learning difficulties that they have some barriers to learning though they still have huge potential to develop skills. So this view asserts that around 95 per cent of the population fall between these two extremes and that with enough motivation, effort and concentration they can become better at almost anything. In her original work, Dweck calls this the 'incremental theory' to suggest the idea that people are capable of making incremental changes in ability and other personal characteristics.

It is important to note that Dweck is not disputing the fact that some people find some types of activities or learning easier than others. What she disputes is that others cannot learn:

> *Just because some people can do something with little or no training, doesn't mean that others can't do it (and sometimes do it better), with training. This is so important, because many, many people with the fixed mindset think that someone's early performance tells you all you need to know about their talent and their future.*

This very simple theory of different views of people has enormous implications for learning and for how teachers and parents interact with young people.

How the mindsets interact with success and failure

For people who have a fixed mindset, success is exceptionally important as it is a way to validate yourself and show how clever and talented you are. It is also a way to prove you are better than others who lack these fixed qualities. Conversely, failure is toxic for those with fixed mindsets as it proves that you are not talented or clever. This means that failure, and mistakes, have to be avoided at all costs. Indeed, Dweck argues that for people with fixed mindsets, 'the loss of oneself to failure can be a permanent and haunting trauma'. By extension, it also means that fixed mindset people feel they must be careful with anything that might be challenging and risky as it may increase the risk of failure and thus show their lack of ability. It is best, according to this view, to harbour thoughts about 'what you could have been' rather than risk failure.

This viewpoint also leads people to be very touchy about any critical feedback as it suggests an innate lack of ability. It also leads to tests being seen as a valuation, not of a specific set of skills, but of how clever or capable you are.

From an educational point of view what is particularly worrying about the fixed mindset is how it sees effort as reprehensible in some way. According to this perspective, people who are naturally clever and gifted do not have to practise and try too hard. So people who need to put effort into something are showing their deficiencies.

People with a growth mindset have a completely different view of success and failure. Of course, they are motivated by success and want to achieve it, but for them success shows that you have mastered something, been stretched and learned new skills: it is not seen as a demonstration of intelligence or talent. This then frees up growth mindset people to see failure not as a negative, undermining judgement on them as people, but as something they need to learn from so that they can succeed in the future. A natural extension of this mindset is to relish, and seek out challenges, rather than avoid them as it is through being challenged that people grow and develop. Failure can often be a painful challenge to growth mindset people but it is still seen as something to learn from rather than something that defines you as an individual.

In the eyes of those with a growth mindset, tests are not measuring your basic intelligence or potential (no test can do that); tests can only give a snapshot of how capable you are at something now. What is more, criticism, particularly from someone you respect and you can learn from, is a gift – a way to accelerate learning – and not something to be feared. Dweck reports that the great Russian ballet dancer and teacher, Marina Semyonova, devised an unusual way of selecting students. During a trial period she watched how they responded to critical feedback. The more responsive they were to 'correction' the more she deemed them worthy of her tutoring. In other words, she was selecting for a growth mindset.

Finally, for people with a growth mindset, learning and development is all about one thing – *effort*. The more you put in the more you will accelerate your learning. What is more, growth mindset people value learning for its own sake, irrespective of the outcome.

These differences between people have been demonstrated by Dweck's research. She describes, for example, how students with the two different mindsets responded to the offer of feedback after completing a challenging task. The fixed mindset students were more likely to refuse the offer of information on how they could improve their performance and chose instead information on how they compared with their peers. The growth mindset students were much more interested in knowing how they could have done better than in finding out how they ranked.

More research findings

Throughout *Mindset*, Dweck quotes findings from extensive research projects on children (usually about the age of ten) which she has carried out with colleagues. One set of research studies asked the children to carry out puzzles. They were then divided into three groups. The first group were given fixed mindset feedback. In other words, they were told that they had done well because they were very clever children. The second group were given growth mindset feedback. So these children were also praised but this time not for anything innate about their abilities – they were only praised for their effort and concentration. The third group, a control group, were only given bland feedback on having done a good job.

Dweck and colleagues found that when these children were then asked if they wanted to undertake harder, more challenging puzzles, virtually all the children in the fixed mindset group refused while most of the children in the growth mindset group accepted the offer. The control group split almost evenly between the two options. Dweck speculates that this no doubt reflected their own tendency to growth or fixed theories of intelligence.

Some of her other research projects also show that children given fixed mindset feedback are less keen to keep trying to improve their learning or their abilities and, if asked to repeat the original task, will often not do it as well. In other words, their performance can often erode rather than improve as a result of being told they are talented or clever. This finding has huge implications for parents, teachers and anyone working with young people.

Lying

Dweck and colleagues found a particular aspect of their research worrying. Following on from fixed mindset feedback, children were asked to tell others of how well they had done. A staggering 38 per cent lied about their score by saying it was better than it actually was. The equivalent figure for the control group was 14 per cent and the growth mindset group 13 per cent. Dweck writes 'What's so alarming is that we took ordinary children and made them into liars, simply by telling them they were smart'.

Mindset and achievement

In *Mindset*, Dweck comes up with a number of powerful examples of people who have succeeded in life through effort, determination, good teaching and effective learning strategies. The basketball player, Michael Jordan, is a good case in point. He is often seen as a 'natural' but, according to his coach, Jordan did not show a great deal of promise initially but he persevered, trained harder than anyone else and particularly worked on his weaknesses. Dweck argues that one of the great ironies about mindsets is that fixed mindset people are often desperate for success to prove how clever and talented they are, however, since they often lack good learning strategies, and are easily stressed by failure, they often do not get to the top. In contrast, growth mindset people are often less fixated on achievement but are more likely to get there. She writes: 'The top is where the fixed mindset people hunger to be, but it's where many growth-minded people arrive as a by-product of their enthusiasms for what they do'. In short, growth mindset people are enthralled by the learning process, not the destination. If they get to the top it is an added bonus, not the point of their engagement.

Praise

An even more important conclusion to draw from Dweck's research is that we have to be very careful about how we praise young people. Dweck quotes research in the USA which shows that 85 per cent of parents think that praise is very important for children's performance and confidence. They are supported in this belief, as we have seen, by the very influential American self-esteem movement. Dweck agrees that 'praise, the chief weapon in their armoury, is a powerful tool'. Dweck also acknowledges that children love being praised for being intelligent and talented but that the benefits are short-lived. Indeed, she argues that 'if praise is not handled properly, it can become a negative force, a kind of drug that, rather than strengthening students, makes them passive and dependent on the opinion of others'.

The problem with praise

Dweck, like Seligman, argues that praise for nothing very much is damaging to children. She argues that children know that if they are given lavish praise for very little it means that nothing very much is expected of them. In other words, unwarranted praise undermines children by communicating low expectations. However, Dweck goes further than Seligman by arguing that praising for high achievement often carries a big risk. As we have seen, her research suggests that when children are praised for how intelligent they are, they become focused on retaining this label rather than on continuing to learn. Dweck argues that praise for intelligence often leads children to become more interested in how they are seen by others than in the learning itself. So praising for intelligence, or talent, may seem a positive thing to do but can distort children's attitude to learning and make them dependent on how they are seen by others. In practice this can mean not opting for challenging tasks or trying new things if it might involve failure.

Positive labels

Dweck argues that many professionals working with children have come to realise the danger of labelling children through criticism; for example saying 'you are a naughty boy' rather than 'that was a naughty thing to do'. But her argument is that positive labels such as 'you are very clever' also undermine children in the longer term as it gets them to focus on things (such as intelligence) that the praise is unwittingly telling them is not under their control. It also erodes their belief that effort is a good thing. Instead of praising for ability or innate talent, Dweck argues we should praise children for effort, concentration and the effectiveness of the strategies they use.

TTT1: How to give praise

- Don't praise unless it is warranted.
- Praise for effort, concentration and good strategies – not for talent, ability or intelligence.
- Be specific – well-judged praise helps young people to learn what they are doing well and what they can build on.
- Don't go over the top with praise – it can lead a young person to feel anxious that they may disappoint you in the future.

The need to challenge children

Like many psychologists, or educational commentators in the US, Dweck is critical of teachers and parents for handing out easy praise to children in the name of building self-esteem, and of lowering standards to allow more children to 'achieve' at school. Dweck is also critical of the way parents and teachers protect children by not giving them accurate feedback on how well they are doing. Dweck is an advocate of giving constructive feedback to young people as a way to hasten their learning and teach them better strategies. This certainly accords with my own views. What is the subtle message we are giving to young people if we constantly avoid criticising what they have done? I believe that the sub-text, which young people easily pick up, is that criticism is so belittling, and so difficult to accept, that we are not giving voice to it. In other words, it makes criticism appear much worse than it is. It also conveys the idea that we expect them to do everything perfectly and that we have no strategies to help them improve. In fact, well-judged, constructive criticism is a gift which can accelerate learning and help young people to develop a growth mindset.

The accompanying example of the pupil in the singing competition (Box 8) shows how Dweck's theories encourage parents and teachers to challenge young people, not spare their feelings, which is ultimately a short-term, counterproductive strategy.

BOX 8: Example from *Mindset*: Spare the criticism and demotivate the child?

Rachel is a fourteen-year old girl who is very keen on singing. For the past year she has attended singing classes and now feels ready to enter a singing competition. She is one of the youngest entrants. At the competition she sings very well but misses a few notes because she is nervous. At the end of the evening she leaves, hurt and despondent, without any prizes or distinction.

What should Rachel's parents or teacher say to her?

1. That they think she sung better than anyone else.
2. That the judges should have made allowance for her age.
3. That singing isn't that important.
4. That she is a talented singer and will win next time.
5. That she didn't deserve to win.

Dweck's theory would lead her to argue the following: that response one is 'insincere' as the parents/teachers and the child know she did not deserve to win. Response two is questioning the judges and the marking system and basically off-loading blame for Rachel's failure on to them. Response three encourages Rachel to devalue something she cares about so it is demotivating. Response four, Dweck argues, is the most dangerous as it makes out that she doesn't have to do anything differently to win next time. For Dweck, response five, although apparently quite hard, is the only serious option. She accepts that the feedback might not be given this boldly, but basically what Rachel needs to hear is that she must practise more and get better so that she doesn't miss notes when she is nervous. But there is an encouraging message here for Rachel and it is this: the other singers did better than her, not because they were innately more talented, but because they were more skilled. If Rachel wants to win singing competitions then she has to practise, practise, practise.

Should we blame children for not trying hard enough?

Dweck is aware that her theory could lead to the conclusion that children from poor, disadvantaged backgrounds are to blame for their lack of achievement because they do not put enough effort in. But she argues that while effort is critical for success, it is much easier for those who come from advantaged backgrounds. Those who lack resources or opportunities in life are much more easily 'derailed'. For example, a pupil who has parents with multiple problems will have more distractions in their life and more reasons for poor school attendance. In her book she does not dwell on the issue, but I think the drift of her argument is such that she would still argue that it is better to use strategies which challenge children, even though they have social problems, rather than to expect little of them. The latter simply condemns them to a cycle of underachievement.

The role of confidence

So in Dweck's theory how important is confidence? Dweck argues that people with the fixed mindset have to 'nurse' and 'protect' their confidence because failure and mistakes knock them off their stride so easily. She cites the tennis champion John McEnroe as an example of someone with a fixed mindset whose confidence was easily undermined during a match. Rather than attending to what went wrong, he blamed others for the adversity. Dweck goes on to argue that people with a growth mindset do not always need confidence to achieve. She explains that growth mindset people will often 'plunge into something wholeheartedly and stick to it'. In fact, she adds that they might become involved and put a lot of effort into something, because they are not good at it. 'This is the wonderful feature of the growth mindset', she writes. 'You don't have to think you're already great at something to want to do it and to enjoy doing it'.

TTT 2: Giving encouragement

Teachers and others working with children often give praise, as they want to appear positive and motivating. However, praise that is unwarranted is counterproductive. It is better to use encouragement instead. For example:

- Show you feel positive about the young person by being interested in them and their work. For example rather than saying 'what a wonderful drawing' it is better to say 'tell me about this person' or 'why did you use this colour of blue?'
- Recognise the effort the youngster is putting in.
- Ask them questions about how they think they are doing, what help they may need, what obstacles they may face and how they can get round them.
- Use a growth mindset and tell them how they are capable of learning with enough effort, concentration and better strategies.
- Encourage them to be optimistic about being able to improve.

Suspending judgement

One of the most compelling aspects of Dweck's work is that she is essentially arguing that we need to stop judging. The fixed mindset leads to a fixation with labels and judgements – he's clever, she's good at sports, she can't count, he's a numpty and so forth. These types of judgements of children's ability are not simply made at school but also by parents at home. It leads children to feel that they are continually being measured. As children are capable of picking up subtle messages, they know that what is really at stake is their worth as human beings. This is why Dweck argues that kids with fixed mindset parents know that their concern with poor grades is not so much about their failure to learn a specific thing but the idea that this shows the child is not smart. Often these young people feel that they never quite live up to their parents' ideal. Even when they are successful they are worried about losing this status if they fail.

It is much better for children if teachers and parents adopt a growth mindset and for Dweck this means 'Don't judge. Teach'. In some of the most powerful passages of her book, Dweck argues that good teachers do not have to love the children they teach but they have to respect them and see them as capable of improvement if they put in effort and employ better strategies. For Dweck the really great teachers are those who do not just pay 'lip service to the idea that all children can learn' but have a 'deep desire to reach in and ignite the mind of every child'. In case any teacher reading this is saying to themselves, 'that's not me. I'm not a great teacher', it is worth reiterating that the mindset theory suggests that any teacher can become much, much better if they have the motivation and desire to learn.

The internal critic

The judgement inherent in the fixed mindset can also be part of our internal dialogue. Dweck argues that people, whether they are conscious of it or not, keep a running account of what is happening in their lives and what they should do about it. Dweck says that their research reveals that people with fixed mindsets create 'an internal monologue that is focused on judging'. These judgements can be about themselves or others and they will tend to be very black and white. Growth mindset people are also attuned to positive and negative messages but they are more likely to look for the learning in them and decide what to do differently, rather than label themselves and others. Dweck argues that techniques such as Cognitive Behaviour Therapy can be helpful in encouraging people to make more realistic judgements. However, she says that such techniques do not necessarily 'confront the basic assumption – the ideas that traits are fixed'. In other words these techniques do not 'escort them out of the framework of judgement and into the framework of growth'.

TTT 3: Giving criticism constructively

Describe the behaviour, not the person. Do not label them – for example, instead of saying 'You're lazy' tell the young person that they are not putting in enough effort. Phrasing criticism in this way allows the person to see that they are capable of doing things differently. (In other words, give criticism from a growth, rather than a fixed, mindset.)

Ask for a specific change. Think through in advance what you want the person to change. There is little point in criticising someone's work or behaviour without having a clear idea of what you want them to do differently.

Don't swamp the person with criticisms. If you have a number of criticisms do not give them all in one go. It is best to decide which changes are the most important for the young person to make. This means that you have to prioritise the criticisms in terms of what would make the most difference.

Ask if you need to do something differently. This allows you to discuss with the young person how they are going to make the change and how you can support them in this.

You may wish to begin or end on a positive note. This may mean starting or finishing by saying what they are currently doing well. However, research shows that people given praise and criticism at the same time are only likely to remember the criticism. This means that you should try at other times to give only positive feedback.

Changing mindsets

Dweck argues that mindset is 'an important part' of a person's personality and she puts forward the idea that much of our mindset is formed from our early interactions with parents and teachers. She cites research which shows that children as young as four display fixed or growth mindsets and those with the former will keep doing easy puzzles rather than moving on to something more challenging. However, it is also important to realise that Dweck believes that mindsets 'can be changed'.

Strategies for change

i. Giving good feedback

Some of the specific recommendations that Dweck suggests to protect young people from the limitations of the fixed mindset are related to praise and criticism and have been outlined within this chapter.

ii. Information on the brain

Another of Dweck's major suggestions is that we need to present young people with information on the brain and its huge potential. This lesson would necessarily include information on how learning allows the brain to form new connections and how these connections become stronger.

iii. Inspiring role-models

Giving young people information on how figures they know, or admire, managed to succeed through effort and good strategies is another useful device in encouraging them to adopt a growth mindset. Positive stories are another method for helping young people to see the potential for change.

The *Curriculum for Excellence*

In this section on good approaches to building confidence I have put this chapter on mindsets first, as I believe the ideas are of fundamental importance to us in Scotland. What Dweck describes as 'the fixed mindset', with its tendency to judge and condemn is in essence what I see as the main barrier to the growth of confidence in Scotland. If we can shift this then we have more opportunity to nurture self-efficacy and optimism: without a growth mindset we shall struggle to get many young people to the starting block.

Key Points

1. Carol Dweck argues that people can be divided into two basic 'mindsets'.
2. The fixed mindset upholds the idea that people's ability is fixed and not open to change and it labels people according to ability and personal characteristics.
3. The growth mindset sees people as essentially malleable and accepts that a small minority of people are born with unusual levels of ability (the geniuses).
4. This simple theory of different views of people has enormous implications for learning and how teachers and parents interact with young people.
5. People with a growth mindset see failure as something they need to learn from so that they can succeed in the future, whereas people with a fixed mindset see it as toxic, as it proves they are not talented or clever.
6. For people with a growth mindset, learning and development is all about one thing – effort.
7. Fixed mindset people are often desperate for success to prove how clever and talented they are, however, since they often lack good learning strategies, and are easily stressed by failure, they often don't get to the top.
8. In contrast, growth mindset people are often less fixated on achievement but are more likely to get there. Growth mindset people are enthralled by the learning process, not the destination.
9. Dweck argues that we have to be very careful about how we praise young people. Dweck acknowledges that children love being praised for being intelligent and talented but that the benefits are short-lived.
10. Praise for intelligence often leads children to become more interested in how they are seen by others than in the learning itself.
11. We should praise children for effort, concentration and the effectiveness of the strategies they use, not for talent, ability or intelligence.
12. Dweck is an advocate of giving constructive feedback to young people as a way to hasten their learning and teach them better strategies.
13. People with the fixed mindset have to 'nurse' and 'protect' their confidence because failure and mistakes knock them off their stride so easily.
14. People with a growth mindset do not always need confidence in order to achieve as they often 'plunge into something wholeheartedly and stick to it'.
15. Mindsets are 'an important part' of a person's personality, however, it is also important to realise that Dweck believes that mindsets 'can be changed'.

8 Self-Efficacy

> *Ordinary realities are strewn with impediments, adversities, setbacks, frustrations and inequities. People must, therefore, have a robust sense of efficacy to sustain the perseverant effort needed to succeed.*
>
> Albert Bandura, 1994

The American psychologist, Albert Bandura, was the first person in his field to advance the idea of self-efficacy. The term refers to an individual's belief that he or she has the skills and knowledge necessary to achieve a particular goal, or could acquire them in the future. The fact that self-efficacy is goal-specific means a student could, for example, feel efficacious about being able to pass the written part of their French exam but not feel efficacious about their ability to perform well in the speaking assignment.

Self-efficacy is not synonymous with self-esteem. The latter is a global and emotional judgement individuals make about their self-worth. In other words, self-esteem refers to feelings about the self overall. Whereas self-efficacy is about agency or the ability to take action and achieve specific goals.

In everyday life when people use the term 'self-belief' they are usually referring to what Bandura means by self-efficacy. Certainly there is much in the theory underlying self-efficacy which underscores the importance of self-belief. Bandura, and other writers on the construct, such as F. Pajares, stress that the key to self-efficacy is self-belief. Of course, skills and knowledge matter but, for reasons presented below, an individual's subjective assessment of their chance of success, and their feelings of optimism, are often much more important than 'objective truth'.

Self-efficacy matters

Research shows that feelings of self-efficacy have a large bearing on our lives. Bandura sums this up when he writes: 'Self-efficacy beliefs determine how people feel, think, motivate themselves and behave'. High feelings of self-efficacy about a goal that is important to an individual not only means that the individual is likely to accomplish something in life which is meaningful to them but also that doing so will enhance their feelings of well-being and life satisfaction. People who are low in self-efficacy are very vulnerable and succumb more readily to stress and depression.

Self-efficacy and optimism

On the basis of extensive psychological research, Bandura argues that self-efficacy, 'human accomplishments and positive well-being' are facilitated by feelings of optimism. Some psychologists argue that optimism can lead people to overestimate their abilities and get them into trouble. In this respect, high optimism can be seen as unrealistic (seeing the world through rose-coloured spectacles) and so a type of cognitive failing. Bandura accepts this can be a problem when the costs of failure are high. Certainly, the dangers of overemphasising one's ability as a rock climber are self-evident. However, he still maintains that generally in life it can be 'a benefit' to overestimate capabilities as this helps individuals to persevere when they meet inevitable adversities – such as failure and rejection. Drawing on research presented by John White in his book *Rejection*, Bandura argues that 'many of our literary classics brought their authors countless rejections'. For example, James Joyce's *Dubliners* was rejected by 22 publishers. Building on this, Bandura argues that the Impressionist painters in France had to organise their own exhibitions because they were initially rejected by the art establishment and in more modern times, pop and rock groups such as the Beatles had to persevere in the face of rejection. Bandura also points out that most innovators in science and technology are, by definition, likely to experience rejection if not derision and only persevere because of what he calls their 'optimistic sense of self-efficacy'.

This mixture of efficacy and optimism is also important for people interested in social transformation. Bandura maintains it is easy to dismiss most social reformers who are intent on changing the world, or improving the lot of those who are unfortunate, as idealistic or unrealistic. While it is true that they often do not fully realise their vision, many often achieve significant goals and without such people our world would be much the poorer.

So for these reasons, Bandura argues that a strong sense of self-efficacy and self-belief should not be viewed as cognitive inadequacy but as the attitude and approach needed for human accomplishment.

Self-efficacy and confidence

This mixture of self-efficacy and optimism is what underpins confidence and is how I defined confidence in Chapter 1 of this *Handbook*. In other words, confidence consists of a strong element of self-belief in goal fulfilment as well as a more generalised positive belief that the future is bright. This means that if teachers are going to deliver the new *Curriculum for Excellence's* desire for more confident individuals they need to be able to cultivate students' feelings of self-efficacy.

TTT 4: Using children's stories to encourage self-efficacy

Self-efficacy may seem like a complex subject but it can be communicated to younger children through stories such as *The Little Engine Who Could* by Watty Piper. First published in the 1940s it has been read to hundreds of thousands of children many of whom were mesmerised by the engine chanting 'I think I can, I think I can, I think I can' – a chant which builds from a whisper to a confident roar.

What encourages self-efficacy?

Bandura argues that there are 'four main sources of influence' on the development of self-efficacy.

i. 'Mastery experiences'

According to Bandura this is the most important of the four sources of influence. Essentially what this means is cultivating a sense of 'mastery' by successfully achieving goals. What is particularly important here is having goals which an individual must work hard to achieve but which are ultimately achievable. Bandura writes:

> *If people experience only easy successes they come to expect quick results and are easily discouraged by failure. A resilient sense of efficacy requires experience in overcoming obstacles through perseverant effort. Some setbacks and difficulties in human pursuits serve a useful purpose in teaching that success usually requires sustained effort. After people become convinced they have what it takes to succeed, they persevere in the face of adversity and quickly rebound from setbacks. By sticking it out through tough times, they emerge stronger from adversity.*

This is why the self-esteem movement's desire to praise children for easy accomplishments, or to protect them from failure, has backfired and robbed children of the opportunities to experience real mastery and build feelings of efficacy. It is important to realise, however, that this does not do away with the importance of psychology for achievement. What often matters is how people feel about their success. It is the feeling of having mastered something, not the actual achievement, that is important.

ii. 'Vicarious experiences'

Essentially what is at stake here is success being modelled by those with whom you can identify. It is not enough for another person to achieve (eg an Olympic athlete) as it is the success of people who are like us in some way that is motivating. Presumably this is why reality TV shows, featuring ordinary people becoming ballet dancers or opera singers, are so appealing. What is more, these role models can help others learn the skills, acquire the knowledge and develop the strategies required for success.

iii. 'Social persuasion'

Bandura argues that individuals' self-efficacy can be encouraged if they are persuaded by others that 'they have what it takes to succeed'. He recognises, however, that it is easier to encourage people to believe that they do not have the skills required to accomplish a task, than it is to strengthen people's belief that they can succeed. Social persuasion is not just about giving verbal encouragement, as we shall see below, it is also about providing the right context for development.

iv. 'Somatic and emotional states'

This refers to people's moods and the way they respond to stress. For example, if people see aches and pains as a sign of weakness rather than a challenge then it will undermine their performance. If they see tension and stress as negative again it will affect their feelings of efficacy. So one of the ways to increase efficacy is to learn how to cope better with stress and improve your emotional state.

The impact of parents on the development of efficacy

> *The newborn comes without any sense of self. Infants' exploratory experiences in which they see themselves produce effects by their actions provide the initial basis for developing a sense of efficacy. Shaking a rattle produces predictable sounds, energetic kicks shake their cribs, and screams bring adults. ... Infants who experience success in controlling environmental events become more attentive to their own behaviour and more competent in learning new efficacious responses, than are infants for whom the same environmental events occur regardless of how they behave.*
>
> Albert Bandura

As is clear from the above quotation, Bandura argues that parents have a key role to play in helping young children to feel efficacious. By being responsive to their infant's behaviour parents can accelerate their child's social, linguistic and cognitive development. Once the child gets older the parents' role in developing efficacious attitudes is augmented by the child's peer group. Bandura argues that 'it is in peer relationships that [children] broaden self-knowledge of their capabilities'. He also argues that a child's level of self-efficacy can affect these peer relationships. Children who have too much can be aggressive and intimidate others while those who have too little can withdraw from social contact and thereby weaken further their faltering sense of efficacy.

Bandura argues that feelings of self-efficacy play an important part throughout an individual's life whether it be through the troublesome time of adolescence, entering the workforce, becoming a parent, dealing with retirement or coping with the impairments which can come with old age. However, he sees school days as the most important for the development of self-efficacy.

The importance of schools

Bandura asserts that schools have a major role to play at a formative period in people's lives in the formation of self-efficacy:

1. Schools expressly develop children's 'cognitive competencies', furnish them with knowledge and develop problem-solving skills.
2. Schools formally evaluate young people's competencies and compare them with others.
3. At school children are exposed informally to other young people and how they model cognitive skills, and compete with others.
4. Schools deliberately try to motivate children with rewards and punishments.
5. The way that teachers interpret and react to success and failure can have profound effects on children's feelings of efficacy.

In effect this means that teachers have tremendous opportunities to influence their students' feelings of efficacy.

TTT 5: Summary of techniques to encourage feelings of efficacy in students

- Be challenging.
- Help students with goal setting.
- Encourage students to see failure constructively.
- Give feedback that encourages good strategies for improvement.
- Give genuine encouragement.
- Encourage students' self-reflection.
- Get students to think and say … I can.

What teachers can do to encourage feelings of efficacy

i. Be challenging

Children develop feelings of mastery by being able to overcome challenges – not from accomplishing easy tasks. Mastery, therefore, requires persistence and some degree of frustration. Being overly sensitive to students by putting too much emphasis on how they feel in the here and now, and not encouraging them to stick with something, despite the frustration, will undermine the development of efficacy. Conversely, encouraging students to persevere with a difficult task, which they are likely to accomplish, will help build self-efficacy. This is not just consistent, but at one, with the spirit behind the *Curriculum for Excellence*. When describing principles for curriculum design, it states:

> *Young people should find their learning challenging, engaging and motivating. The curriculum should encourage high aspirations and ambitions for all. At all stages, learners of all aptitudes and abilities should experience an appropriate level of challenge, to enable each individual to achieve his or her potential.*

ii. Help students with goal setting

Bandura argues that failing at a task can undermine self-efficacy particularly 'if failures occur before a sense of efficacy is firmly established'. This means that teachers have an important part to play in helping young people set sufficiently challenging, yet realistic, goals. A. Woolfolk Hoy, in a paper called 'What do teachers need to know about self-efficacy?' recommends that teachers have regular goal setting and goal review meetings with students. Other experts on self-efficacy and education, Schunk and Parajes, contend that 'learning goals that are specific, short-term and viewed as challenging but attainable enhance students self-efficacy better than do goals that are general, long-term and not viewed as attainable'. This type of goal setting is a key part of Assessment for Learning and will be discussed more fully in Chapter 12.

iii Encourage students to see failure constructively

Even if teachers help students to set attainable goals students are still likely to encounter failure. They can be encouraged to take a more constructive view of failure, if the teacher does not link failure with fixed traits, such as IQ or physique, or other matters beyond the young person's control. Instead, the teacher should encourage the student to link failure to weaknesses which they can put right with effort and the application of better strategies. Alan McLean highlights the importance of this when he writes:

> *The primary cause of disengagement from learning is repeatedly putting failure down to stable, personal, uncontrollable, and global factors that suggest failure is inevitable. Students with a lethal cocktail of pessimistic explanations of progress, fixed ability*

ideas, a strong performance attitude to achievement and low competency beliefs are especially vulnerable to a spiral of failure avoidance.

iv. Give feedback that encourages good strategies for improvement

Zimmerman and Cleary, two experts on adolescents and 'personal agency', argue that this constructive view of failure must also be incorporated into teachers' feedback. Feedback can be defined as a structured response – either written or verbal – that aims to inform the learner about how they are doing and what steps they must take to achieve their desired goal. Zimmerman and Cleary argue feedback is important 'because it focuses a student's attention on important learning strategies'. Later they add that 'thinking in the "language of strategies" motivates adolescents to view success and failures in terms of using "controllable" strategies rather than innate, unchangeable factors such as ability'.

v. Give genuine encouragement

Bandura, Woolfolk Hoy and other experts on self-efficacy argue that social persuasion is important but that the potency of persuasion depends on the credibility, trustworthiness and expertise of the persuader. This is not a new notion. In the 1950s Eric Erikson warned 'children cannot be fooled by empty praise and condescending encouragement'. Nonetheless, this still means that a trusted teacher or coach can influence young people's effort. Woolfolk Hoy argues that the intervention of a good teacher or coach may be enough to encourage a student to make the effort which leads to improvement. As the French writer Anatole France once remarked: 'Nine tenths of education is encouragement'.

vi. Encourage students' self-reflection

Experts agree that an important aspect of self-efficacy is self-reflection. This means that teachers can help students develop self-efficacy if they encourage them to try to make sense of their personal experiences and their beliefs, and to evaluate themselves and their behaviour. Following this self-reflection the young person can then take steps to behave differently.

vii. Get students to think and say … I can

The language of self-esteem is 'I feel' whereas the language of self-efficacy is 'I can'. Such 'can-do' attitudes are the antithesis of Martin Seligman's helpfully defined 'learned helplessness'. It is very empowering for adults in Scotland, let alone young people, to focus attention on what they are able to do in life: to see themselves as active agents able to shape their own destiny. Again this is in tune with the *Curriculum for Excellence*. The *Progress and Proposals* document states that a key feature of the *CfE* approach is that it describes experiences and outcomes from the learner's point of view, using terms like 'I have …' for experiences and 'I can …' for outcomes.

Three barriers to building self-efficacy in Scotland

As we have just seen, there are many different strategies that individual teachers can employ immediately in their classrooms to help cultivate feelings of self-efficacy in their students. However, it is also important to recognise that there are certain barriers which are outwith their control.

i. Modelling

Research by Schunk, Harrison and Cox indicates that modelling (one of the four main ways to encourage feelings of efficacy) is most effective when models are similar in terms of age, ability and gender. In Scotland, the chances of students having male teachers to model ability and behaviour for them are low. Scottish Executive figures from 2005 show that three-quarters of teachers in Scotland are women; the gender imbalance is likely to increase, given the rise in applications from females to university education faculties. It should be noted, however, that a study of eleven-year-olds in a national sample of English primary schools by the University of Durham in 2005 found that teachers' gender was unrelated to children's attainment. So it is likely that the problem of gender imbalance may be one for secondary, rather than primary schools.

ii. The need for more curriculum choice

Self-efficacy experts such as Bandura and Pajares recognise the importance of intrinsic motivation. This happens when we are doing something for its own sake or because it gives us a sense of satisfaction or stimulation. Extrinsic motivation comes from rewards (such as payment), punishments or from our desire to please others.

It is much easier for a teacher to nourish a young person's feelings of efficacy around tasks that are in tune with their intrinsic motivation. One of the problems facing many teachers is that they are trying to involve young people in subjects that are just not of interest to them. Alan McLean, an expert on disengaged young people, highlights the problem when he writes: 'Disengaged students need alternative learning contexts to start from, and build on, their interests and goals. Learning needs to be connected to students' lives, involving real life challenges and experiences'.

Fortunately, this need for varied and relevant education is being recognised by education policy makers and leaders in Scotland. The HMIE 2005 document *Improving Scottish Education* claims there is a need for 'vocational education' to become 'integral to the education of all pupils'. The vision here is not 'two separate types of education' and a struggle to maintain 'parity of esteem' but to create a system which provides 'an appropriate education for all'. This means more relevance in the curriculum, at least for some learners. This is a welcome change.

iii. Teacher efficacy

Research shows that teachers' self-efficacy affects their students. A teacher with a high level is more likely to create mastery experiences for students, whereas a teacher who feels powerless, and lacks efficacy, is more likely to undermine his/her students' belief that they can achieve.

There have been many welcome developments in Scottish education in the past twenty years. Teachers have had to absorb and cope with many changes but while teachers' professionalism improves, their confidence and feelings of powerlessness appear to be an issue. This quickly emerges if you talk to probationary teachers about their experience in schools, to teachers themselves and to education managers. So if teachers are to deliver the *CfE's* commitment to create 'confident individuals', teachers themselves will need to become more confident. This may mean more exposure to ideas on how to increase their own efficacy and optimism but it will also require changes within the system which empower teachers rather than direct them.

The importance of basic skills

Clearly I passionately believe that teachers should take steps to attend to their students' confidence and well-being. However, I also think that these aspirations need to be kept in perspective. The most important function schools need to perform is teaching young people basic literacy and numeracy skills. In our modern world it is very difficult for people to survive economically and socially, let alone feel confident, if they are unable to read, write or count. Yet this is the challenge facing twenty per cent of the Scottish population – once the most literate country in the world.

Years ago I volunteered as an adult literacy tutor. My student was a man named John who was good with his hands and was working for himself as a builder. He was a likeable man with good social skills and lots of drive. But it was clear that his problems with literacy and numeracy were huge barriers for him. When he attended a course on starting up in business, he went along with his arm in a sling in case he was asked to write. He permanently had problems giving people quotations for work, working out quantities and charging fees. There is not a technique in this book that would have helped John more than being able to read, write and count.

John's failure to learn these basic skills was not about poor teaching. His mother had a chronic illness and frequently kept him off school. He was not particularly motivated by school so he was happy to stay off. It was the system, and a lack of support, that let John down. Many of the young people who are currently performing badly at school are much more the victims of deprivation and multiple social problems than the lack of good teaching.

Changing the system to tackle deprivation and to help vulnerable young people learn basic skills, and develop 'can-do' attitudes, will require a strong sense of collective and optimistic efficacy. Some of the techniques and attitudes outlined in this book could help people to work together to achieve these goals.

Assertiveness skills

Finally, one of the best techniques I have encountered for building confidence is assertiveness training. This is often described as a way of developing self-esteem, however for me this is a by-product. The main benefit of assertiveness training is that it encourages self-efficacy in a very important area of life – communication and negotiation skills. Feeling that you can communicate better, and deal with difficult situations, raises efficacious feelings, hence confidence.

Here is an illustration of what I am talking about. An individual's goal may be to walk across the desert. Ostensibly, the skills required for this feat have nothing to do with assertive behaviour as such and have more to do with fitness and survival skills. The ability to endure a challenging task on your own is also central to the realisation of this goal. However, most tasks in life cannot be accomplished alone and require us to communicate and negotiate with others. Indeed, even in the example of the trek through the desert, assertiveness skills may have been required in negotiating with employers, parents, travel companies or government agents. Failure in these negotiations may bring the goal to a premature end. So accomplishing just about anything in life is easier if we have the ability to communicate well with others and know how to negotiate. These skills are important in all walks of life but of crucial significance to teachers who have to be assertive both in and outside the classroom.

Giving more information on assertive behaviour or techniques on how to behave more assertively are outwith the scope of this *Handbook*. However, anyone interested in knowing more can download materials on assertiveness from the Centre's website.

Key Points

1. Self-efficacy is not synonymous with self-esteem: self-esteem refers to feelings about the self whereas self-efficacy is about agency or the ability to take action and achieve specific goals, along with self-belief.
2. Self-efficacy beliefs determine how people feel, think, motivate themselves and behave.
3. People who are low in self-efficacy are very vulnerable and succumb more readily to stress and depression.
4. Bandura argues that self-efficacy, 'human accomplishments and positive well-being' are facilitated by feelings of optimism.
5. The newborn comes without any sense of self and parents have a key role to play in helping young children to feel efficacious.
6. Bandura argues that schools have a major role to play at a formative period in people's lives in the formation of self-efficacy and that 'it is in peer relationships that [children] broaden self-knowledge of their capabilities'.
7. Children develop feelings of mastery by being able to overcome challenges – not from accomplishing easy tasks. Conversely, encouraging students to persevere with a difficult task, which they are likely to accomplish, will help build self-efficacy.
8. Learning goals that are specific, short term and viewed as challenging but attainable enhance students' self-efficacy better than do goals that are general, long-term and not viewed as attainable.

9. Teachers can help students develop self-efficacy if they encourage them to try to make sense of their personal experiences and their beliefs, and to evaluate themselves and their behaviour.

10. The language of self-esteem is 'I feel' whereas the language of self-efficacy is 'I can'.

11. The main benefit of assertiveness training is that it encourages self-efficacy in very important areas of life – communication and negotiation skills.

9 Optimism and Hope

Optimism is faith that leads to achievement. Nothing can be done without hope or confidence. ... No pessimist ever discovered the secret of the stars, or sailed to unchartered land, or opened a new doorway for the human spirit.

Helen Keller

Optimism

An optimist is commonly thought of as someone who sees the silver lining in every cloud and views the world through rose-tinted spectacles (or a glass that's always half full). Some of these attitudes can be witnessed in optimists, but with more than twenty years of solid scientific research into the subject, it is clear that optimism goes much deeper than was previously thought. Alongside self-efficacy optimism is a core ingredient of confidence and important for well-being and quality of life. In short, it is a topic that certainly warrants attention in this *Handbook*.

Why optimism matters

More than 100 studies have shown the impact of optimism and pessimism on people's lives. Professor Chris Peterson, a leading Positive Psychologist, likens optimism to 'velcro' in that it is attached to all the ingredients which promote well-being, happiness and, as we will see below, the confidence to act. As may be seen in Box 9, whether young people think optimistically or pessimistically has important implications for their life both in and outside of school.

BOX 9: Relevance of optimistic and pessimistic thinking to young people's lives

Optimistic thinking	Pessimistic thinking
Persisting in the face of difficulties or after failure	Giving up; expecting failure
Feeling confident	Feelings of helplessness and vulnerable to depression
Effective problem-solving strategies – particularly factoring in a number of variables	Expecting the worst so not taking action and working on solutions
Achieving more in school, enterprising activities or sport than IQ or aptitude tests would predict	Doing less well than intelligence and skills aptitude tests predicted
Good health	Poorer health outcomes; more prone to infection and less able to make good health decisions
Popular, strong social ties	Socially isolated

One of the main reasons pessimism is often insidious is that it causes people to lose heart and give up. This is understandable: if you think the outcome is doomed to be bad then why bother doing anything?

Research indicates that as many as seven to ten years of life expectancy may be at stake in whether a person is an optimist or a pessimist. This is more significant for life expectancy than smoking a pack of cigarettes every day. One of the reasons advanced for why optimists tend to be healthier than pessimists is that negative emotions release certain hormones, which undermines well-being.

In psychology there are two main ways to define optimism: Scheier and Carver's dispositional optimism, which refers to people who generally 'look on the bright side of life'; and Professor Martin Seligman's concept of 'explanatory style'. Since the latter approach is linked to evidence that leads to different ways to increase optimism, this is the version we shall focus on here.

Explanatory style

> *The basis of optimism does not lie in positive phrases or images of victory, but in the way you think about causes.*
>
> Martin Seligman

Professor Martin Seligman is author of *Learned Optimism* and co-author of *The Optimistic Child*. He argues that each of us has our own 'explanatory style', a way of thinking about the causes of things that happen in our lives. We develop our explanatory style during childhood and, unless deliberate steps are taken to change it, it will last for the whole of our life, acting as a prism through which we explain to ourselves why things, good or bad, happen to us.

Seligman argues that there are three central dimensions that we use to interpret events in our lives; these dimensions are permanence, pervasiveness and personalisation.

i. Permanence versus temporary (always/not always)

People whose explanatory style is pessimistic will assume that when something goes wrong, then it will always go wrong. If they deliver an inadequate talk in the classroom, they assume that they will always be poor at public speaking. 'There is no point in me volunteering to talk, I'll always screw it up', they tell themselves.

Those who have an optimistic explanatory style will simply tell themselves that it will go better next time, that it is just a temporary setback. 'Maybe my talk wasn't that great and I dried up a bit. But some boys in the class asked me things about it later. Next time I'll do more preparation.'

Dr Karen Reivich, co-author of *The Resilience Factor* and *The Optimistic Child*, is a colleague of Dr Martin Seligman and has worked with him and other researchers on a wide range of studies. She shares Seligman's conviction about the importance of explanatory style and has developed the model further. Her version of the permanence dimensions of optimism/ pessimism she calls 'always versus not always'. In other words, how lasting across time do you understand the cause of the problem to be? So a student who explains an exam failure by saying 'I'm stupid' has an 'always' view of their problem, seeing it as lasting across time, and will probably take a pessimistic approach to the re-sits. Eventually this negative belief becomes permanent. Their class-mate who also fails but says 'I didn't do any studying before that exam', has a 'not always' explanation and is likely to take an optimistic view of their next test. The optimistic student sees the problem as temporary – something that can change.

ii. Pervasiveness versus specific (everything/not everything)

When things go wrong for pessimists, they tend to catastrophise. They see their failures as all-pervasive, or global:

- I'll never be any good at sport
- I'm a total failure
- no one in the class likes me.

Optimists don't like failure either, but they see it as a specific setback rather than all-pervasive:

- I didn't play well on Saturday, but I missed a lot of training because of my sore knee
- this year I've not been doing as well at school
- some of the folk in the class don't like me but I've got friends in other classes.

Reivich describes this dimension as 'everything versus not everything'. She too sees this as being whether you tend to globalise, to catastrophise, to see a problem as flowing through many aspects of your life. If you do see setbacks in one area of your life as permeating others, then you are an 'everything' person. But if you tend to compartmentalise and come up with very specific explanations for what caused a negative event, then you are more of a 'not everything' thinker.

iii. Personal – internal versus external (me/not me)

This axis is about deciding where to attribute responsibility when things go wrong. Pessimists will blame themselves, thus internalising the problem. Optimists will often consider a greater number of factors – including external events, others' action and so on. Those who tend to blame themselves for everything that goes wrong often have low self-esteem, while those who find external reasons for setbacks will generally feel more positive about themselves.

Recently, Seligman has had second thoughts about whether it is worth focusing on the personal dimension, since doing so can encourage people merely to blame others for what goes wrong – something that is rife in contemporary society. However, this remains an important aspect of Reivich's work. She prefers to use the labels 'me'/'not me', and argues that this dimension is not about whether you blame yourself or other people, it is about adding new information when considering what went wrong. If you are a 'me' person then you are likely to blame yourself for what went wrong, but if you usually believe that the cause of things that go wrong is 'not me' then you will seek an external explanation. If you are late for a meeting and you put it down to unusually high traffic congestion, then that is a 'not me' explanation, whereas 'I never leave myself enough time to get to meetings' is a 'me' explanation. 'I don't believe you can be an effective problem solver if you don't consider where the cause of the problem lies. And so my goal isn't to take someone who's a "me" person and say "okay simply point the finger outwards and blame everyone else"', she says.

Her argument is that if you are a 'me' person you should notice everything that you did that led to this problem. But you should also consider other things that contributed to the problem. 'Similarly if you're a "not me" person and you're always blaming others, my challenge to you would be to say "great, you notice everything about the weather and everyone else, but is there one thing you did?" I don't think we can just dismiss this dimension', she says.

So an optimistic thinker is someone who, when problems arise, tends to say, 'not me', 'not always', 'not everything'. So when bad things happen, their style of thinking focuses them on the causes of the problem, particularly circumstances that are changeable and that are very specific and not going to lead to lots of other problems in their life. Optimism is – 'not me', 'not always', 'not everything'.

If, however, when things go wrong or adversity strikes, and a person usually sees the causes of the problems as being: about them, hard to change, long-lasting and likely to cause problems in other parts of their life, then they have a more pessimistic thinking style.

Interpreting good events

Explanatory style is not just relevant to how you view bad events but also to how a person interprets the good things that happen in life. What we see is a reversal of the pattern described above. Optimists see good fortune, such as passing an English exam with flying colours as permanent (I'm going to keep doing well in English), pervasive (I'm going to keep doing well at school) and something about them (I really worked hard/I'm good at English). Whereas pessimists are more likely to see something good as temporary (the work will get harder next year), specific (it was just a one off) and something they are not responsible for (it was a fluke, I was lucky).

Good news for pessimists

Addressing the Centre for Confidence and Well-being's Vanguard Programme in 2006, Dr Reivich emphasised the fact that we can learn to become more optimistic:

> *I want to stress that these are thinking styles, these are not personality traits. And because they are thinking styles, they are changeable. So even if today your style is to be more of a pessimistic thinker, we have strong data to suggest that by learning some resilience and optimism skills, you can absolutely increase your ability to focus on other causes of the problem, particularly those that are more changeable and are more local.*

How optimism develops

> *There is no sadder sight than a young pessimist.*
>
> Mark Twain

Research into twins in recent years has revealed that personality traits and the disposition for optimism and pessimism, for example, are much more genetically determined than previously thought. Identical twins, even if raised apart and subject to different influences when growing up, are remarkably similar in terms of levels of optimism and happiness. This still means that the other 50 per cent are shaped by external factors.

Parents, teachers and coaches have, after genetic inheritance, the biggest influence on whether young people develop an optimistic or pessimistic explanatory style. It is from these sources of influence that children learn how to interpret good and bad events. Seligman and Reivich say that these important adults must be particularly careful in how they criticise children and young people, and should encourage them to adopt a positive, optimistic outlook. The prevailing culture is also important, as this may have influenced the explanatory style of parents and teachers. This is the argument I advanced in Chapter 3 when I reasoned that Scottish culture encourages people to adopt a pessimistic explanatory style.

Seligman also argues that single, highly significant events can shape a child's explanatory style. The death of a mother when the child is under eleven increases the risk of depression in later life. Such a catastrophic event is both permanent and pervasive, affecting many aspects of the child's outlook. In such cases, '...all setbacks are soon catastrophised into permanent and pervasive losses', he says. Other childhood issues tending to create a pessimistic outlook include physical and sexual abuse, or strife between parents, and divorce.

TTT 6: Giving 'optimistic' criticism

One of the most important steps parents and teachers can take to increase young people's optimistic explanatory style is to be careful in how they criticise children. For example, instead of saying 'At this rate you're never going to pass any of those exams', it is much better to say 'If you did your homework you'd pass your maths exam'. By using criticism that offers a specific strategy for change (do your homework) and which is non-pervasive (it's just the maths where your problem lies) the child is encouraged to be more optimistic. Criticism should also be accurate; exaggerating faults only induces unnecessary levels of guilt and shame.

A quick and easy way to think about using criticism optimistically is that we should:

- be very careful about using the words 'always' and 'never'
- make any critical remarks as specific as possible
- try to factor in a variety of causes when things go wrong.

Programmes to increase young people's optimism

The Penn Resiliency Program (PRP) is a school-based intervention, designed to build resilience, increase optimism, promote adaptive coping skills, and teach effective problem-solving in children. It was devised in Pennsylvania by Professor Martin Seligman, Dr Karen Reivich and Dr Jane Gillham. A major goal of the programme is to promote optimistic thinking to help children and adolescents. Research shows that it is effective in helping buffer children against the effects of stress, including more serious levels of stress such as anxiety and depression. Many of the ideas underlying the programme can be accessed in *The Optimistic Child*. An Australian programme called *Bounce Back*, which is examined more fully in the next chapter, also teaches young people how to develop a more optimistic explanatory style and has also proved to be effective. Helen McGrath and Toni Noble, the *Bounce Back* authors, have come up with a useful technique to encourage people to attribute responsibility in a fair and accurate manner; this is outlined in Tools, Tips and Techniques 7.

Personal responsibility

When things go wrong it is common for people to do one of two things – either blame themselves for the problem, even when they are not totally responsible, or blame other people and absolve themselves of all responsibility. Neither approach leads to a positive outcome. Blaming ourselves unfairly, and not factoring in other variables, leads to pessimism and a loss of feelings of self-worth. However, blaming others for problems is also counterproductive as it often undermines relationships and prevents us from learning from our mistakes. In short, it retards our development.

Techniques to increase optimism

The technique favoured by Professor Seligman to teach optimism skills is the ABCDE technique devised by Albert Ellis, founder of Rational Emotive Behaviour Therapy, which is similar to Cognitive Behavioural Therapy. However, this is a fairly complicated technique to use and so here I am going to simply outline some of the key elements of enhancing optimistic thinking. This will allow readers who are usually optimistic to become more aware of how they maintain optimistic thought processes. Heightening self-awareness in this way allows optimistic teachers to pass on these skills more readily to others, including young people. It will also help those with a proclivity to pessimism to become aware of the shift in thinking that would help them to become more optimistic. *(Information on how to learn about the ABCDE technique is contained in the resources section.)*

Disputation

Most people in countries around the world admit, when asked, to having an internal voice, which often says fearful and critical things. Professor Martin Seligman argues that commonly people, if they are roundly and unfairly criticised by others, do not meekly take it but argue back using various facts that dispute the criticisms. However, Seligman argues that when the criticism is being put forward internally by ourselves we often just accept that it must be true and do not question its validity. After all, we know ourselves better than anyone else so the criticisms must be true. Seligman, a self-confessed pessimist, maintains that pessimists either have more vocal, critical inner voices or pay more attention to what is being said, than do natural optimists.

So a central technique in increasing optimism is for people to become more conscious of their internal, critical voice and to detach themselves from it. Seligman says it is helpful if people with a proclivity for pessimism can teach themselves to see this inner critic as an enemy who is out to make life as difficult for them as possible.

The next stage in the process is to engage in a 'disputation' with this critical voice. Bearing in mind the tendency in pessimists to see problems as long-lasting, pervasive and somehow their fault, what is involved here is trying to come up with factual information which disputes the pessimistic charge of the inner critic. Note that this does not mean the type of wishful, affirmative approach often advanced by positive thinking courses. For example, if you have handled a class very badly, positive thinking courses may suggest that you keep telling yourself

'I am a wonderful, professional teacher'. However, the problem with this approach is that it is often difficult to fool ourselves in this way. The inner voice is simply likely to intrude and say 'aye, right'.

TTT 7: Allocating responsibility using Responsibility Pie Charts (RPC)

An RPC is a concrete way for students to understand that all negative situations can be said to occur as a result of a combination of three factors:

- Their own actions: How much did their own behaviour or others contribute to the situation (me)?
- The action of others: How much did the behaviour of others contribute to the situation (others)?
- Random unpredictable factors: How much did bad luck or circumstances (eg weather, timing, coincidences, lack of knowledge, illness) contribute to the situation (random factors)?

The RPC can either simply be drawn on a piece of paper or a moveable device created (see resources section).

When students are asked to allocate responsibility following an incident or event, it is a good idea to allow them to allocate no responsibility to 'others' or to 'random factors' or bad luck. But they must always allocate at least 10 per cent to their own actions (me).

Some students are likely to allocate too much responsibility to themselves and not enough to other factors and you can point this out to them and discuss whether they want to amend their percentages. Other students allocate too little to themselves and you might want to discuss this with them as well.

It is useful when discussing responsibility with young people to try and avoid the words 'blame' and 'fault' and use the following terms instead:

How much was ... responsible for what happened?

How much was what happened due to ...?

How much did this happen because of ...?

How much does ... explain what happened?

Helen McGrath and Toni Noble recount that schools using the *Bounce Back* programme have made moveable pie chart devices and used them, to great effect, in the playground when they need to debrief various incidents.

Adapted from *Bounce Back*, by Helen McGrath and Toni Noble

Disputation gets round this problem by encouraging the individual to stick to facts, or at least to alternative, realistic ways of viewing the problem. Much of pessimistic thinking is driven by fear, not fact, and so what we need to do is to build a more optimistic perspective by generating alternative interpretations. In the case of handling the class badly there may be extenuating circumstances, such as being particularly tired that day because of additional commitments, or the fact that this class (or student in it) is presenting difficulties for other colleagues as well. Even if you have to admit to yourself that class discipline is not something that you are particularly good at you can still 'decatastrophise' the difficulty by looking at how you could get help with this problem and so improve. If you have to admit it is a serious difficulty you can still look at your options, which may include leaving teaching for another profession where this type of discipline issue would not present a problem. In other words, instead of seeing the problem as a catastrophe, acknowledging and containing it can help you to see that while it presents difficulties these will be short-lived and do not have to cast a long shadow either into your future or other domains of your life. This is what pessimistic thinking tends to do and it can be dispiriting and de-energising.

As Karen Reivich explains, in becoming more optimistic people have to become much more attuned to how they are using the formulation of 'always', 'everything' and 'me' when they meet difficulties in life.

TTT 8: Helping young people to become more optimistic

Teachers have an important part to play in helping young people become more optimistic, simply by modelling an optimistic explanatory style. However, teachers and other professionals can become more alert to pessimistic tendencies in young people and actively challenge these. Essentially, what teachers and others need to do is listen carefully to how young people recount bad events, particularly listening for explanations that suggest the difficulty is permanent, pervasive and related to something unchangeable about them. However, you have to be aware of the fact that pessimists often express their negative views subtly. For example, here are two different ways young people could respond to a poor examination result:

Student A: I'm not surprised I failed. I'm not good at exams.

Student B: I'm not surprised I failed. I just waffled and wrote garbage. Mince. None of my questions came up. I'm rotten at history.

Student B's response although apparently more negative and self-deprecating, is much more optimistic. S/he explains the problem in ways that are not permanent and pervasive whereas Student A's views are much more pessimistic.

If we become alert to pessimistic formulations then it is possible to start challenging them. The trick here is to help dissolve faulty thinking and beliefs by really concentrating on facts. Asking student A to recount exams they have passed would be useful, as would finding out the exact source of their problem. Is it because they don't study enough or haven't developed good study skills? Is it nerves? By breaking it down in this way students can be helped to see how problems can be overcome and so optimism increased.

Optimism and health

As we saw earlier, there are clear health and well-being implications of being optimistic and this is particularly important for Scotland, given some of our poor health record. Pessimistic thinking has been linked to low life expectancy – a feature all too prevalent in poor areas of Scotland. In some deprived areas of Glasgow, the life expectancy for men is 54 – lower than it is in many third world countries. In the wealthiest areas of Scotland it is 78 years. Scotland's Chief Medical Officer, Dr Harry Burns, argues that many of Scotland's health inequalities are driven by feelings of hopelessness. Changing life circumstances for poor people, through employment schemes or better housing, is part of the solution. But he thinks that we also have to tackle the underlying psychology as well.

There is a simple explanation for the link between our explanatory style and the things that happen in our lives. Dr Karen Reivich points out that if we look at a 50 year-old man who smokes, drinks a lot of alcohol, eats a lot of red meat and has had a first coronary episode, we shall find that his explanatory style has a big impact on his ultimate health outcome. Pessimists tend to be passive in the face of bad news, rather than spurred into action to change their lifestyle and improve their health. Reivich explains it in the following terms:

> *The doctor says 'you need to quit smoking, quit drinking and change your diet'. But if you're a 'me', 'always', 'everything' type, then what will pop into your head? Most*

likely you'll say to yourself something like 'it's in my genes, my father died of a heart attack, his father died of a heart attack, I'm just destined for this'. And if that's your belief then that's going to dictate your behaviour, and you're going to be less likely to follow doctor's orders. So there's nothing magical about the pathway through which explanatory style leads to real world outcome, explanatory style drives behaviour – and behaviour is what leads to outcomes.

Research led by Dr Mika Kivimaki in Finland concluded that optimism may reduce the risk of health problems and actually help a person to recover after experiencing a serious life-changing event, such as death of a spouse or child. Following a major life crisis, pessimists tend to take more time off work than optimists. According to Kivimaki, 'Pessimists frequently distance themselves from emotional events and this coping strategy may be less effective than using active problem-focused coping immediately after an uncontrollable severe event such as death of a family member'.

People who think pessimistically face the real risk of giving up in the face of adversity, of passively accepting that they were born to draw the short straw in life. But we do not need to live like this. When bad things happen we can take action by striving to find the 'not me', 'not always', 'not everything' explanations, then focus our energy there.

For some people this could mean the difference between life and death.

Optimism and sport

Sports enthusiasts at every level are intuitively aware that the 'mental' part of performance can be just as important as the physical. Gymnastics are often said to be 90 per cent mental and 10 per cent physical. Other sports see 'intangible' factors, such as confidence and a 'cool' head under pressure, make up more than 50 per cent of success.

Many will talk about 'being in the zone' when they perform at their peak. Olympic 100 metre gold medallist Linford Christie described his focus on the starting line as being like looking down a long, straight tunnel. His ability to blank out other competitors, the roar of the crowd, the flashbulbs, gave him those extra centimetres over his rivals.

In sport, psychology matters – and at every level. If you go onto the tennis court telling yourself that you have never beaten Jill before and that you are not going to beat her today, then the result is very predictable.

Optimism boosts sporting performance, both at team and individual levels. Research into baseball and basketball teams in the USA revealed that teams have their own explanatory styles. The explanatory style used by teams after a defeat or when under pressure in the last few minutes of a game will determine future performance, regardless of the quality of the team. Those who are optimistic in the face of defeat are more likely to be successful in their next game; those who explain setbacks negatively will perform more poorly. Research into swimmers revealed that the same trend holds for individual athletes. Quite simply, when under pressure optimistic sportsmen and women try harder.

How to use optimism appropriately

A note of caution is required however. Like all things in life, optimism can be overdone. People who are overly optimistic can take unacceptable risks or be called foolhardy, cavalier or just plain foolish. Thinking that the worst may happen has a protective function. It keeps us alert to possible danger and is part of our survival instinct. If we are in risky situations where the cost of failure is high then it pays to be pessimistic rather than optimistic. Seligman talks about 'realistic optimism' and gives specific advice for when to use optimism techniques.

TTT 9: When to use optimism techniques with young people

Here is some guidance, based on Professor Martin Seligman's work:

When to encourage optimism in young people

- If the young person is in a situation linked to achievement (tackling a challenge, winning a game, performing in a test)
- If the child is concerned about how they feel (fighting off depression, keeping up morale)
- If the situation is apt to be protracted and physical health is an issue
- If they are in a position to inspire or lead others – eg captain of a team, prefect.

When to avoid using optimism techniques

- If the child's future is risky or uncertain and when the cost of failure is high
- If your goal is to counsel children whose future is dim don't use optimism initially. If you want to appear sympathetic to a child's troubles don't begin with optimism although you can work towards it when their confidence picks up.

Measuring optimism

There are a variety of tests to measure optimism. One of the main ones is Scheier and Carver's Life Orientation Test (Revised) – LOT-R. This comprises a ten-item scale that includes three filler questions. It is easy to score and administer (for further information see Resources Section). This is a straightforward test to measure how optimistic an individual is about the future and is the one the Centre is currently using, simply on grounds of practicality. However, Professor Martin Seligman has devised an optimism test which you can complete free on the Authentic Happiness website (www.authentichappiness.com). The advantage of this test is that it is not a simple measure of optimism but breaks responses down into categories related to explanatory style, such as pervasive and permanent. It also makes a distinction between optimism in the face of bad and good events.

Critics

As is always the case in psychology not everyone agrees with the way that Martin Seligman views optimism or his belief that it can be changed. Some argue that it is more dispositional than he makes out and that it is not easy to teach people who are naturally pessimistic how to become more optimistic. However, it must be said that Seligman never claims that it is possible to take someone who is very pessimistic and turn them into an optimist. He is arguing that it is possible to make their explanatory style more optimistic by 20-30 per cent.

Defensive pessimism

An American psychologist, Julie K. Norem, argues that there are people who do not benefit from being told to become more optimistic. She calls them 'defensive pessimists'.

> *Defensive pessimists expect the worst, and spend lots of time and energy mentally rehearsing, in vivid, daunting detail, exactly how things might go wrong. Before a business presentation, they worry that PowerPoint might fail, that the microphone will go dead, that – worst of all – they will stare out at the audience and go blank. Before a dinner party they imagine that the new neighbours will clash with the old, and the sushi will give everyone food poisoning.*
>
> Julie K. Norem

In her book *The Positive Power of Negative Thinking* Norem argues that those who fret a lot about what might go wrong can actually forestall the disastrous outcomes they fear. She says that always seeking the worst outcomes can help defensive pessimists harness their anxiety, allowing them to perform at their peak. The optimistic news for dyed-in-the-wool pessimists is that they need not struggle to find the silver lining. 'Trying to squeeze everyone into an optimistic perspective can be both uncomfortable and unproductive, like struggling to stuff a queen size body into petite size pantyhose,' says Norem.

Trying to be positive when we are feeling anxious can backfire, because we are discounting our real feelings. By acknowledging and controlling their worries, pessimists can unleash the positive power within their negativity. By trying to predict everything that could go wrong, they can identify strategies that have a good chance of working effectively and of helping them achieve their goals. Norem argues:

> *Defensive pessimism isn't different from good planning in terms of the ultimate results. It is different because of its role in getting to those results: Defensive pessimism is the process that allows anxious people to do good planning. They can't plan effectively until they control their anxiety. They have to go through their worst-case scenarios and exhaustive mental rehearsal in order to start the process of planning, carry it through effectively and then get from planning to doing.*

Her theory is not an attack on optimism and its importance; it is an important insight into the fact that some people are at their most effective when they fear the worst and plan strategies to minimize the disastrous outcomes they envisage, thus seizing victory from the jaws of defeat. Teachers, colleagues, managers, family members and others can help by understanding that those who see the world through a glass darkly can sometimes be more effective if they convince themselves that the worst might happen.

Hope

> *If you lose hope, somehow you lose the vitality that keeps life moving, you lose that courage to be, that quality that helps you go on in spite of it all. And so today I still have a dream.*
>
> Martin Luther King

In everyday life it is common to see hope as an emotion – as a feeling, often contrary to harsh reality, that a good outcome is possible. In other words, hope is often seen as little more than wishful thinking, a naïve crossing of fingers, and so somehow detached from the eventual outcome. However, this is not to say that hope is disparaged. Hope is also commonly seen as a good thing - as a virtue that sustains the individual and allows them to experience positive emotion in dark, difficult times.

However, research undertaken by a psychologist, Professor C. R. Snyder, portrays hope in a different light. He claims that hope is not an emotion but a cognitive ability. He maintains that 'hopeful thought reflects the belief that one can find pathways to desired goals and become motivated to use those pathways'. So those who are hopeful have the ability to imagine different approaches to problems and to be able to keep going until the problem is solved. This definition reframes the hopeful so that they are no longer simply wishful thinkers but problem-solvers who are able to motivate themselves to achieve goals which others may think impossible.

Some hope theorists refer to 'conceptual hope', which is applicable to abstract concepts such as 'world peace'. They also talk about 'operational hope', which refers to one's own life. It is this type of hope that we mainly look at here.

Hope is incredibly important for human beings and for well-being. It is hope that gives life meaning and purpose and without it we often feel powerless and adrift. Research shows that those who have high hopes are healthier and have good relationships with others. They also achieve more academically and in sport.

Good personal relationships early in life that foster trust appear to be critically important in nurturing hope in young people. Unlike optimism, for example, which seems to be partly genetic, hope is generally seen as something we learn. In short, it is part of our socialisation.

TTT 10: Encouraging young people's hope

Here are a few simple ways to get young people thinking more hopefully:

- Give young people opportunities to articulate their dreams for the future. This could be done in class essays or projects.
- Introduce young people to the idea of pathways to goals and the importance of having different paths so that it is possible to switch paths and keep going when some pathways are blocked.
- Hope theory need not be presented formally. It could be conveyed via discussion of films or literature featuring historical or fictional characters. Nelson Mandela is a good example of someone who lived with hope.
- The focus on hope need not be for the individual student. The class could discuss their general hopes for the future and then try mapping out ways they might begin to achieve some of these goals collectively. This could provide energy and interest for some charitable or sponsorship projects.

Young people and hope

Children and young people are generally full of hope. Their hope is not easily extinguished, but it can be easily hidden. Often children and young people hide their hopes, even from themselves and certainly from others. Even after years of separation, children of divorced parents still hope for some reconciliation. Children often have unrealistic hopes about their futures – few will end up being the dashing football star, the celebrity singer or model.

Professionals, teachers and others must always remember that the lives of children and young people are not dominated by their attendance at school or their engagement with professionals. School is not their life. And young people's hopes are grounded mainly in their life experience outside of school and in their own personal ambitions. These ambitions depend on their 'ambit', the scope of the world they inhabit. The best teachers are often those who help to open up a child's ambition and the breadth of their world view and manage to support the young person's hope of operating successfully in that expanded world. This is as true of pupils striving to study medicine or philosophy as it is of children with learning difficulties. The hope of the world is closely wrapped up in the expansion of children's ambition.

Hope theory

Snyder's definition suggests that there are two processes at work when an individual is being hopeful – 'pathway thinking' and 'agentic thinking'.

i. Pathway thinking

This is the belief that we can move towards and reach goals by working out possible routes to get there. Snyder argues that the more possible routes a person generates the better their chances of reaching their goal. Indeed, Snyder's research shows that one of the characteristics of individuals who are highly hopeful is that they generate many more of these pathways to desired goals than do people who are low in hope.

ii. Agency

Someone high in hope does not simply envisage multiple pathways to their goals, they also believe they can keep going if pathways are blocked. So hope involves not just the ability to generate pathways but the belief that motivation can be sustained in the face of obstacles and difficulties. In short, a hopeful person sees him or herself as an agent who is able to achieve their goal.

Those who lack hope, by contrast, not only generate few pathways to desired goals but are likely to collapse – or give in/feel overwhelmed – if they find a pathway blocked and non-negotiable. Difficulties can also present themselves when someone persists too long on a blocked pathway rather than giving up and finding a more encouraging route.

Key Points

1. Optimism plays an important part in people's lives. More than 100 international studies have shown that optimism is linked to good health, educational and sporting achievement and good relationships.
2. There are two main ways to define optimism. One is to define it as the disposition to see things in a positive light. The other is to see it as part of an individual's 'explanatory style'. It is this second definition which we use in this *Handbook*.
3. Explanatory style refers to how a person interprets good and bad events. Optimists see bad events as temporary, restricted and not necessarily their fault. Pessimists see problems as long-lasting, worse than they are and often due to their own shortcomings. For good events, this pattern is reversed. So, for example, optimists see good fortune as something which will last.
4. Various programmes have been devised to teach young people to think more optimistically.
5. One of the main ways to teach the skills of optimistic thinking is called 'disputation'. This is the opposite of wishful thinking as it encourages people to concentrate on evidence. Often pessimistic thinking is based on fear, not fact.
6. Teachers can encourage young people to be more optimistic if they are careful about how they attribute the cause of good and bad events.
7. Optimism can be overdone. Pessimism has a purpose as it helps us to pay attention to possible dangers. We should not encourage others to be optimistic if the costs of failure are high.
8. There are various scales to measure optimism.
9. Some psychologists are critical of the concept of 'explanatory style' and doubt if optimism can be taught.
10. Julie K. Norem has advanced the idea of 'defensive pessimism'. She argues that some people find they do their best if they think the worst might happen as this is what galvanises them to prepare by studying, for example.
11. Hope is important to the quality of our lives.

10 Resilience

If I regarded my life from the point of view of the pessimist, I should be undone. I should seek in vain for the light that does not visit my eyes and the music that does not ring in my ears. I should beg night and day and never be satisfied. I should sit apart in awful solitude, a prey to fear and despair. But since I consider it a duty to myself and to others to be happy, I escape a misery worse than any physical deprivation.

Helen Keller

Understanding resilience

Even for the best cared-for child, the world can seem full of adversity. Think back to some of the big challenges in your young life: your first day at school, establishing friendships, your performance for the sports team, your role in the Christmas show, sitting tests, graduation to secondary school – then it starts all over again. Other major challenges for young people include coping with introductions to alcohol, drugs, sex and bullying. The ability to cope with these challenges varies considerably from individual to individual.

Over the last 30 or 40 years psychologists have realised that if we can find and identify the elements of natural resilience, then ways of helping those with low resilience could be developed. In a stressful, fast-changing world, boosting resilience in individuals and communities could help inoculate against depression and other mental illness, while boosting self-confidence, achievement levels and productivity.

So the concept of resilience, and an understanding of what develops it, is hugely important for the creation of 'confident individuals' encouraged by the *Curriculum for Excellence*. Indeed the new curriculum in Scotland expressly mentions 'resilience' as one of the key ingredients of 'successful contributors', along with an enterprising attitude and self-reliance.

A short history of resilience

All definitions of resilience incorporate some reference to an individual's ability to 'overcome odds' and to demonstrate personal strengths to cope with hardship or adversity.

Helen McGrath and Toni Noble

When we talk about resilience, most of us use the word fairly loosely. Often it is intended to convey the same meaning as words such as hardy, tough, irrepressible, stamina, 'stick-ability' etc. But psychologists use the word with much more precision. For example, the psychologists Luthar, Cicchetti and Becker give the following definition: 'Resilience is predicated on exposure to significant threat or adversity and on the attainment of good outcomes despite this exposure'.

The study of resilience started only 40 or 50 years ago. Back in the 1960s and 1970s, psychologists studying children growing up in high risk environments realised that a proportion of the youngsters developed well despite the adversity they faced in life. Those who appeared to be thriving psychologically, despite the impact of poverty, poor parenting, hunger or war, were quickly seen as being 'resilient', 'stress-resistant', 'survivors', or even 'invulnerable'.

Whatever the label, some children were clearly able to adapt to, and cope with, their adverse circumstances. The search was then on to find the ingredients that make up resilience. To develop as human beings, we need to be able to cope with what life throws at us, adapt to the situation and continue to develop. As a result, the study of resilience has quickly become an important area of social and psychological research in its own right.

All young people need resilience

Early resilience research mainly focused on young people deemed to be living in very risky social or physical environments, but over the last couple of decades professionals working with young people have come to recognise that the demands of growing up mean that all young people need to cope with life's challenges and inevitable ups and downs. As a result, the study of resilience has expanded significantly and now encompasses practical applications as well as theoretical studies. What is more, many of the pioneers of resilience research rejected the notion that they should simply be looking for children with 'problems' and sought a more positive line of inquiry. For example, William Frankenburg, one of the fathers of resilience research, remarked:

> *Researchers and care providers alike have been caught up in a pathological model of looking at children. We have focused on looking for problems, a negative approach that may sometimes have the undesirable effect of making us think negatively about children.*

Positive resilience

Frankenburg preferred an approach that would build on, and strengthen, resilient traits. Positive resilience theory rejects the idea that risk is something to be avoided. Instead, it focuses on those factors that promote well-being in individuals faced with adversity. Rather than take a defensive stance against risk, resilience theory takes the view that life, with all of its ups and downs, is there to be embraced – and that coping with risk and bouncing back from adversity are positively good for us.

Why resilience is becoming more important for young people

i. The rise of mental health problems

Another reason why resilience is increasingly on the agenda is that professionals working with young people are concerned about the rising tide of mental health problems. While it is important to see growing up as a time of inevitable change and development (hence some stress), research data suggest that young people are suffering more mental health problems than before. For example, a 2001 research study concluded that 11 per cent of youth aged 16–24 in the UK have a major depressive disorder. Anxiety disorders, which often precede or accompany depression, are found in approximately 3 per cent of children aged 5–15 and 15 per cent of youth aged 16–24 in the UK. Other indications of rising mental health problems can be seen in the increases in suicide, self-harm and eating disorders. Scotland has particularly high suicide rates for young men. However, mental health problems for young people are apparent throughout the western world.

ii. Social and cultural changes

Various social and cultural explanations are advanced for these trends. Such explanations can be reduced to the following types of factors.

- The impact of the mass media/advertising on young people's perceptions of themselves and their expectations.
- The growing fear in society at large as a result of the rise of terrorism, the media's portrayal of crime, the challenges of global warming and the growing disenchantment with politics.
- Family/community break-down. This can be seen in the high level of divorce in modern society, one-parent families, the decline of extended family and neighbourliness and the decline in organisations such as guides and scouts.
- Increased expectations of, and pressure on, young people (eg more exams and tests and more emphasis on going to university).

These trends can be summarised as an increase in individualism and an obsession with an individual's success in life, along with breakdown in family ties, social support and belief in collective action to improve living conditions.

Critics like Professor Frank Furedi, whose thesis was summarised briefly in Chapter 2, would argue that these mental health problems are the result of a culture which undermines resilience, disrespects autonomy and encourages 'help-seeking'.

iii. Over-protection of young people

As these social/cultural pressures on young people have increased, the way that children are brought up may, unwittingly, be undermining their ability to cope and so is adding to the problem. Some of the factors involved in changes in parenting and teaching styles which may be undermining young people have already been set out in the section 'Learning from America's mistakes'. However, they are summarised below along with some additional factors.

- Contemporary parents and teachers often put too much emphasis on the idea that it is important to feel good and happy all the time. This leads young people to focus too much on themselves and their feelings. This then unwittingly leads them to feel very vulnerable when things go wrong and they experience negative feelings.
- Parents' and teachers' attempts to protect children from negative feelings mean that they often reduce competition and restrict the opportunities for failure and mistakes. This then erodes young people's capacities to overcome bad feelings, learn from them and cultivate resilience.
- Children's opportunities to play outdoors, walk to school on their own, or go on independent outings have also been restricted by parents who are overly fearful of the dangers of traffic or of child molesters. In school too, children's activities for play and exploration in the playground are more curtailed as a result of authorities' fear of claims for negligence. Again, by protecting children in this way, we are robbing them of the opportunities to encounter problems, solve them and develop their resiliency skills.

iv. The prevalence of resilience

The International Resiliency Project directed by Edith H Grotberg investigated the factors used by parents, teachers, carers (and children themselves) to develop resilience in young people. Some fifteen adverse scenarios were devised, and the reactions to them by children and carers from fourteen countries were analysed. One of the major findings was that more than half of the responses showed no, or only partial, use of resilience factors.

What conditions encourage resilience?

Research reveals that those who have most resilience often share certain characteristics such as having:

- a support network in the shape of family, friends, colleagues, teachers, etc
- confidence that they can face up to new and challenging situations
- enjoyed previous successes on which they can fall back to remind them that they have overcome adversity in the past.

Bonnie Benard, of the University of Minnesota's National Resilience Resource Center, is a resilience expert who focused on how substance abuse can be prevented or reduced among young people. Her positive attitude, her strategies for improving the lives of young people, and her conviction that adults have a duty to do more for children, have made her a popular figure among professionals and volunteers who are working to reduce substance abuse in the US.

She believes that there is a 'critical need for the prevention and education fields to change the framework from which they often view youth, to see children and youth, not as problems which need to be fixed but as resources who can contribute to their families, schools and communities'.

Features of resilient children

According to Bonnie Bernard's research, resilient children display the following characteristics:

i. Social competence

They are more responsive than non-resilient children; they can elicit more positive responses from others; and they are more active and adaptable than other children, even in infancy. Other attributes include a sense of humour (including the ability to laugh at themselves), empathy, caring, communication skills and so on. As a result, they find it easier to form friendships. Studies on young people who face problems with drugs, alcohol, crime and so on reveal that they often lack social competence.

ii, Problem solving skills

The capacity for abstract thought, reflection, flexibility and a willingness to attempt alternative solutions are all signs of resilience. Research into some of the most disadvantaged youngsters in the world – street children – reveals strong planning skills, which help them if they are to survive the daily dangers, hassles and setbacks that life throws at them.

iii. Autonomy

This is about the ability to have a sense of your own identity, the capacity to act independently, and to exert some control over your environment. This is especially important for children living in dysfunctional families where drug addiction, alcohol abuse, mental illness and so forth make life very tough. The ability to separate themselves psychologically from their dysfunctional family, to see themselves as separate from their parents' illnesses or addictions, or behaviours, gives such children a buffer that can allow them to continue their own development. Psychologists call this 'adaptive distancing'.

iv. A sense of purpose and future

Ambitions, goals, a desire for achievement, motivation, a desire for educational success, optimism and hope – all are part of the make-up of the resilient child. Children with a strong ambition – such as achieving sporting excellence – are more able to resist peer pressure to experiment with drugs and alcohol.

Werner and Smith, who carried out a 35-year study into resilience in children, summed up their findings by saying:

> *The central component of effective coping with the multiplicity of inevitable life stresses appears to be a sense of coherence, a feeling of confidence that one's internal and external environment is predictable and that things will probably work out as well as can be reasonably expected.*

And they point out that the above attributes are the direct opposite of the 'learned helplessness' so often found in people suffering from mental illness or social problems. Other factors linked to resilience include being healthy and being female, since girls generally are more likely to show resilience than boys. Our resilience level can be significantly enhanced, or depressed, by the attitudes of the people around us. As a result, research has been seeking 'protective' factors that can build resilience in young people – ways of helping them to face up to, and even thrive in, times of adversity, including when coping with peer pressure. Teachers modelling a resilient attitude could help build young people's resilience.

The resilience of Scottish teachers

Research undertaken by the University of Edinburgh, published at the end of 2006, indicates that 90 per cent of secondary school teachers in Scotland viewed their profession as 'quite' to 'very' stressful. The survey also found that 33 per cent of secondary teachers in Scotland reported symptoms similar to those of clinical psychology outpatients. Almost half reported feelings of hopelessness or worry. As many as a quarter reported severe symptoms of depression and anxiety. The top five stressors for teachers were reported as being indiscipline, paperwork, time pressures, work load and pupils' manners. Lack of control is generally seen as stressful for employees, and teachers, rightly in my view, often feel they do not have enough control over what they do in the classroom. No doubt there are practical steps that can be taken to help teachers deal with the stress facing them, such as more support with difficult pupils.

But stress management approaches generally recognise there are two different ways of dealing with stress: one is to reduce exposure to what is causing stress (which can be difficult) or to view the situation differently so that it seems less negative or threatening. Even in the figures quoted above it is possible to see that some teachers, although challenged by their role, are not ground down by it or suffering as a consequence. They too have to fill in the paperwork and cope with the pressures of the modern school but are more resilient than some of their colleagues. Helen McGrath and Toni Noble, the creators of *Bounce Back,* claim that one of the benefits of exposing teachers to the concept of resilience and how it can be developed in young people is that they can utilise these ideas in their own professional and personal lives.

The main ingredients of resilience

Dr Karen Reivich is co-author of *The Optimistic Child,* with Professor Martin Seligman, and co-author of *The Resilience Factor*. In 2005 she gave a lecture for the Centre for Confidence and Well-being in which she talked about her work on resilience. She recounted that when she first started to study the topic she assumed that people were either born resilient or not. However, as she and her co-researchers became more involved in the topic they realised that 'resilient people have the ability to stay resilient'. From their research they identified a number of abilities that resilient people are strong in. One of them is humour. However, as there is no known way to encourage people to become more humorous, Reivich *et al* dropped this characteristic and focused instead on seven other abilities which she says are 'changeable, learnable skills'. While all of them are important, Reivich argues that optimism is the most important. She sees it as 'a motivator' – it's what keeps people going.

Reivich stresses that this is not an exhaustive list and that you do not need to score highly on each of those seven in order to be given the 'stamp of resilience'. Indeed, she argues that to increase resiliency people simply need to consider which of the factors on this list they are strong on, and to play to these strengths as much as they can.

She also argues that the importance of empathy in this list is at odds with what people often think about resilient individuals. Reivich argues: 'Contrary to some of the myths around resilience, resilient people don't go it alone, when bad stuff happens they reach out to the people who care about them and they ask for help'. Empathy is vital as it 'is the glue that keeps social relationships together'.

It is important to reiterate that Reivich argues that while some individuals are naturally inclined to such behaviour and attitudes, everything on this list can be increased by individuals if they put their minds to it and are prepared to learn.

The Penn Resiliency Program

Professor Martin Seligman and his colleague and co-author Karen Reivich have devised a programme called the *Penn Resiliency Programme* (PRP). It is a school-based intervention curriculum designed to increase resilience, 'promote adaptive coping skills', and teach young people effective problem-solving. The PRP combines the work of figures like Martin Seligman, and his concept of 'explanatory style', with the Cognitive Behaviour Therapy models of Aaron T. Beck and Albert Ellis. A major goal of the PRP is to promote optimism. Other modules cover assertiveness, negotiation and decision-making skills. Seligman and his colleagues have tested the efficacy of the PRP. Their research shows that after two years, the students in the PRP condition were half as likely as students in the usual-care condition to report moderate to severe levels of depressive symptoms.

BOX 10: Dr Karen Reivich: The seven 'learnable' skills of resilience

1. Emotion awareness or regulation
   This is primarily the ability to identify what you are feeling and, when necessary, the ability to control your feelings.
2. Impulse control
   Highly resilient people are able to tolerate ambiguity so they don't rush to make decisions. They sit back and look at things in a thoughtful way before acting.
3. Optimism
   This means having an optimistic 'explanatory style' (see previous chapter). However, it is 'realistic optimism' that is important, not pie-in-the-sky optimism. People who are blindly optimistic and stick their heads in the sand, for example, do not have a brand of optimism which facilitates problem solving: in fact, it interferes with it. So for optimism to help resilience, it needs to be 'wedded to reality'.
4. Causal analysis
   This means the ability to think comprehensively about the problems you confront. Folk who score high in resilience are able to look at problems from many perspectives and consider many factors.
5. Empathy
   People who score high on emotional awareness and understand their own emotions tend also to score high on empathy – the ability to read and understand the emotions of others. This is important for resilience for two reasons: first, it helps build relationships with others; and second, it gives social support.
6. Self-efficacy
   This is confidence in your ability to solve problems. This is partly about knowing what your strengths and weaknesses are and relying on your strengths to cope. Reivich stresses that this is different from self-esteem. In other words, it is not just about feeling good about yourself, it is what she calls 'a skills based mastery based notion of coping'.
7. Reaching out
   By this Reivich means being prepared to take appropriate risk. People who score high on resilience are willing to try things and view failure as a part of life.

Bounce Back

Bounce Back is a classroom resiliency programme devised by two Australian psychologists – Dr Helen McGrath and Dr Toni Noble. As both are former teachers who now work in teacher training colleges it is a very practical, teacher-friendly programme and its efficacy has been demonstrated by research. The *Bounce Back* programe is outlined in an accompanying *Teacher's Handbook.* There are also three *Teacher's Resource Books.* The books can be used as stand alone resources but there is also a two-day training programme to facilitate teachers' learning about how to use the concepts and materials in the classroom. The Centre hosted a course, facilitated by Dr Toni Noble, in Glasgow in February 2007. The response was extremely positive and more may follow.

Bounce Back has been designed for upper primary and lower secondary pupils but its authors say that once teachers or other professionals grasp the basics they can easily adapt the materials to other stages or contexts – eg social care. While adolescence is obviously a time of stress for young people, McGrath and Noble argue that it is more effective to introduce ideas about resilience before they reach adolescence. However, they also believe it is better to introduce them at adolescence than not at all.

Bounce Back is based on a two-pronged approach to resilience: evironmental factors and personal coping skills.

Environmental factors

The first prong recognises the importance of external factors in a person's life that help them feel resilient and able to cope with life's inevitable ups and downs. Drawing on research, McGrath and Noble include the following in these environmental factors for young people:

- feeling connected to the school
- positive family–school links
- feeling connected to peers
- supportive teacher and classroom environment
- sense of worth from the family environment
- one caring adult outside the immediate family
- involvement in community life
- part of a religious community.

McGrath and Noble acknowledge that many children do not have these positive links with families or with their communities. This then leads them to the argument that schools have a vital role to play in fostering resilience in young people:

> *Next to families, schools are the most likely place where students can experience the environmental conditions and learn the personal coping skills that foster resiliency. For students who are alienated from their families, schools take on an even greater importance as a place that offers the conditions and opportunities in which to develop resilience.*

McGrath and Noble devote a considerable section of their *Teacher's Handbook* to ways to ensure that the classroom and the whole school facilitate, rather than impede, young people's development of resilience. These include:

- teachers ensuring that they are optimistic and resilient and act as role models for pupils
- establishing peer support structures
- using co-operative learning
- holding classroom meetings
- using 'circle time'
- building good relationships with pupils
- taking extra time with pupils who seem to lack resilience
- having high expectations of pupils.

The authors also devote a whole chapter on how to tackle bullying, which they see as one of the main planks in creating a safe environment for young people at school. They also reinforce the idea of taking a whole-school approach and developing an ethos that supports the classroom based programme. Finally, they suggest ways to develop good school parent connections and how to present the resiliency material at parents' meetings.

Personal coping skills

The second prong in the *Bounce Back* approach to building young people's resilience in the classroom is to develop their personal coping skills.

i. Optimism

Like Dr Karen Reivich, McGrath and Noble see having an optimistic explanatory style as one of the most important features of resilient individuals. They set out their argument in ways that are similar to what has been outlined in the previous chapter of this *Handbook*. However, they also add the concept of 'normalising, instead of personalising' as one of the indirect aspects of optimism. By this they mean the ability to understand when problems occur that this is a relatively normal occurrence and has little to do with who you are as an individual. If a young person does not see this they will often think there is something wrong with them:

> *In normalising we say 'that happened to me because it is one of those things that happen to many people in their lifetime, not just me. If others can deal with it, so can I'. Over time, young people who personalise everyday difficulties develop a negative self-perception or a belief that they are jinxed, doomed or inadequate.*

TTT 11: Helping young people to 'normalise' difficult experiences

When people experience difficulties in life it is common for them to make out that somehow this is something that is much more likely to happen to them. For example, they might say: 'That's typical of me', 'that's just my luck' or something along the lines of 'what's wrong with me?' or 'why me?' when difficulty strikes. This type of thinking leads people to feel that they are victims and doomed in some way. This thinking style does not foster resilience.

So it is useful for adults working with young people to listen to their conversations to see if they are construing difficulties in their lives in this way. Without trivialising the young person's feelings, it is useful to ask the young person to consider 'Is what I am going through totally uncommon or does this happen to other people as well?' The point of this is to encourage the young person to see that lots of people have to confront difficulties in their lives – that this is normal rather than abnormal.

The central lesson you hope the young person will learn is that people cope with bad things happening in life and so there is no reason why they can't cope as well. This realisation can help build optimism and hope.

ii. Humour

McGrath and Noble, again like Reivich, identify humour as a major weapon in the resilience armoury but unlike her they believe that people can be taught and encouraged to use humour more.

The *Bounce Back* authors cite the work of theorists such as H.M. Lefcourt who argue that humour may have important survival value for us as it helps us cope with unbearable circumstances. It may also be an antidote to anger and aggression and act as one of the factors making it easier for human beings to live together. There is also evidence of how laughter is positively good for our immune systems and helps us distance ourselves from our problems and so cope with them more effectively. In short, humour is good for the individual personally and beneficial for relationships.

McGrath and Noble go on to list the ways that humour builds relationships, including building group cohesion through sharing and experiencing positive emotion; the fact that self-deprecating humour often draws in others; and that using humour can be a sign of affection and the strength of the relationship. Humour can also act as an ice-breaker, help to defuse difficult situations where there might be conflict, and generally oil the wheels of social interaction, making it easier to get to know people. However, McGrath and Noble are aware that humour can be negative as well. It can, for example, be used to ridicule and put down others. It can also be used to belittle people and their problems. Also, if people continually make light of problems it often saps motivation to confront the issue and deal with it.

The Scots pride themselves on their sense of humour and I am sure we can all think of people whose resilience is evidenced in the way they can make a joke of their problems. However, humour often has a dark side in Scottish culture. When visitors come to Scotland they are often taken aback at the prevalence of our put-down humour. This has been satirised to good effect in the BBC Scotland television series, 'Chewing the Fat'. So when discussing humour with classes, teachers must make a distinction between beneficial humour, which helps us cope with life's adversities, and the type of humour which is destructive and damages not only others' dignity but also social relationships.

iii. Acceptance

The Prayer of Serenity:

> *God grant me the serenityto accept the things I cannot change;*
> *courage to change the things I can;*
> *and wisdom to know the difference.*

Reinhold Niebuhr

It may sound trite but there is indeed wisdom in the idea that there are many times in life when it is useful to accept those things which we have absolutely no power to change. If people spend too much time dwelling on negative things that they cannot influence, then they can feel helpless and depressed. It is much better if people devote time and energy in their lives to the things which they can do something about. It is very useful for young people's resilience if we can help them to understand that *everyone* has some areas of influence in their life as well as matters which they just have to accept. These types of lessons in life can be pointed out in various classroom scenarios or in response to stories about people in history or literature.

This is undoubtedly a subjective and tricky area. Some people will see something as hopeless and something they have to accept while others may still think that change is possible, and something which they could bring about via various pathways. However, the general point still stands, that there are times in life when we have to accept certain situations and adapt to them rather than waste energy moaning and experiencing our powerlessness.

Bounce Back acronym

McGrath and Noble add to optimism and humour a number of other coping skills that are vital for resilience. Interested readers can get more information from the *Bounce Back Teacher's Handbook*. To help young people remember the key learning points, these have been distilled into the acronym BOUNCE BACK.

Using literature to teach resiliency skills

One of the best aspects of *Bounce Back* is that it is a programme designed by people who understand how important it is to produce material which is usable in the classroom or in other settings. The authors argue that many resilience messages can be communicated via the use of general literature. Tools, Tips and Techniques 13 lists a few of the questions the authors suggest can help young people to focus on resilience as a result of reading a story. Story telling is also a useful way in which teachers can explore the subject of resilience with young people.

Resilience and looked after/vulnerable children

Our natural outrage about child abuse drives us to develop ways of protecting children who experience abuse and neglect. But Professor of Social Work at the University of Dundee, Brigid Daniel, argues that our sense of outrage can get in the way of providing the best means of helping children develop strategies for avoiding being abused, or to cope when abuse happens. She says that we become 'preoccupied with vulnerability, and that fails to honour and build on human qualities for survival'.

TTT 12: The *Bounce Back* acronym

Bad times don't last. Things always get better.

Other people can help if you talk to them. Get a reality check.

Unhelpful thinking makes you more upset.

Nobody is perfect – not you and not others.

Concentrate on the positives (no matter how small) and use laughter.

Everybody experiences sadness, hurt, failure, rejection and setbacks sometimes, not just you. They are a normal part of life. Try not to personalise them.

Blame fairly. How much of what happened was due to you, to others and to bad luck or circumstances?

Accept what can't be changed (but try to change what you can first).

Catastrophising exaggerates your worries. Don't believe the worse possible picture.

Keep things in perspective. It's only part of your life.

Detailed guidance on using this learning with young people, in particular how to ensure a supportive classroom environment to reduce the feeling of threat, is included in the *Teacher's Handbook*.

TTT 13: Examples of questions to encourage resilience through the use of literature:

- What were the 'hard times' in this story? Which ones are the sorts of hard times that everyone faces at some time in their life? Which ones were the sorts of hard times that many people your age experience? Which ones were rare?
- Was there any part in this story where a character coped better because they talked to someone else about their problem and their feelings?
- Did anyone in the story jump to conclusions without good evidence?
- Did any character use humour as one of the ways in which they coped?
- How much of what happened was because of what this character did? How much because of another character? How much due to bad luck or circumstances?
- Were the bad times only temporary and got better?
- To what extent did the character in the story just have to accept what happened or did they have the ability to change things?
- When one unhappy time happened for this character, which parts of their life were still OK?

For more questions see *Bounce Back Teacher's Handbook*

Her point is that, thanks to research into resilience and other areas of psychology, we now know what children need if they are to thrive, as well as the kind of nurturing environments that promote healthy development.

In a lecture for the Centre for Confidence and Well-being she argued that we should also focus on a child's inner strengths and on the support factors they can obtain from their environment, rather than concentrating totally on protection and vulnerability. She proposes a simple grid in which the first axis comprises extrinsic issues in a child's life, ranging from 'protective factors' to 'adversity'. The second axis comprises intrinsic factors that affect a child's outcome, these range from 'vulnerability' to 'adversity'.

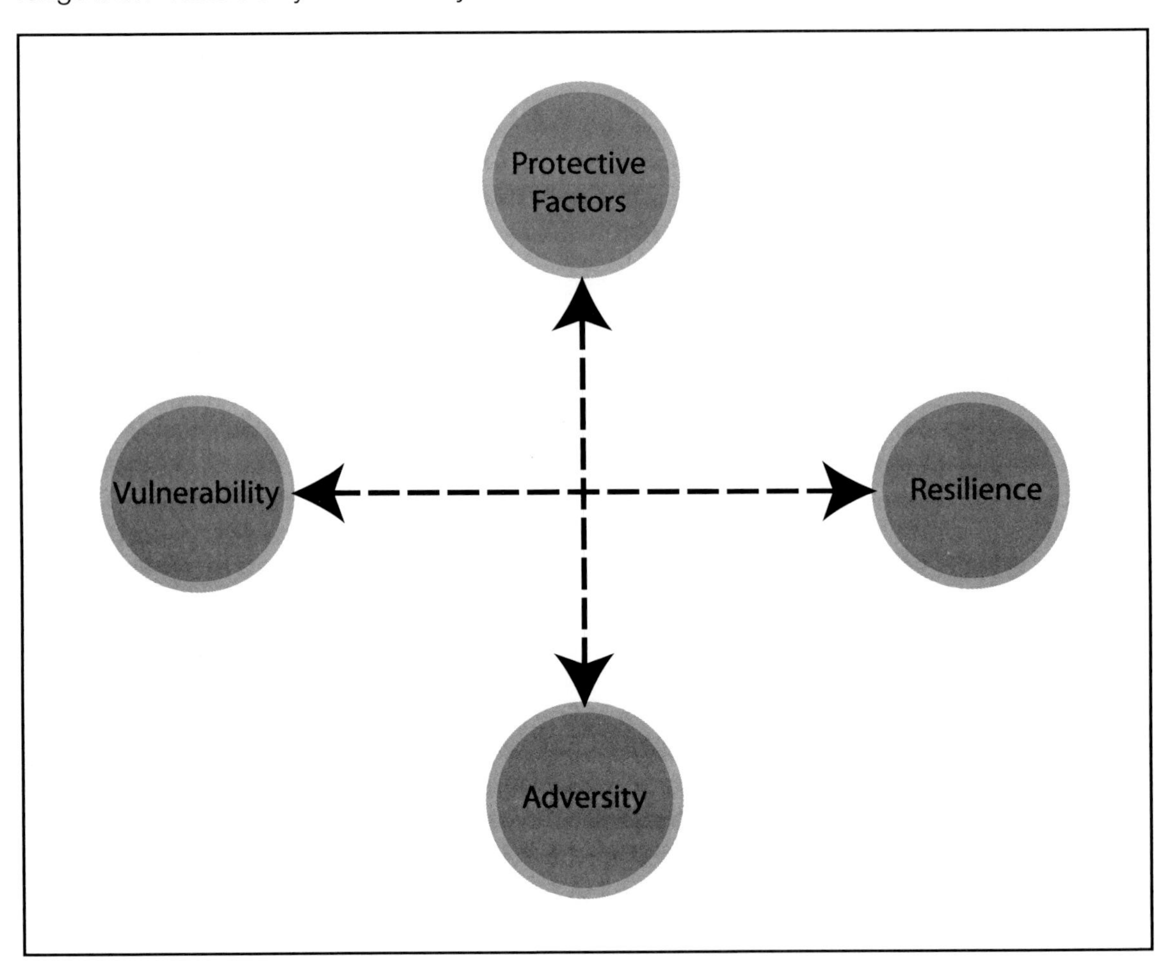

The resulting grid enables practitioners to locate the different factors that may be affecting a child, then aim to identify and support any protective extrinsic resources – while nurturing the child's inner capacity to make use of resources. She lists three protective factors and three key resilience factors.

i. The three key protective factors (extrinsic) are:

- at least one secure attachment relationship
- access to wider support, such as extended family and friends
- positive experiences at nursery school or in the community.

ii. The three key resilience factors (intrinsic) are:

- a sense of security, whereby the child feels a sense of belonging and of being loved
- an internal sense of worth and competence, along with a sense of the worth of others
- self-efficacy, which means a sense of mastering control, along with an accurate understanding of personal strengths and limitations.

Professor Daniel has also drawn up a list of six areas of children's lives where social workers, teachers, medics and others with an interest in nurturing a child's resilience can intervene, or offer encouragement, to foster resilience in the child.

The six areas comprise:

Secure base – where the focus is on secure attachment relationships

Education – where school is a place where teachers are seen as people and learning is seen as a process

Friendship – where the ability to get on with peers is supported

Talents and interests – where opportunities to boost self-efficacy and flow are nurtured

Positive values – where kindness to others is encouraged

Social competencies – where the ability to behave appropriately is developed.

In her lecture Professor Daniel reports:

> *We've been exploring the use of this framework with practitioners in local authorities and voluntary organisations, and with carers who are supporting children who have very difficult experiences. We've found that practitioners appreciate the positive approach the concept of resilience offers. They work in very challenging situations and can sometimes lose sight of the positive things that they can do to help children thrive. The approach also provides the theoretical basis to underpin the creative work they're already doing. Working to increase children's resilience offers workers hope for these children's future.*

Word of caution

There is a need to undertake some amount of resiliency training with young people in schools because in the past few decades various developments appear to have undermined young people's mental health and their ability to cope. Some of these developments have been induced as a result of a fascination with psychological constructs, most notably, the fixation with self-esteem. At the Centre for Confidence and Well-being we think that there is a newer generation of work being undertaken under the emotional intelligence/literacy/well-being banner which, paradoxically, could undermine resilience even though it claims to build it. Our reasons for arguing this will be set out fully in Chapter 15.

Key points

1. Boosting resilience in individuals and communities can help inoculate against depression and other mental illness, while boosting self-confidence, achievement levels and productivity.
2. All definitions of resilience incorporate some reference to an individual's ability to 'overcome odds' and to demonstrate personal strengths to cope with hardship or adversity.
3. Positive resilience theory rejects the idea that risk is something to be avoided and instead states that coping with risk and bouncing back from adversity are positively good for us.
4. Resilience is becoming more important for young people for various reasons; these include a rise in mental health problems, social and cultural changes and an increase in the over protection of young people.
5. According to resilience researcher Bonnie Bernard, resilient children display the following characteristics: social competence, problem solving skills, autonomy and a sense of purpose and future.

6. Dr Karen Reivich argues that there are seven learnable and changeable skills of resilience: emotion awareness or regulation, impulse control, optimism, causal analysis, empathy, self-efficacy and reaching out.
7. Optimism is the most important aspect of resilience, according to Reivich.
8. Dr Helen McGrath and Dr Toni Noble who designed the Bounce Back programme take a two-pronged approach to resilience: environmental factors and personal coping skills.
9. Professor Brigid Daniel argues that we cannot let our sense of outrage about child abuse or neglect get in the way of helping children become more resilient by focusing on protective factors such as doing work at school or having hobbies and interests outside of school.

Fostering Teacher–Pupil Relationships

11

An inclusive teacher never makes you feel like a second class citizen. They listen to you and don't just ignore what you think.

Scottish secondary school pupil

Talk to people who have done something different with their lives and you will usually find that somewhere along the line they had an influential, often inspiring, teacher. It was the teacher's influence that encouraged the young person to do something against the grain of their upbringing, such as being the first in the family to go to university or college, studying a minority subject or becoming a writer or artist. For example, writing in the *Sunday Herald* recently, columnist Sylvia Patterson explained there were two reasons why she became a writer. One was because her dad took her to the library when she was young; the other was because she had 'a brilliant English teacher'.

In short, teachers have a large part to play in helping students to become more confident. In the course of the book I have already outlined a number of ways that teachers can do this through adopting a growth mindset, using optimism and so forth. They can also help to inspire students through a love of their subject. However, in this chapter I simply want to point out the importance of teachers' personal relationships with students.

Quality relationships

Next to physical survival, the greatest need of a human being is...to be affirmed, to be validated, to be appreciated.

Stephen R. Covey

Research across many different fields highlights the importance of relationships. Gallup, for example, has undertaken extensive research into employee engagement and concludes that the most significant factor in how an employee feels about their job is the quality of the relationship with their manager. This is why Gallup has come up with the memorable line that individuals join organisations but 'leave managers and supervisors'.

Other research confirming the importance of relationships comes from more unexpected quarters. For example, research teams in the USA trying to find out which doctors are sued and why, studied tapes of doctors' interactions with patients. What they discovered was that doctors who do not get sued do not give better information or better medical advice than doctors who do get sued. What protects them from litigation is that they build good, respectful, empathetic relationships with their patients. This means that if things go wrong, or the doctor makes a mistake, then the patient does not seek redress. Doctors who have not cultivated relationships in this way are much more vulnerable. What is important in fostering a good relationship is partly time but also tone. Researchers discovered that if they showed independent people tapes of doctors talking to patients, and the sound on the tapes was so distorted so that all that could be picked up were qualities such as warmth, hostility, dominance and anxiousness (rather than individual words) observers were still able to predict which doctors were more likely to be sued. The most important factor was whether the doctor sounded dominant; in other words, whether their tone of voice did, or did not, convey respect. Doctors who talked down to their patients and used a condescending tone were much more likely to be sued if things went wrong.

The four horsemen

This research echoes the findings of John Gottman – a clinical psychologist at the University of Washington, who studies married couples. Gottman has received considerable publicity in the press as he is able to predict with 90 per cent accuracy, from listening to a couple's conversation about a difficulty in their relationship, whether they will be together fifteen years later. Gottman says that when he sees what he dubs 'the four horsemen' in a couple's conversation then he knows the prognosis is not good. Gottman's four horsemen are 'criticism, contempt, defensiveness and stonewalling'. By far the most important of the four, according to Gottman's research is 'contempt'. This includes sarcasm, cynicism, eye-rolling, sneering, mockery and hostile humour. Contempt is so corrosive as it conveys to the other person disgust at their behaviour. Another variation of contempt is 'belligerence' – being aggressively provocative.

What this research with doctors, and with married couples, tells us is that one crucially important aspect of relationships is our need to feel valued and respected. This is consistent with an influential contemporary school of psychology called 'Self-Determination theory'. Based on international, empirical research on the fundamental requirements for human well-being, Self-Determination theorists argue that people have needs for: affiliation (close relationships with others); competence (feelings of self-worth from being able to act in the world) and autonomy (the ability to make decisions for oneself). It is only if individuals' basic psychological needs for affiliation, competence and autonomy are met that they will flourish. So it is not difficult to see why relationship breakdown involving contempt is so toxic, as it does not simply threaten our needs for closeness and affection (affiliation) but our very competence as human beings.

Teacher/pupil relationships

Numerous studies in education conclude that as far as learning is concerned not only do teachers make all the difference but positive relationships between students and teachers are fundamental to success at school. Dutch academics Wubbels, Brekelmans and Hooymayers have examined learning environments internationally and demonstrate the importance of teachers to students' performance. Two factors are particularly important: what they call teacher 'influence' – the teacher being assertive and in control in the classroom – and teacher 'proximity' – the teacher being open and understanding.

Over the years Professor Brian Boyd has written a great deal about how pupils feel about teachers. In his article on Scottish pupils in the definitive tome *Scottish Education* edited by T.G.K. Bryce and W. M. Humes, Boyd summarises the conclusions of a group of senior pupils from Largs Academy on what makes a good teacher. According to them a 'good' teacher:

- is competent and achieves the best results from his pupils
- is able to generate mutual respect
- is able to mix discipline with fun
- is adaptable, communicates well and has empathy for all his pupils
- is enthusiastic, knowledgeable and compassionate
- is genuinely interested in young people
- is patient, well-organised and self-disciplined
- makes time for individuals
- has a likeable personality and allows it to come through
- takes part in the wider life of the school.

What is interesting about this list is the way that it blends professional and interpersonal skills. It is about the teacher having good teaching strategies as well as the ability to form good respectful, encouraging relationships with pupils. This resonates with Wubbels *et al's* assertion that what teachers need to be most effective is a judicious blend of influence and proximity.

The young people who compiled this list are senior pupils and so have benefited from the education system. What about the views of those who are more likely to be failed by it? In a more recent piece written with Paul Hamill about young people's attitudes to behavioural support, Brian Boyd quotes disaffected youth at risk of exclusion. They are remarkably consistent in their complaints about unfairness and injustice and the sense of being written off. But one young man's comments are particularly telling:

Good teachers help you and spend time with you. They understand how you feel, they respect you and give you a chance. Bad teachers don't listen, treat you like dirt, pick on you, think they are always right and boss you around all the time.

The sense of being superior – a better class of person – emerges in Boyd and Hamill's article as one of the main complaints that disruptive young people have about what they consider 'bad teachers' – an uncanny echo of the attitudes of American doctors at risk of litigation, or the contempt between couples destined for the divorce courts. For some young people the superior, judgemental view of some teachers no doubt contributes to their feelings of worthlessness. For others it ignites feelings of anger and a desire to strike back (belligerence – another form of contempt), thus ensuring more trouble for them in the future. In neither case is a teacher's judgemental, superior approach good for learning or fostering feelings of can-do, confidence.

If Self-Determination theorists are right and affiliation, competence and autonomy are pre-requisites for well-being then we can see from the quote above why this type of 'bad' teacher should be so toxic for young people. The 'bad' teacher not only fails to form a healthy relationship with the young person based on trust and respect but they also undermine the young person's feeling of competence by labelling or making negative judgements about them. What is more, as is clear from the quote, the young person feels their autonomy is completely overwhelmed and they are simply bossed about.

Of course, this relationship breakdown is not only about teachers and their interaction style. Relationships are two-sided affairs. Some young people can be hostile and unco-operative. School subjects can be a turn-off and students can become bored and disengaged. However, it is not uncommon for disaffected students to get on with some teachers. Boyd and Hamill in their report about inclusive education write:

... as far as these young people are concerned, the teacher is the key. They accepted that some young people can be so disruptive that they are unwilling to respond positively to any teacher but they were also well aware that teachers varied considerably in their ability to relate to young people.

Giving detailed information on how to establish and maintain good teacher–pupil relationships is outwith the scope of this book. However, over the years I have covered this topic with a range of teachers and discovered that there are a few insights or techniques which they have found helpful in developing their own thinking on the topic.

The importance of positive emotion

Generally, people think that good relationships are based on how we help other people through negative experiences. Do we support the person who is going through a difficult time? Do we allow and encourage the person to talk about their difficulties? Obviously it is important to have friends, partners, colleagues (or even teachers) who are supportive in times of need – who are dependable and not just fair-weather friends. But research carried out by psychologist Shelly Gable and colleagues shows that supporting people when they experience positive events is very important for well-being and for the relationship. They refer to this mechanism as 'capitalization'. What they mean by this is that 'telling others about a positive event in one's life' amplifies it. They propose that this is important because the communication generates 'additional positive affect, over and above the positive affect associated with the event itself'. They think this happens for three main reasons:

- sharing a positive story involves retelling, and therefore reliving or re-experiencing the positive experience.
- by talking about a positive experience a person is more likely to pay attention to it and commit it to memory
- sharing good events with others fosters positive social interactions and increases positive feelings, which can reinforce relationships.

Gable has devised a technique to amplify positive emotion by responding to another's story of a good event. It is called 'active and constructive responding' (see Tools, Tips and Techniques 14).

Responding in a positive way to a young child's good news is one of the traditional hallmarks of a good primary school teacher. 'Show and tell' sessions are often designed to encourage children to experience their own enthusiasm and positive emotion. But given Shelly Gable's research about how 'capitalizing' on good news can be important for well-being and relationships, secondary school teachers should become more consciously aware of the importance of responding actively and constructively to their students' positive stories.

TTT 14: Enhancing positive emotion and relationships with 'active constructive responding'

What is involved here are two different ways in which we can respond to someone's good news: we can be constructive or destructive in what we say or do and we can convey this approach actively or passively. Someone who is 'active and constructive' uses positive body language and is constructive in their approach to the other's good news. Someone who is 'passive and constructive' may say something positive but with not much enthusiasm or energy. An 'active and destructive' response involves going out of your way to respond negatively to what the person has told you while 'passive and destructive' is about lacking interest and saying nothing – this can be experienced as destructive by the person who has shared their positive news.

What is important about 'active and constructive' responding is that it is not necessarily about praise. The individual hearing the news need not convey any distinct judgement on the good news such as 'well done' or 'you deserve it'. Their positivity can be communicated through interest and encouraging the other to tell the story and thereby experience their feelings. In other words, it can be about asking questions – an act which encourages the other to talk more about what's good about their news.

Active and constructive

You give the other a positive verbal response. This need not be praise but it requires focused positive interest through, for example, the asking of questions. Your positive response is also apparent by your positive body language such as maintaining eye contact and the display of genuine positive emotion such as smiling.

Active and destructive

You give a negative verbal response which is also conveyed in negative body language such as frowning, or in your critical, negative tone of voice.

Passive and constructive

You give some positive verbal acknowledgement but it is limited and not accompanied by positive body language – eg your energy is low-key and you may look away and your face does not register any emotion.

Passive and destructive

You give no verbal acknowledgement of what the other has said and you may also turn away and give attention to something else, thus conveying the idea that you are not interested in, if not contemptuous of, what the person has said.

Investing in relationships

One of the most useful ways to think about relationships, and how to ensure they flourish, is contained in Stephen Covey's international best-selling book *The 7 Habits of Highly Successful People*. Covey encourages us to see relationships as something we invest in. Entering into a relationship with someone is like opening an 'Emotional Bank Account'. Into this account we can make 'deposits' and 'withdrawals'. When we have made more deposits than withdrawals our relationship is warm and healthy. When we have taken out more than we have put in then the relationship is in 'overdraft' and thus is in danger. Covey argues that there are six types of major deposits which individuals can make into their emotional bank accounts: 'understanding the individual', attending to 'the little things', 'keeping commitments', 'clarifying expectations', 'showing personal integrity' and 'apologizing sincerely' if you make a withdrawal.

Despite the reduction of relationships to financial imagery, this is a metaphor which works well as it can help people think more constructively about what they have to do to encourage relationships to flourish. I have used this often with teachers, and the types of things they suggest as equivalent to classroon credits and debits are summarised in TTT 15.

TTT 15: 'Investing' in classroom relationships

Credits	Debits
Acknowledging the student by giving them some attention (eg, making eye contact at least once in a period); nodding to them outside of class.	Ignoring the student. If you have to talk to them you do not make eye contact.
Using the student's name when talking to them.	Not listening, interrupting, jumping to conclusions.
Listening to what the student has to say (particularly when there has been an incident).	Using sarcastic remarks or put-downs.
Being responsive to what the student does or says.	Being unresponsive to what the student does or says.
Showing interest in their opinions/work/ asking questions about their work.	Labelling (eg, you're a troublemaker, you're useless at maths).
Giving genuine praise or compliments.	Only focusing on what's wrong/being overly critical.
Taking the time to give constructive criticism/helpful input on strategies for improvement.	Shouting/losing temper/being irritable.
Valuing their contribution in the class.	Talking down to students/patronising or belittling them.
Assuming the student has potential and can get better with effort and concentration.	Not treating the student as an individual.
Taking their views into consideration (eg, through consultation) when making decisions which affect them.	
Apologising if you make a mistake.	

This table helps to solve what for some people is a conundrum. Why is it that some people can occasionally shout at others or lose their temper and yet it does not *irretrievably* damage the relationship? The answer is that the person, when they are not short-tempered, is investing enough in the relationship with their positive behaviours that if they do lose their temper and shout, their negative behaviour does not tip them into overdraft. This is often why parents can shout at their children without it being damaging to the relationship in the longer term. This is not to say that teachers shouting in class is acceptable, simply that it will not necessarily undermine their relationships with students if it is counteracted with considerable amounts of relationship-building behaviour.

Once when I covered this with a group of probationary teachers, one young man looked at the list we had created and said: 'But we could just re-label this as "good teacher" and "bad teacher"'. But this is far too simplistic. Even teachers who are generally on the credit side of the balance sheet have off days and then may shout, be sarcastic or irritable. No human being is perfect. So long as they are not like this much of the time their positive behaviour should carry them through.

Some teachers practise lots of credit behaviour but only with some students that they take to. This comes out clearly in the Boyd and Hammill article on inclusive education in secondary schools. What such teachers need to do is use this behaviour more with all students – not just a select few. If they have not got off on this footing with some students it can be difficult to suddenly change gears, but one improvement they can make is to resolve to be more creditworthy with all new students in their classroom.

Encouragement versus compliments and praise

> *Flatter me, and I may not believe you. Criticize me, and I may not like you. Ignore me, and I may not forgive you. Encourage me, and I will not forget you.*
>
> William Arthur Ward

When you talk to people about Positive Psychology or confidence, as I often do, it is commonplace for them to think what you are talking about is praise and compliments. In other words, they think it is about individuals giving others feedback on how well they are doing or a pat on the head.

Certainly, the right type of praise can be motivating (see Chapter 7 for specific advice). Receiving a compliment can also enhance positive feelings and let us know what we are doing well – so it can be instructive. Paying a compliment can also induce positive emotion in the giver, allowing them to experience positive feelings of generosity as a result.

But praise has drawbacks as well. By definition it is top down. It is about someone who is older or more knowledgeable telling someone else that they've done well. This is why in the workplace some people dislike praise and find it patronising. They only like to be praised by people they particularly admire or respect. Some people also find praise or compliments embarrassing, particularly if they are given in front of others. Praise can also be used as a way to control young people and teach them that they must constantly seek approval from adults.

The humanistic psychologist Abraham Maslow once declared 'If the only tool you have is a hammer, you tend to see every problem as a nail'. For me this sums up how some people use praise – it is the principal tool they use to create or sustain:

- positive relationships
- a positive atmosphere
- motivation
- confidence
- self-esteem.

This is why teachers and parents are so tempted to give out praise even when it is unwarranted.

But as we have seen in this chapter, and elsewhere in this book, positive relationships and confidence can be fostered in other ways. Much of this boils down to encouragement. Encouragement is about showing an interest in someone. Encouragement is about being interested in other people and putting energy into your interaction with them. Of course, it is aided by time but there is something about the quality of the interaction which is even more important.

In his book *The Motivated School*, Alan McLean admirably sets out the importance of encouragement for building young people's confidence when he writes:

> *Encouragement is affirming in that it helps students feel valued just for being themselves. With encouragement students learn to appreciate their special qualities and to feel capable. This kind of interest in a student's work is more appreciative than complimenting a trait. It not only rewards students for their work but teaches them values and gives them confidence that will serve them well in the future.*

Key points

1. Numerous studies in education conclude that as far as learning is concerned teachers make all the difference. This is partly about good teaching strategies but also about forming good, respectful, encouraging relationships with pupils.
2. For some young people the superior, judgemental view of some teachers can contribute to feelings of worthlessness. This approach is neither good for learning or for fostering feelings of can-do, confidence.
3. There are various ways in which teachers can invest in their relationships with students in order to create a better climate for learning and the building of confidence.
4. Giving people attention when they experience positive events is as important for relationships as supporting people through negative events.
5. Responding actively and constructively to positive stories can enhance positive emotion and relationships.
6. Encouragement helps students to feel valued for being themselves. It rewards them for their work and also provides them with positive values and supports the development of their confidence.

12 New Educational Approaches

> *Our vision is of a world class school system founded on excellence, in which all young people, regardless of their background, have the opportunity to learn the skills required to take their place as citizens in the learning society which is modern Scotland. Our young people are our greatest asset; by targeting excellence, we will ensure that they are all given the opportunities to reach their full potential.*
>
> Donald Dewar

Scottish education, particularly primary, has gone through a transformation process in recent years. When I was at school pupils were belted for fairly minor misdemeanors and for failing at classwork. The whole system was also designed to make pupils know their place – even where you sat in the classroom in primary school reflected your academic ability. The system was also very top-down and hierarchical. We were only expected to speak if spoken to and pupils had little chance to express themselves. A former teacher of English, Alexander Scott, summed up this aspect of Scottish education dryly when he penned one of his famous two line poems:

Scotch education

I tell't ye
I tell't ye.

I am sure that there are vestiges of this approach still around in Scottish education. Nonetheless, the system, its attitudes and ethos have changed substantially in the past few decades. And in writing this *Handbook* I do not want to give the impression that no useful changes have occurred or helpful initiatives launched that are likely to build young people's confidence. So the purpose of this chapter is to acknowledge a few of these changes and to examine why they may encourage confidence to rise.

Enterprise education

Enterprise activity is low in Scotland. It is not terrible but it is lower than in some other sections of the UK or comparable small countries and it is lower than would be expected, given Scotland's reputation for innovation. There are a number of plausible explanations for this including the opportunities available and the climate for business. The Global Entrepreneurship Monitor for 2006 estimates than on research conducted between 2002 and 2005, 'Scots born and resident in Scotland had significantly lower TEA [enterprise] rates, at 4.1 per cent, than either in-migrants from the rest of the UK (10.8 per cent) or immigrants (9.3 per cent)'. Since a substantial number of Scottish business births are delivered by people who are not Scottish this seems to indicate that the problem is partly about the Scots' attitude to entrepreneurship, their failure to see opportunities or their lack of confidence or skills.

There is little doubt that entrepreneurs need confidence – both self-efficacy (ie the belief that they can meet their desired goal) plus a strong feeling of optimism. Without this confidence would-be entrepreneurs would fall at the inevitable hurdles they have to negotiate in their attempt to set up in business.

The Scottish Executive's 'Smart, Successful Scotland' strategy is designed to counteract any cultural impediments to entrepreneurship. It sets out in the long term 'to build an enterprise culture in Scotland. To give young people a better chance of realising their full potential. To give the economy of Scotland the skills, new ventures and entrepreneurs it needs for growth'.

'Determined to Succeed'

Determined to Succeed (DtS) is the Scottish Executive's attempt to instil the necessary 'can do, will do' mentality required to create a more entrepreneurial, ambitious culture in Scotland. Between 2003 and 2008 the Scottish Executive plans to invest £86 million in Scottish education to deliver progress on four key themes: 'enterprising teaching and learning, entrepreneurial learning, work-based vocational learning and appropriately focused career education'. Local authorities have been given responsibility to deliver on a number of recommendations and all students are now guaranteed some exposure to DtS themes as part of their schooling. Partnership with business and employers is also a key feature of the DtS programme. Many have given support to various elements of the programme and in some cases are helping to fund it.

DtS has largely arisen out of the Scottish Executive's economic and enterprise agenda. However, the initiatives are not restricted to making/selling activities or even to projects involving money. Much of the impetus behind DtS is about encouraging a more creative, active, problem-solving approach in schools among both students and staff. The types of activities encouraged by DtS are about making things happen, and thus teach students about ideas generation, project planning, evaluation and team working. This approach encourages young people to think for themselves, to link more into the wider community and to have a better understanding of business and work. For students who are not that interested in the academic curriculum, DtS projects can also bring a welcome emphasis on practicality and the real world.

DtS has spawned a great deal of activity in many schools and there are many projects, competitions, newsletters, etc. At an anecdotal level many business people are impressed by many of the projects. Numerous business people have told me how inspired and moved they are when they hear young people from schools, particularly in deprived areas, talking about their projects. I also know a few young people who think their enterprise project was one of the most memorable things they did at school.

School staff too are generally positive about DtS. A recent research publication by York Consulting on the impact of DtS reports that 88 per cent of head teachers believe it is an 'excellent initiative' and 86 per cent of teachers are 'confident that DtS is having a positive impact on students'. Indeed, what is significant about this report is just how positive staff mainly are about the likely impacts of DtS.

However, the same report is unable to evidence any real changes in students as yet. The consultants have now devised a new way of measuring enterprising behaviours and hope their current research will provide a baseline so that changes can be detected in the longer term. Another report was published in January 2007 on research into a pilot project jointly funded by the Hunter Foundation and DtS between January 2004 and March 2006 in two learning communities in East Ayrshire. Much of the activity carried out with students and staff was related to creativity and involved input from Tony Buzan, of mindmap fame, and the Tapestry partnership. The researchers found that 'small' measurable changes were apparent, at least in the short term, at primary but not at secondary school level. What is important about this study is that it shows that following a year's worth of enterprise education and activity, the results showed a drop between S1 and S2 in the characteristics the authors deem to be the essential elements of enterprising attitudes. These characteristics are: self-confidence, organisational confidence, motivation, determination, responsibility, curiosity, persistence, and vocational confidence. The drop was less evident in boys, whose results stayed fairly constant except for a decrease in 'vocational confidence'. The results for girls were much more worrying. The girls' results were lower across the board. The authors write: 'The results for the girls are of concern in every area, with the exception of determination and organisational confidence'. This report also shows that there was a significant drop in the 'total enterprise' score for students between S1 and S4.

What is particularly important about this report is that the project researchers were evaluating a 'whole school approach' to enterprise. In education, delivering initiatives via a whole school approach means that the intervention is much better than standard – in short, it is more of a Rolls Royce than a Mini. It is, of course, too early to say that this report shows that the DtS activities carried out have little value. Some of the work done in this project was leadership development for teachers and head teachers and may not bear fruit for considerable time to come.

The researchers say that unemployment in East Ayrshire is above the national average and that in recent years there has been a particular decline in manufacturing jobs in the area. This may account for the particular drop for boys and girls in 'vocational confidence'. If that is the case, then optimism, hope and resilience training may have been beneficial.

The relevance of this book

DtS has commissioned various reports on enterprise education and all acknowledge the importance of confidence. Confidence features in all the different indices that consultants have used to measure enterprise activity. So it is not difficult to see why many of the topics covered in this *Handbook* could be helpful in supporting the DtS agenda. Various chapters have looked at how to support or nurture the types of attitudes and behaviours involved in taking risks, setting goals, working with others and coping with setbacks and failures.

Assessment for Learning

Tests and examinations have been the predominant form of assessment in Scotland's schools for some time. External exams have long been a necessary part of life in the upper stages of secondary education; when national testing of five to fourteen year olds in English and mathematics was introduced in the early nineties, primary schools also discovered the impact of tests on learning, especially for children unsure of their ability.

This kind of assessment is called 'summative' because it is supposed to sum up what has been learned so far. Although using test and exam results to measure individual attainment and monitor standards in schools generally has become the norm in Scottish schools, recent research has questioned the extent to which we should accept the results of a single test as an accurate indicator of performance.

Just as regularly inspecting a plant's roots is not the best way to assess its health, so we are beginning to realise that frequent testing can actually be damaging to children. In 2002, a Scottish Executive initiative called Assessment is for Learning was launched to create a better balance between summative assessment and other kinds of assessment, particularly those more likely to support learning as well as monitor it.

Foremost among these is 'assessment for learning' or formative assessment as it is sometimes called. The most influential account of formative assessment was set out in *Inside the Black Box*, published in 1998 by Paul Black and Dylan Wiliam from King's College, London. Its subtitle is 'raising attainment through classroom assessment' and its main messages are about the importance of helping students to see that attainment depends more on effort than innate ability and that, to improve, they need to take greater responsibility in assessing their own progress. *Inside the Black Box* also began to show teachers how they could develop the use of classroom assessment to achieve this, mainly through improving the quality of interactions between teachers and their students. The first area for improvement is about whether students actually understand the learning purpose underlying any specific activity. Setting a task without indicating what should be learned by performing it is a bit like having a meeting without first setting an agenda; in both cases the event can be confusing and the outcome unpredictable.

So the clarity with which teachers communicate what they actually want students to learn when engaged in some activity is an important starting point in developing effective classroom assessment. Only if students have some clear understanding of their learning objectives and of the criteria for recognising success in achieving them, can they begin to engage in their own learning.

If students understand clearly what they are trying to learn and what success might look like, then their next priority should be to look for and gather evidence to show they are getting there. If of high quality, classroom dialogue between teachers and students can provide valuable evidence of learning. Asking better questions and asking questions better are both important in this and research suggests that there is considerable room for improvement in how we frame questions and then use them to explore the quality of learning in the classroom. Good questions and questioning approaches provide rich information about students' understandings and more importantly misunderstandings. The evidence of learning gathered by skilled questioning provides teachers and students with the raw material for identifying appropriate next steps.

Gathering evidence of learning in this way leads naturally on to giving students the feedback they need to improve their learning, the third and final area of what Black and Wiliam call 'the evolution of good teaching'. The emphasis here is on the kind of feedback that students need to close the gaps in their learning. In 1989, Royce Sadler pointed out:

> *When anyone is trying to learn, feedback about their efforts has three elements – the desired goal, the evidence about their present position, and some understanding of a way to close the gap between the two. All three must to a degree be understood by anyone before they can take action to improve their learning.*

This provides a succinct statement of the role of feedback in shaping students' learning and again evidence from research studies provides insights into how we can improve the effectiveness of the feedback we give children. Some of these insights run counter to common conceptions. For example, research reported by the educational psychologist R. Butler shows that marking, despite its voracious appetite for teachers' time and energy, is often too little and too late to contribute in a meaningful way to a student's progress.

In each of these three areas, being explicit about learning, gathering evidence of learning and focusing feedback on improvement, the practice of formative assessment can be developed through a plethora of different practical classroom strategies, tactics and techniques, which have captured teachers' (and students') imaginations.

However, while the teacher's use of good questioning and feedback techniques are important in assessment for learning, it is ultimately more important to encourage children to do it for themselves by helping them to find meaningful ways of thinking about what they are learning and how they are learning it. When children and young people learn how to assess their own work, they begin to understand that their present state is not the result of some pre-determined and innate ability but actually down to factors over which they have some control. Evidence gathered by Black and Wiliam and others points to significant gains, particularly for those in the long 'tail' of low attainment where much potential talent is lost.

Assessment for Learning and confidence

> *Teachers using formative assessment have changed the culture of their classrooms, putting the emphasis on helping students feel safe to take risks and make mistakes and to develop self-confidence in the classroom.*
>
> OECD publication

Many of those who write about the impact of assessment for learning mention that it increases student confidence. For example, an evaluation of Assessment is for Learning carried out for the Scottish Executive by the Institute of Education and published in 2004 reports that 'students were better motivated and demonstrated more positive attitudes towards learning. Many were more confident'. This assertion was not based on actual measurement of confidence but on reports by teachers on changes in their students' attitudes and behaviour.

It is certainly not difficult to see why assessment for learning would build confidence as it accords with many of the methods encouraged by this book. For example, assessment for learning:

- encourages the development of self-efficacy through feedback and goal-setting
- requires students to take responsibility for their learning
- encourages learners to see failure as an inevitable part of learning
- encourages learners to develop an ethos of continuous improvement.

Another way to express these benefits is to say that assessment for learning encourages what Carol Dweck calls a 'growth' rather than a 'fixed' mindset. Indeed, Dweck's research on different attitudes to achievement was influential in the development of Black and Wiliam's ideas on assessment set out in *Inside the Black Box*.

Reading teachers' accounts of using assessment for learning also makes clear that it helps build their relationships with students by making them much more responsive to learners' needs. It also helps to develop teachers' confidence. If teachers are more confident this will help them model confidence for young people – again boosting the confidence-building potential of this assessment tool.

The Motivated School

> *In the motivated school pupils want to learn for interest and enjoyment rather than because of rewards and punishments. Children are curious from birth and are naturally inclined towards learning. They are intrinsically motivated to meet their needs for knowledge and understanding, a sense of competence, self-determination and involvement with others.*
>
> Alan McLean

Motivation has become an important focal point in Scottish education as a result of the pioneering work done by Glasgow-based educational psychologist Alan McLean. In 2003 he published his first book called *The Motivated School*, which has now been translated into several languages. Educationalists in other countries, including Ireland and New Zealand, are now putting into practice some of his ideas. He has set out his theories on motivation in a training resource, sponsored by the Scottish Executive, and many schools across Scotland are now working with his ideas in the classroom.

Writing for the Centre for Confidence and Well-being's website, McLean presents motivation in the following terms: 'Motivation is what moves a person to action; to motivate means you provide a motive to do something. It is useful to think of motivation specifically in terms of the capacity to cope with challenges, setbacks and obstacles'. He argues that motivation is also about how individuals marshal 'feelings of enthusiasm, confidence and persistence'.

As McLean's ideas are readily available to readers in Scotland in his book, training resources and on websites, I do not intend to outline his main ideas. Rather, I intend simply to point out how his ideas are relevant to confidence and to the topics covered in this *Handbook*.

The Motivated School and confidence

As was indicated in Part 2 of this *Handbook*, 'Learning from America's Mistakes', Alan McLean is critical of attempts to boost self-esteem artificially through unwarranted praise as they simply do not work. He urges us to forget about self-esteem as a way to motivate or build confidence and concentrate instead on what he calls 'the most important "feel good" factor, ie self-efficacy in goal achievement'.

McLean argues that if we want to build other people's confidence there are two different things we can do. The first is to encourage people to 'adopt a self-improvement rather than a "prove yourself" attitude'. The second is to help people 'make sense of progress in a way that builds their self-belief'. This means that confidence building teachers 'treat mistakes as opportunities to learn by linking failure to factors that people can repair. They instil the belief that ability is not fixed'. This is entirely consistent with what Dweck now calls the 'growth mindset'. Dweck is one of the psychologists who have had a large influence on McLean's work.

McLean is a great believer in the importance of feedback, believing it to be 'the motivation power-tool'. Again, writing for the Centre's website he conveys this succinctly when he writes: 'Perhaps the greatest potential to nurture confidence and well-being lies in the direct impact we can have over others' sense of agency through the feedback we give them'.

Alan McLean's work on motivation is innovative, as he expands current ideas on mindset, feedback and so on and presents different 'classroom climates'. He also sets out various positions students often adopt in the classroom which he calls 'the learning stances'. Increasingly he is interested in personality and motivation. In a column for *The Times Educational Supplement (TES)* in 2006 he gave some insight into his new ideas:

> *Some aspects of the curriculum strain elements of particular pupils' personalities leading to severe distress while it resonates with others. So shy children dread social dancing*

at Christmas; extraverts thrive in the school show. Timed tasks are thought to motivate boys but this mainly applies to extravert competitive boys. Some personalities are more reluctant than others to self-disclose and this limits their creative writing. Some children are by dint of their personality concise and so struggle to understand the need to elaborate to achieve full marks.

The achievement gap between children with the personality characteristic of poor self-control and the rest has been found to be the equivalent to one year of school. Personality must be considered because it is powerful in predicting achievement.

Alan McLean's book *The Motivated School* is also a useful source of ideas on how gender differences impact on the classroom and how to motivate boys and girls. He is consistently interested in how to involve those who are least engaged and in danger of being excluded from the system.

The approach taken by this *Handbook* is very much in tune with *The Motivated School*. Indeed the advice given on specific techniques, such as praise, is quite consistent with McLean's views.

Co-operative Learning

The truly committed co-operative learning group is probably the most productive tool humans have.

David W. Johnson and Roger T. Johnson

Traditional schooling has been competitive and individualistic. Students are in competition with one another to show who is the brightest and the best in any chosen field. Yet learning is inherently a social activity – our brains are programmed to learn from one another. We learn better, and ultimately achieve more, with other people than we do on our own. The blue tit and the robin story is a lovely illustration of this point (see Box 11).

BOX 11: Robins and blue tits

Arie de Geus, a Dutch businessman and author of *The Living Company,* tells a wonderful story to remind us of the social nature of learning:

In the early part of the twentieth century milk was delivered to doorsteps throughout the UK. The milk bottles were uncovered and so birds had easy access to the cream which rose to the top. The main contenders for this rich food source were blue tits and robins. Between the wars, there was mounting concern about hygiene and so milk distributors ensured that milk bottles were covered with aluminium tops. By the early 1950s blue tits throughout the length and breadth of the UK were pecking through these tops to access the cream. This was not the case with robins. Here and there an innovative robin learned how to access the cream but this learning was not passed on to other members of his species. Why?

The answer is quite simple. Robins – both male and female - are extremely territorial, competitive birds. They do not like sharing their patch with another bird of their species. This meant that if one clever robin learned how to access the milk from covered bottles this technique was not passed on to other robins. Blue tits by comparison are gregarious birds. Outside the breeding season they move about in flocks. Once one clever blue tit had learned how to access milk it was only a matter of time before his or her mates learned the trick too.

The moral of this story is simple – birds that flock learn faster. So should we not be encouraging more sharing activity in the classroom?

What is Co-operative Learning?

Co-operative Learning is an educational methodology which has been around for the past 30 years but has only come to prominence in the UK since 2000. According to David and Roger Johnson, the originators of Co-operative Learning, it is mainly an offshoot of 'social interdependence theory'. This can be traced back to the great German thinker of the 1920s and 1930s Kurt Lewin, who is credited as being the father of action research and the participative group methodology commonly used in training. Lewin's ideas on the importance of co-operation and group learning were extended by his student Morton Deutsch and eventually taken up and applied to education by Johnson and Johnson at the University of Minnesota.

Johnson and Johnson argue that Co-operative Learning works because it encourages social interdependence and facilitates relationships:

> *Caring and committed friendships come from a sense of mutual accomplishment, mutual pride in joint work, and the bonding that results from joint efforts.*
>
> *The more students care about each other, the harder they will work to achieve mutual learning goals. Long-term and persistent efforts to achieve do not come from the head; they come from the heart. Individuals seek out opportunities to work with those they care about. As caring increases, so do feelings of personal responsibility to do one's share of the work, a willingness to take on difficult tasks, motivation and persistence in working toward goal achievement, and a willingness to endure pain and frustration on behalf of the group. All these contribute to group productivity.*
>
> *In addition, the joint success experienced in working together to get the job done enhances social competencies, self-esteem, and general psychological health.*

How does Co-operative Learning work?

Put simply, Co-operative Learning requires students to work together to achieve shared goals. Following teacher input of various kinds, groups work together to complete tasks structured in such a way that all members will understand and gain mastery over the material.

Every child and every teacher knows that the quality of the relationships within a classroom impacts on the child's ability to learn. When we consider the impact of a young person's emotional state on learning we can readily see that if their relationships are flawed, many youngsters will not achieve their best work. Yet the development of 'team' is very often ignored. Classes are left to sort themselves out and so the results are rather hit or miss. Co-operative Learning consciously develops the sense of team and thus the security and safety within which young people can learn. As well as that it offers a framework in which young people can learn social skills explicitly. Connection with others is a key aspect required for young people to thrive and, without direct teaching of these skills, little will be accomplished.

Co-operative Learning recognises that learning is a social activity; that effective learning results from a conversation and deep learning is achieved when material, concepts and skills are 'digested' and transformed by the individual. Co-operative Learning offers tight learning structures that ensure opportunity for such conversations and transformation. Students are grouped in interdependent learning groups for sections of their learning. This does not replace instruction, or ICT input, or indeed input from any resource. What it does is create opportunities for efficient 'digestion' of new material and ideas and ensures that thinking is tested against input from others.

The five 'elements' of co-operative groups

We have all been in groups where people have worked together, but they have not always been productive or co-operative. According to Johnson and Johnson, teachers have to encourage group working with the following five 'elements' of co-operation:

i. Positive interdependence

This means that each and every individual is clear that they have a contribution to make and that it is their responsibility to learn and to ensure that other members of the group learn. Positive interdependence also means that the group succeeds or fails together at a single task. In other words, everyone sinks or swims.

ii. Individual accountability/personal responsibility

Written into the structure of groups is the idea that everyone in the group is accountable for the group's work and answerable in some way for its performance. This is important to eliminate the strong possibility of individuals not pulling their weight or what Johnson and Johnson call 'social loafing'.

iii. Face to face, promotive interaction

This means that all individuals in the group are engaged in high levels of interaction, which facilitate and support other learners and the accomplishment of the task.

iv. Group process

The group needs to spend some time reflecting and processing how it is functioning.

v. Appropriate use of social skills

Social skills are included along with the academic skills and are debriefed, or processed, at the end of the task. Without these skills group members will not be able to work co-operatively together.

Putting these ideas into practice

Teachers who understand these basic elements of Co-operative Learning can create their own methods for interaction. A large number of methods are available in texts and on the internet to support teachers who are keen to use Co-operative Learning. Two simple examples are included in this chapter.

TTT 16: Two Co-operative Learning techniques

Think, pair and share

This is a delightfully simple method which can be undertaken quickly. It involves nothing elaborate like movement or special equipment. Basically, the teacher asks a question or sets a small task. For example, she might ask pairs of students to recall three points from the previous lesson. Students think for approximately 30 seconds and then share and agree the best answer. Either of the pair will be asked to answer, thus ensuring that both take responsibility for answering. Learning partners will often work together for a space of time and there will be an ongoing social skill such as 'listening to one another' or speaking in a quiet voice or disagreeing respectfully and this will be debriefed from time to time.

Think, pair and share is often used by teachers at the start of a lesson and the great advantage of it is that all students are involved in thinking and answering. It is much more engaging than the traditional method of simply asking for a show of hands in response to a question.

Jigsaw

This is a slightly more complex and very powerful method of working with material.

The jigsaw involves setting up expert groups who then take turns to teach the other members of the group. Here is how it works: The teacher gives each member of the group a different portion of material. Group members then team up with other students, from another group, who have the same material. They then digest the material and become 'expert' before returning to teach the other members of their group. The teacher also sets a final task requiring that either the whole group, or the individual members, demonstrate their understanding of the material.

Criticism of Co-operative Learning

Inevitably Co-operative Learning has a downside and a number of critics. It is predicated on the idea of sharing group tasks. But inevitably some young people, particularly in the early days of using the methodology, do not want to participate or pull their weight. This then means that the responsibility for the group's efforts falls on the shoulders of the most conscientious. Another criticism is that it may hold back the achievement of the brightest who are put in the role of bringing on the less able. And finally, some critics believe that it relieves teachers too much of their responsibility to teach. However, Co-operative Learning, well delivered, is very demanding of teachers as it requires considerable forethought and organisation.

The proponents of Co-operative Learning rebut most of these criticisms by pointing to the evidence which underlies this methodology.

The evidence behind Co-operative Learning

Co-operative approaches have been shown to benefit individuals in a number of different ways: achievement, relationships/social skills, psychological well-being and confidence/self-esteem.

i. Achievement and productivity

Johnson and Johnson report that 'between 1898 and 1989 researchers conducted over 375 research studies with over 1700 findings on social interdependence and productivity and achievement'. A subsequent meta-analysis conducted by Johnson and Johnson found that 'the average person co-operating performed at about 2/3 of a standard deviation above the average person learning within a competitive … or individualistic situation'.

Support for these findings can be found in the current drive in organisations, even commercial companies, to promote team working. This is recognition of the fact that people achieve more together than they do individually; something that is particularly important in the very complex environment in which we all work these days.

Johnson and Johnson also report research which shows that co-operation encourages individuals to persist more, to retain what they have learned, to use 'higher-level reasoning' and to come up with more creative solutions. What is more, individuals are able to take away skills they have learned from the group and use them on their own. According to Johnson and Johnson, 'both competitive and individualistic structures, by isolating individuals from each other, tend to depress achievement'.

ii. Relationships and social skills

Another benefit of learning co-operatively is that it enhances our relationships with others. People who are required to co-operate, rather than compete, in their learning not only like each other better but are also more likely to offer personal and academic support. Research shows that this type of social support is also important for achievement and physical health. Co-operation also encourages social skills to develop. This is not only important for the modern workplace but also of fundamental importance within the family and community.

iii. Psychological health and well-being

Johnson and Johnson report that four studies have directly measured the impact of social interdependence on psychological health. They report that the results showed that working co-operatively, and valuing this co-operation, are 'highly correlated with psychological health'. They maintain that a whole number of positive indices of mental health such as 'emotional maturity', 'strong personal identity', ability to cope with stress and a positive, trusting attitude towards others was fostered through co-operation. Working in competition with others had some negative, and some positive, correlations with positive psychological health. Individualistic working practices were, they claim 'negatively related to a wide variety of indices of psychological health'.

iv. Self-confidence and self-esteem

An important ingredient in psychological health is positive feelings about the self and self-confidence. Again, these too have been positively related to co-operative practices. Johnson and Johnson report that over 80 studies since the 1950s have compared the varying impact of co-operative, competitive and individualistic experiences on self-esteem and they write:

> *Co-operative experiences promote higher self-esteem than do competitive or individualistic experiences. Our research demonstrated that co-operative experiences tend to be related to beliefs that one is intrinsically worthwhile, others see one in positive ways, one's attributes compare favourably with those of one's peers, and one is a competent, and successful person. ... Competitive experiences tend to be related to conditional self-esteem based on whether one wins or loses. Individualistic experiences tend to be related to basic self-rejection.*

Johnson and Johnson also report that evidence shows that co-operation fosters feelings of self-confidence.

Co-operative Learning in Scotland

In Scotland, North Lanarkshire is leading the way on Co-operative Learning. A few years ago they researched pedagogy in a number of countries outwith Scotland and were particularly impressed by what they witnessed in Durham District in Ontario where Co-operative Learning has been the key method for the delivery of the curriculum for a number of years. Their results showed sizeable improvements in both academic achievement and a number of social factors. These results persuaded North Lanarkshire staff to begin a co-ordinated roll out of training to use Co-operative Learning across the authority. North Lanarkshire is now adopting the Durham model of training all teachers, managers and support staff in the techniques and strategies of Co-operative Learning. To date, some 2000 members of staff from across all sectors and stages have been trained.

Staff at North Lanarkshire report that students are enthusiastic about how much more enjoyable learning is with this new methodology. Teachers also like the method and believe that both attainment and whole-school ethos have improved. Her Majesty's Inspectorate of Education (HMIe) have commented positively on the benefits of Co-operative Learning in school reports, and a great deal of interest has been shown nationally. The North Lanarkshire project is now being evaluated.

Numerous studies have shown that Co-operative Learning can also be used with great effect for post-school education. Recently I observed a two-day course for university students on personal development where co-operative groups were used and the students were not only engaged but enchanted. Their evaluation of the course could not have been more positive.

The fit between this *Handbook* and Co-operative Learning

One of the main messages from the earlier section called 'Learning From America's Mistakes' is that we must guard against too much of an individualistic focus and an obsession with how people feel in the moment. There we also encountered the empirical work of Professor Jennifer Crocker which shows how the pursuit of self-esteem goals can undermine well-being. This is very much echoed in the research, which shows that, unlike competitive or individualistic activities, co-operation is positively beneficial for people's well-being and relationships and ultimately encourages achievement as well. So we think there is undoubtedly a role for Co-operative Learning techniques in the classroom and that they work well alongside some of the other approaches we outline in this *Handbook*.

Other useful approaches

In this chapter I have looked at four current initiatives in Scottish schools and showed how they may be helpful for building confidence. However, this list is not meant to be exhaustive and there are other approaches, such as Critical Skills training or philosophy courses which may also encourage young people's feelings of self-efficacy.

Key Points

1. Scottish education was traditionally seen as being very top-down and undermining of young people's confidence.
2. Scottish education has changed substantially in the past few decades and most of these changes have been good for the development of young people's confidence.
3. In trying to create more 'confident individuals' we can build on some of the initiatives that are currently taking place in Scottish schools.
4. Scotland still has lower levels of entrepreneurial activity than other equivalent countries. Determined to Succeed, a school-based enterprise initiative, has been devised as a way to create more enterprising attitudes in Scotland.
5. The activities undertaken in schools, under the banner of DtS, are good for building confidence as they are generally about building skills and fostering can-do attitudes.
6. Assessment for Learning is the name given to the development of formative assessment in Scottish schools. Formative assessment is different from summative assessment as the assessment does not simply happen at the end of the learning cycle but is part of the learning process itself. Good feedback and questioning techniques are a fundamental part of AfL. These are also useful ways to build young people's confidence.
7. Many Scottish schools are now using techniques to encourage young people's motivation as a result of the work undertaken on this theme by Alan McLean, a Glasgow-based educational psychologist.
8. McLean's work is in step with the Centre's definition of confidence: he too is critical of self-esteem and emphasises the importance of self-efficacy and self-belief.
9. Learning is essentially a co-operative activity; human beings are hard-wired to learn from one another.
10. Co-operative Learning is the name given to an educational methodology devised primarily by David and Roger Johnson. This methodology is now being taken up in various schools throughout the UK.
11. Co-operative Learning is based on a specific type of group work that encourages interaction and the development of social skills. Its efficacy has been demonstrated in various empirical studies.
12. Co-operative learning is beneficial for the development of relationships and social skills; psychological health and well-being; and self-confidence.
13. There are other new approaches in Scottish schools, such as philosophy, which are also likely to be beneficial for the development of confidence in students.

Activities to Foster Confidence

13

> *A classroom education is largely a two-dimensional education, a life in Flatland, and the experience is as flat as drinking lemonade without the fizz.*
>
> R.F. Mackenzie

As the definition of confidence used in this *Handbook* is self-efficacy (belief you can reach a specific goal) plus optimism, it should be clear that confidence does not exist in a vacuum. It is confidence to *do* something. This could, of course, mean learning to read or write an essay in French, but clearly it is helpful if school provides a range of opportunities for students to pursue different types of goals and different types of learning experiences.

Sport and fitness

Sport is a particularly good way to build confidence, as participating in sport teaches people the types of attitudes and skills necessary to succeed at other things in life. People participating in individual, competitive sports such as tennis or badminton have to learn to get better at what they do, as well as to cope with failure and mistakes; this learning equips them with the skills to succeed in life both in and out of the sporting arena. Particular mental skills, and a feeling of strength, are obtained from endurance sports such as long distance running or mountaineering. Learning positive mental approaches is also relevant in team sports such as football, hockey or rugby. A further advantage with team sports is that they also require co-operative and team working skills.

As well as teaching students the attitudes and skills required to build confidence, sport can also provide an important way for young people, particularly those who are not so academically inclined, to experience what it is like to achieve and be successful.

Finally, research shows that being fit generally helps people's mental and physical well-being. This is partly because exercise releases endorphins – feel good hormones – which can help ward off depression and counteract stress. Fitness also helps individuals to feel more powerful and able to cope with life's challenges – this too has a confidence building effect. And being fit affects how people feel about their bodies. Research shows that becoming fitter can actually boost people's self-esteem.

Outdoor education

> *Must we always teach our children with books? Let them look at the mountains and the stars up above. Let them look at the beauty of the waters and the trees and flowers on earth. They will then begin to think, and to think is the beginning of a real education.*
>
> David Polis

For decades people have felt passionate about outdoor education. John Muir, the Scottish born naturalist who created America's national parks, once claimed 'a day in the mountains is worth a mountain of books'. Traditionally, in Scotland outdoor education has referred to a range of activities, often carried on outside school hours, with either an adventure or environmental emphasis.

Outdoor education has recently been given a shot in the arm in Scotland. In June 2005 the then Minister for Education, Peter Peacock, initiated a two-year development programme called 'Outdoor Connections'. What this envisages is that all learners – from three to eighteen – will learn outside the school in a variety of different settings. This could be school playgrounds, parks, woodlands, at the sea, in designated outdoor centres or in a variety of different settings. At the heart of this new policy shift is the idea that teaching young people outdoors is a beneficial way to further a number of key aspects of the curriculum. The National Foundation for Educational Research (NFER) reviewed studies from round the world during the decade 1993 to 2003 and found that outdoor learning has much to commend it for helping young people learn across a range of curriculum areas. Part of the argument in its favour is that learning outdoors stimulates the senses, enhances a positive emotional response to education and therefore helps young people retain more of what they have learned. Learning and Teaching Scotland's (LTS) website usefully lists the ways in which outdoor education can help not just in boosting confidence, but with the four capacities (see Box 12).

Another reason why the Scottish Executive is keen to get young people out of the classroom and participating more in the natural world is concern about ecological issues and sustainable development. The thinking here is that if young people experience more of the natural world then they are more likely to value it.

David Spence, the Chief Executive of Scottish Centres, an organisation dedicated to giving young people in Scotland access to outdoor education, has been arguing for some time that the work they do can help deliver the new *Curriculum for Excellence*. He maintains that his organisation is able 'to help young people to develop' their:

- self-esteem
- emotional intelligence
- pride in achievement
- joy in learning
- thrill of challenge
- respect for values
- eco-literacy
- confidence to take control over and responsibility for life-shaping decisions
- enterprise skills
- communication skills.

In his book *Therapy Culture*, Professor Frank Furedi is dismissive of the fact that outdoor educators are now justifying their activities on the grounds that they help to build young people's self-esteem. However, who can blame them? If this is now on the education agenda then it is important that outdoor educators reinforce the idea that this may well be achieved by these types of activities and that we do not always have to resort to psychologically-based interventions. One of the issues confronting outdoor educators, however, is being able to provide evidence that their work is making a contribution to developing young people in this way.

Creative endeavours

> *Children are more imaginative, more artistic than adults, who have generally had the artistry hammered out of them.*
>
> R.F. Mackenzie

As with sport and outdoor education, artistic and creative activities can provide people, particularly those who are not interested in academic pursuits, with the opportunity to succeed and experience themselves in new ways. One of the main advantages of creative endeavours such as art, drama, photography or video work, is that they provide people with a vehicle to express something about themselves that would have lain dormant without this outlet. Music too can provide this opportunity. Together with a sense of achievement, this creative endeavour can provide opportunities to build feelings of efficacy.

The power of classical music to promote positive attitudes, including enhanced self-esteem and internal locus control, was observed in a large study of children in Venezuela. Interestingly, studies showed that the positive effect of being in the orchestra, or involved in the music school, also rubbed off on their parents (see Box 13).

BOX 12: Potential impact of outdoor learning on the four capacities

Successful learners

- Outdoor learning develops knowledge and skills in ways that add value to learners' everyday experiences in the classroom.
- It has a positive impact on long-term memory.
- It reinforces links between the affective and the cognitive, with each influencing the other and providing a bridge to higher order learning. It fosters the development of specific academic skills, as well as improved engagement, achievement and stronger motivation to learn.

Confident individuals

- Outdoor learning impacts positively on young people's attitudes, beliefs and self-perceptions: for example, independence, confidence, self-esteem, locus of control, self-efficacy, personal effectiveness and coping strategies.
- It yields benefits in the promotion of positive behaviour and improved physical self-image and fitness.

Responsible citizens

- Outdoor learning has a positive effect on social development and greater community involvement.
- It raises learners' attainment, improves attitudes towards the environment, and creates more positive relationships with each other, with teachers and with the wider community.
- It renews learners' pride in their community and fosters a greater sense of belonging and responsibility.

Effective contributors

- Outdoor learning impacts positively on young people's interpersonal and social skills, such as social effectiveness, communication skills, group cohesion and team work.

TTT 17: Building confidence and psychological capital via activities

All the types of activities outlined here could be beneficial for building young people's confidence. However, this is much more likely to happen if the instructors/facilitators are operating in ways that are consistent with the messages at the heart of this *Handbook*. It is particularly important that instructors/facilitators do three things:

- Ensure that they employ a 'growth mindset' so that they continually point out how students can get better at the activity if they put in effort, concentrate and learn good strategies. It may be useful to have a repertoire of stories that make this point.
- Introduce students to the concept of 'flow'. Flow refers to that sense of engagement in activities that are absorbing and challenging. Being able to experience flow in life contributes substantially to a sense of happiness and well-being. It is also through flow that we build psychological capital and the skills necessary to feel confident in life. More information on flow will be covered in the next chapter.
- Use these activities to teach young people the value of positive mental strategies to deal with stress and pressure and to cope with inevitable failure. This will also equip them with important confidence lessons for life.

BOX 13: Young People's Orchestras in Venezuela

30 years ago a pioneering Venezuelan economist, politician and musician, José Antonio Abreu, set up the State Foundation for the National System of Youth and Children's Orchestras of Venezuela (FESNOJIV). Venezuela now has 125 youth orchestras, 57 children's orchestras and 30 adult performing orchestras. There are also music schools located throughout the country. Over 250,000 children are involved in urban and rural areas.

Over the years, FESNOJIV has produced a number of internationally renowned classical musicians; but cultivating musical talent is not the main aim. Abreu's vision has always been to use music as a development tool that would teach children about responsibility, hard work, respect and sacrifice. These are all necessary to achieve anything in life. Abreu's intention was always for the orchestras to have most impact on the life of young, poor, marginal young people from the slums – the 'barrios'. Many have become involved, having come from juvenile detention centres or from living in the streets.

Children do not require any previous musical experience to become involved. They are given an instrument – usually a violin – to start with. If this doesn't suit then they try out others until they find the one that suits them best. There are also opportunities to support the orchestra in other ways, for example, by mending instruments.

As this initiative is a tool of human development it is funded by the Ministry of Health and Social Development, not the Ministry for Culture.

A major research study into the impact that participation in the orchestras has on young people revealed that their involvement does indeed support the development of positive attitudes. For example, self-esteem rises and so does internal locus of control and motivation. Interestingly, the research also shows similar increases in the parents of the children who take part.

Other benefits have been reported. Making music has now become part of the daily lives of many families. This may not have made them better off economically but it has created 'spiritual affluence'. Other studies have shown that the young people who take part are much less likely to get involved in crime or drug taking. In the communities that have young people's orchestras, studies have shown that deliquency and drug abuse has fallen by about 30 per cent. One important reason is that so much of children's time – often as much as six hours a day – is taken up by the orchestra.

Extra-curricular activities

Traditional extra-curricular activities such as debating or chess clubs also provide young people with opportunities to learn and grow in a structured activity in skills which, traditionally at least, they did not get the chance to use very much in the classroom. There is little doubt that many politicians not only cut their teeth but began to grow their confidence in school debates.

This chapter is not aiming to be an exhaustive list of all the activities that could be helpful in building young people's confidence, but is simply illustrating ways in which activities such as these can provide opportunities for building confidence.

Key Points

1. The belief that you can reach a specific goal is fundamental to our definition of confidence. Schools can help nurture young people's confidence by offering a choice of activities that are good for fostering self-belief.
2. Sport and fitness activities are very good ways of encouraging a rise in young people's confidence and for teaching important skills and attitudes.
3. Another type of useful activity for confidence building is outdoor education.
4. Creative endeavours such as art, drama, photography, video and music are good vehicles for building confidence as they give young people the opportunities to learn skills and express themselves in different ways.
5. Extra-curricular activities such as debating or chess are also good for building confidence.

PART V
well-being

14 Positive Psychology

> *At this juncture, the social and behavioural sciences can play an enormously important role. They can articulate a vision of the good life that is empirically sound while being understandable and attractive. They can show what actions lead to well-being, to positive individuals, and to thriving communities. Psychology should be able to help document what kinds of families result in children who flourish, what work settings support the greatest satisfaction among workers, what policies result in the strongest civic engagement, and how people's lives can be most worth living.*
>
> Martin Seligman and Mihaly Csikszentmihalyi

In October 2006, the leader of the new Positive Psychology movement, Professor Martin Seligman, was the keynote speaker at a conference in Edinburgh organised by the Centre for Confidence and Well-being. The theme of the event, inspired by the new *Curriculum for Excellence*, addressed the question of what actions to take to create confident individuals. A long-term critic of self-esteem, Seligman was at pains to distance himself from the type of approaches to confidence that the self-esteem movement suggest. In recent years he has been positive about the concept of confidence as it carries the sense of agency, self-efficacy and optimism. But at this event he argued that he no longer thinks that we should be focused on specific concepts such as optimism, happiness or confidence, and should instead focus on describing the circumstances for people to live good, flourishing lives. Since the *Curriculum for Excellence* is taking a broad view of the four capacities teachers should aim to develop these in young people; Positive Psychology, with its emphasis on optimal functioning, flourishing and well-being, has much to offer.

Here we set out the background to the Positive Psychology movement, its key ideas and its relevance to education and the new curriculum.

The development of Positive Psychology

The vision for psychology outlined in the opening quote was set out by the founders of the new Positive Psychology movement – Martin Seligman and Mihaly Csikszentmihalyi. Writing in January 2000 they considered this new 'Positive Psychology' a far cry from run of the mill psychology, which had little knowledge of what 'makes life worth living' and was more interested in diagnosing and fixing damage and disease. Now many more psychologists are rallying behind this banner. The new course on Positive Psychology at Harvard University has attracted so many students that it is the most popular course in Harvard's history. Interest is also growing in other disciplines such as economics and population health as well as in business, social services and education. Indeed, there is interest in every area of life where human development, flourishing or motivation matter.

Much of the momentum behind Positive Psychology comes from Martin Seligman. Since his ground-breaking 'learned helplessness' experiments in the 1960s, he has towered over psychology both in the US and internationally. His research into what makes people helpless led him on to study depression and from there to research into optimism and pessimism. In 1998 he became President of the American Psychological Association. As presidents usually have a theme they pursue during their year of office, Seligman was casting about for what his might be. It came in the form of an epiphany while gardening with his five-year-old daughter. This consisted mainly of an understanding that raising children should not be about fixing what is wrong with them but about recognising and building on their strengths.

Seligman believed that this insight did not fit with the usual preoccupation of psychology: his discipline had become increasingly focused on what is wrong with people and paid scant attention to what is right. This had not always been the case. Until the 1940's psychology had three main areas of interest: understanding ordinary human life to help people become more productive and fulfilled; understanding and nurturing genius; and the study and treatment of mental illness. But after World War II, in the US and the UK, new government spending priorities allowed psychologists to make a living treating or researching mental illness. This meant that a disease focus came to dominate psychology. Thus Seligman and Csikszentmihaly write of this era of psychology that 'practitioners went about treating the illnesses of patients with a disease framework by repairing damage: damaged habits, damaged drives, damaged childhoods, and damaged brains'. This deficit model, they argue, has also influenced the thinking of other professional groups.

It is important not to confuse Positive Psychology with 'positive thinking'. The former is a development in social science supported by extensive empirical research while the latter is a branch of personal development, often with little supporting empirical research, that often glibly promotes the notion we should be trying to be positive all the time through such techniques as affirmations. Positive Psychology, by contrast, stresses the power and the pull of the negative.

BOX 14: Four main pillars of Positive Psychology

Much has now been written on Positive Psychology but the following are four of its main pillars:

- It is interested in what it calls 'the science of optimal human functioning'.
- It wants to learn what works from studying human success rather than human failure or weaknesses.
- It focuses attention on positive subjective experiences such as happiness and well-being as well as on positive human characteristics such as strengths and virtues.
- It is not interested just in individuals but in how group structures such as organisations, families or cultures can induce positive emotion and encourage the use of strengths.

The negativity bias

> *... with nothing to do, the mind is unable to prevent negative thoughts from elbowing their way to center stage. ... Worries about one's love life, health, investments, family, and job are always hovering at the periphery of attention, waiting until there is nothing pressing that demands concentration. As soon as the mind is ready to relax, zap! the potential problems that were waiting in the wings take over.*
>
> Mihaly Csikszentmihalyi

Some contemporary psychologists of happiness, such as Professors Ed Diener and David Myers, stress that research shows that most people report being above neutral in mood for the majority of the time. The leaders of the Positive Psychology movement – Seligman and Csikszentmihalyi – acknowledge this, but emphasise the fact that the brain tends to prioritise negative information. As is clear from the quote above, Csikszentmihalyi believes that, unless we are occupied with other thoughts, worrying is the brain's default position. This is why he argues we must constantly strive to escape such 'psychic entropy' by learning to control our consciousness and directing our attention to activities which provide 'flow' – activities which give positive feedback and strengthen our sense of purpose and achievement.

Professor Seligman points out that the brain is 'hard-wired' for negativity; that it is all too easy for the brain to concentrate on worries and fears and for gloomy thoughts to dominate. Why? His argument, which draws on the work of evolutionary psychologists, is this: To have survived the geological epoch known as the Pleistocene, where the weather was bad and life uncertain and fraught, our ancestors needed to be alert to danger to survive. So it is the genes of the gloomy, pessimists of Pleistocene times that we have inherited – not their happy-go-lucky relatives, as they were more likely to have been washed away in an unexpected flood.

From a simple survival point of view it makes sense for our brains to prioritise negative information rather than positive. This means, for example, that we pay much more attention to criticism than praise: to the bad things that happen in life rather than the good. This is also why research shows that people experience more negative emotion if they lose $100 than positive emotion if they win $100. It is also why bad news can easily undermine a good mood whereas good news rarely has the capacity to eliminate a bad mood. Psychologists now refer to these types of facts as the 'negativity bias'.

In short, negative emotion always has the ability, as Seligman describes it, 'to trump' positive emotion. This is also why Seligman, Csikszentmihalyi and others argue that we have to 'learn' to keep negative emotion in check and amplify positive feelings.

The role of positive emotion

> *Positive affect – positive emotions, positive moods and positive attitudes – may in fact be the single most important active ingredient in the recipe for human flourishing.*
>
> Barbara Fredrickson

Until the advent of Positive Psychology, most empirical psychologists had little interest in positive emotion. In fact, they viewed feelings of positive emotion, such as joy or happiness, simply as an indicator that an individual was not suffering from depression! While it was easy for psychologists to understand the role of negative feelings, they found it very difficult to understand positive emotions. This meant that psychologists could not easily explain why human beings have the capacity to feel joy, contentment, pride and so forth.

The 'broaden and build' theory

Ground-breaking work by Professor Barbara Fredrickson has now provided an explanation for the role of positive emotion. Her work is known as 'the broaden and build theory of positive emotion'. Fredrickson's thesis is that positive emotion does not simply signal well-being and the absence of negative emotions, but has the capacity to encourage well-being and flourishing. Negative emotions narrow people's perspective and keep them focused on the specific difficulty. For example, you do not want to notice the colour of the sky if you are running away from a ferocious animal. However, Fredrickson's research shows that positive emotions 'broaden' people's thoughts and actions as well as their behaviour. In other words, when we are experiencing positive emotions we have more 'behavioural flexibility' and this allows us to build 'intellectual and psychological resources'. So if we are feeling positive we are more likely to be curious, to learn, to explore and be creative than if we are negative. If we experience a negative emotion, such as fear, we are more likely to withdraw and avoid. So it is when we are experiencing positive emotions that we are able to build personal resources which have lasting benefit to us and hence help us to cope better with adversity. It is also when we are in a positive frame of mind that we are more likely to build relationships with others. One reason for this is that it is easier to read others' body language and so be empathetic when you are in a positive mood. In Chapter 9 we encountered research that shows that optimists can live, on average, seven to ten years longer than pessimists, so there are distinct health benefits from experiencing positive emotions such as optimism.

It is for all these reasons then, as the above quote shows, that Fredrickson argues that being in a positive frame of mind is the essential ingredient in 'human flourishing'.

Fredrickson's thesis has evolved from, and is supported by, various experiments. By inducing different emotional states in participants (either contentment and joy or fear and anger) Fredrickson and her colleagues have shown that those who were feeling positive had a 'broadened attentional focus' and so, for example, were less likely to display a race bias when shown faces of people from different racial groups. They also found that positive emotion has the ability 'to undo' the effect of stress and so encourages resilience. Indeed, Fredrickson's research shows that the hormones released when we feel loved and looked after can counteract the negative effects of stress hormones such as cortisol.

BOX 15: Comparison of the effects of positive and negative emotions

Positive emotion	Negative emotion
• Broadens attention	• Restricts the focus of attention
• Allows 'behavioural flexibility'	• Aids narrow, analytical thinking
• Encourages curiosity, exploration, creativity and learning	• Encourages us to withdraw and avoid
• Allows us to build 'intellectual and psychological resources'	• Allows us to focus on the immediate (eg, something dangerous)
• Helps us build relationships with others	• Impedes empathy or being in tune with others
• Good for our health	• Bad for our health
• Helps to undo the affects of stress and so builds resilience	• Undermines well-being
• Essential for 'human flourishing'	

The Positive Psychology paradox

There is a paradox at the heart of Positive Psychology and it is this: the brain finds it very easy to be negative but it is very important for human beings to experience positive emotions, as this emotional state promotes good physical health and helps us to foster relationships and build intellectual and psychological reserves.

Such a paradox leads ultimately to the conclusion that it is crucially important for human beings to learn how to side-step the natural negativity of the brain and to experience more positive emotion. Positive Psychologists believe that the research into happiness and other emotional states now gives people access to information on how to minimise negativity and live a more positive and fulfilling life.

Positive emotion in the classroom

Positive Psychology research provides evidence for what we have known intuitively for a long time – people are more likely to learn if they are in a positive atmosphere. Negative emotions such as fear, anxiety or pessimism detract from learning. Given this evidence there is now more onus on teachers to become aware of the classroom climate and deliberately take steps to encourage a climate which is positive. Positive Psychology provides a useful reference point for this.

Research into teams and organisations shows that to keep an atmosphere positive we need a ratio of positive to negative of at least 3:1. Equal amounts of negative and positive remarks, for example, are likely to create a negative atmosphere, as negative emotion always trumps positive. However, 100 per cent positivity is not good either as it blocks out critical thinking and views. Some of this is needed to create an opening for new ideas and doing things differently.

The mistake that many teachers could make on hearing how important a positive atmosphere is for learning is to see praise as the main tool they have to achieve this. The accompanying box suggests different methods to create a positive climate in the classroom.

TTT 18: Creating a positive classroom climate

In the course of this *Handbook* various techniques have been set out that are useful for teachers who think they may need to take steps to create a more positive climate for learning. The ones that are most relevant for this purpose are as follows:

Giving praise (page 67, Chapter 7)

Giving encouragement (page 69, Chapter 7)

Helping young people to become more optimistic (page 86, Chapter 9)

Encouraging young people's hope (page 90, Chapter 9)

Active and constructive responding (page 108, Chapter 11)

Investing in classroom relationships (page 109, Chapter 11)

Using signature strengths in the classroom (page 143, this Chapter)

Happiness

> *Feeling positive emotion is important, not just because it is pleasant in its own right, but because it causes much better commerce with the world. Developing more positive emotion in our lives will build friendship, love, better physical health, and greater achievement.*
>
> Martin Seligman

Seligman is an empiricist and his views on positive emotion, often described as happiness, correspond with research. A raft of recent research projects shows that happy people are healthier, harder working, more involved with their friends and families and tend to be more successful in life. In short, their lives are more fulfilled and they are less likely to divorce, become long-term sick, long-term unemployed, or to commit crime. For those who want to see a healthier, well-educated, fully-employed society, an increased level of happiness now looks as though it could make a significant contribution.

People in western democracies have never been so wealthy. Even poor people are better off materially than the poor in previous times. However, while we have never had so much, our houses, cars, holidays, and designer clothes are not making us any happier. Traditionally, the politician's response to signs of unhappiness in society was to improve the economy, boost our spending power and tell us that we have never had it so good. But it is now becoming clear that an ever higher income is not the recipe for increased happiness. Indeed, research shows that once your basic economic needs are met (eg, you have a roof over your head and food on the table) additional income adds very little to your level of happiness.

Partly as a result of Positive Psychology research, academics across the social sciences are beginning to take happiness seriously. Of course, happiness has been a subject of serious study for millennia. Some 2000 years ago, Aristotle pondered the subject of happiness. He concluded that most of the things we desire are really about happiness. Our hankering for power, prestige, wealth, fame, good looks, material possessions – even confidence – arise because we think that by acquiring these things we will be happier. Aristotle therefore concluded that happiness must be the ultimate goal of our lives, superseding all other desires.

Aristotle's musings on happiness also led him to reject the idea that happiness is about pleasure (hedonism) and he argued that the aim of life should be eudemonia – a meaningful life.

Seligman's levels of happiness

In his most recent book, *Authentic Happiness*, Seligman also focuses attention on the real meaning of happiness. Ultimately he concludes that there are three different types of happiness.

BOX 16: Martin Seligman's hierarchy of happiness

1. The Pleasant life: pleasure and positive emotion.
2. The Engaged life: participation in activities which are intrinsically interesting and rewarding for the individual and induce 'flow' .
3. The Meaningful life: serving a goal bigger than yourself, particularly using your 'signature strengths'.

Level 1 Happiness: The pleasant life

This is how Seligman describes the type of happiness which comes from positive emotion. Such pleasure can come from a variety of different sources such as sensory experience (good wine, sex, massage) or emotions induced by relationships or achievements (joy, love, exuberance, pride, etc.) 'The pleasures are delights that have clear sensory and strong emotional components ... they are evanescent, and they involve little, if any, thinking', writes Seligman. Much of what we are encouraged to desire in modern consumer society belongs to this type of happiness – big houses, cars, expensive clothes, music players, sex and entertainment. However, while these experiences can be intensely pleasurable the problem is that they are transitory and so add little to a lasting feeling of satisfaction in life. This is exactly the problem that Robert Burns described in his verse from Tam O'Shanter more than 200 years ago:

But pleasures are like poppies spread
You seize the flow'r, its bloom is shed
Or like the snow falls in the river
A moment white – then melts forever

One of the main reasons why pleasures do not last is that, as human beings, we have incredible powers of adaptation. Novel experiences, such as driving a new car, may make us feel great but soon the novelty wears off and we hardly notice the experience any more. The new car, kitchen, suit or whatever just becomes part of our lives and loses its capacity to bring us pleasure. This is one of the reasons why, within a year of winning, lottery winners' level of happiness is no higher than it was before the win.

Positive emotion is not, however, to be dismissed out of hand as it can add substantially to the quality of our lives and our health and well-being. Pleasure and positive emotions are part of the formula for happiness. There is no need to be hair-shirt ascetics. But as we shall see below, Seligman certainly does not see pleasure and the accompanying positive emotions as the main ingredient of happiness.

Seligman makes a distinction between positive emotion in the past, in the present and in the future.

The past

Positive emotion about the past refers to how positively we think about our life experiences. When we remember our childhood, for example, do we think of all the bad things that happened to us or do we remember positive experiences? When we think of individuals in our life do we feel gratitude for what they have done for us or do we focus on what people did not do? Do we forgive people who wronged us or do we hang on to feelings of transgression? Modern Positive Psychology research shows the importance of feelings of forgiveness and gratitude. Feelings such as these allow individuals to amplify positive emotion and thereby gain benefits to their health, happiness and well-being.

TTT 19: Three good things

One of the exercises which Professor Martin Seligman suggests to increase happiness is this: when you go to bed at night, write down on a pad three good things that have happened in your life that day and which you feel grateful or thankful for. Keep doing this for a couple of weeks. His research shows that for many this simple exercise can increase happiness slightly and even counteract mild to moderate depression. Essentially it works by re-educating your attention to look for what is good in life.

At the Centre we are trying out a variation of this exercise with S2 pupils in a positive writing exercise in the classroom. We are taking pre- and post-measures of life satisfaction, happiness and so forth. At the time of writing the results have been mixed and we are now undertaking more research to see what the benefits may be of this exercise.

As we do not have the evidence to show that it will be beneficial for students in Scottish schools, we suggest that you only try this exercise for yourself, as it is possible that it could lead some students to feel more dissatisfied if they do not think they have enough positive things happening in their lives.

Please check the Centre's website (www.centreforconfidence.co.uk) for information on the final research report.

The present

Positive emotion in the present means experiencing good feelings in the here-and-now. This may seem easy but, as seen above, it is all too common for pleasure to diminish with familiarity. What is more, the fast pace of modern life means that we are often too busy planning what we are going to do next to really pay attention to the present. It is not too difficult to see how not paying attention to food when we are eating may encourage us to eat more than we need; an important message in a country like Scotland where a growing number of young people are obese.

We can, however, learn how to maximise pleasure in our life if we learn techniques which enhance savouring. The two researchers involved in this field, Fred B. Bryant and Joseph Veroff, outline the types of things we can do to amplify the pleasure we get from everyday life (see TTT 20). We can also experiment with spacing our exposure to things we enjoy. So, for example, if we really enjoy wearing a particular perfume, or eating a particular food, rather than encountering this pleasure every day it may be beneficial to keep these pleasures for special occasions rather than to undermine them through everyday use. The same may apply to music, paintings, places we visit or even the route we take to work in the morning. This could mean deliberately taking our time over a meal, for example, or heightening our experience by talking about it. It may also mean keeping things we enjoy for special occasions rather than making them part of our everyday lives. Learning that we shall get more pleasure from spending money on experiences, or things that stimulate us, rather than many consumer goods, is another way that we can increase positive feelings in our lives.

The work of happiness researchers like Professor Ed Diener show that for the majority of people happiness is mainly about relationships. The people who consistently score highest for happiness are those whose lives are very centred around families and friends. Part of the reason for this may be because we get more pleasure in life when we do things with other people.

As we saw in Chapter 11, research into marital relationships and friendships shows that the best relationships are ones where there is a high level of positive to negative remarks. In other words, for every criticism or complaint there are lots of positives. What also matters is that we support friends and partners not just through bad times, but good times. This is why we outlined an important technique to facilitate this support called 'active and constructive responding' (see Chapter 11).

TTT 20: Introduce students to the concept of savouring

Fred B. Bryant and Joseph Veroff have undertaken extensive research with American students on what enhances pleasure and some of their techniques have been adapted for the following exercise.

1. Involve students in a discussion about the type of food they find pleasurable and how much they pay attention to what they are eating.
2. Give each class member something to eat – eg, an apple. (Have an alternative in case some students do not like apples.)
3. Encourage the students to become totally immersed/absorbed in tasting what they are eating. It can help if they close their eyes.
4. Ask them to take another bite and begin to describe the flavour. Encourage them to go into real detail about this.
5. Involve them in a discussion on ways that they can enhance their experience of pleasure – eg, through being involved with others. This is why eating with others is much more satisfying than eating alone. Research says that sharing with others is the most important factor in how much pleasure we experience in life.
6. Discuss with students other ways to maximise the pleasure they can get out of experiences/activities – eg, consciously trying to create memories they can draw on in the future or having some kind of physical souvenir of the event if this is appropriate.
7. Brainstorm with students the types of small things which give them pleasure and which they could use to enhance feelings of gratitude and thanksgiving.
8. Use this type of exercise with very different activities, such as listening to music, reading a poem, looking at a beautiful painting, going for a walk in the countryside and so forth.

The future

There is one word to describe positive emotion about the future and it is optimism. Given the importance of experiencing positive emotions, and keeping negativity at bay, it is easy to see why people who have a tendency to think optimistically have an advantage over pessimists. In Chapter 9 we saw not only that people can learn to think more optimistically but also the basic techniques for doing this. Optimism is a major plank in Positive Psychology.

Level 2 Happiness: The engaged life

According to Seligman another way we can find happiness in life is not through pleasure and positive emotion but through engagement. What Seligman has in mind here is essentially the concept of 'flow'. This is a term coined by Mihaly Csikszentmihalyi as a result of studies he undertook on what gives people enjoyment. What he found is that people of all ages, nationalities and interests in life report their involvement in activities in a similar way. In a nutshell 'flow' happens when we become so absorbed in an activity that we lose ourselves and our sense of time is altered. When we are engrossed we often have so little sense of ourselves that we do not feel happy – in fact we feel nothing. (Or indeed we may even experience physical discomfort; as may be the case for a mountaineer or athlete.) But afterwards we have such a strong sense of gratification that we construe the activity as enjoyable and satisfying and so such experiences contribute substantially to our feelings of happiness and well-being.

Activities which can induce flow are varied and numerous. It can come from reading a book, playing a sport or having an engrossing conversation with a friend. Commonly it is something that we find challenging. This is why many people experience flow easily in competitive sports where challenge and feedback are intrinsic to the activity. If the talents of the players are mismatched – one is a beginner chess player, for example, and the other is a Grand Master then neither is likely to experience flow. For one opponent there is no challenge and for the other it is too daunting and so not easy to lose oneself in the activity.

Another aspect of flow is that it is intrinsically rewarding and therefore motivating. We may be involved in the activity because it is our work, and so we are being paid to do it, yet if we are in flow with the activity we get the feeling that we would be involved even if we were not being paid.

It is useful to see flow as a process where the issue is not whether someone is in flow or not but the degree to which he or she is experiencing flow.

TTT 21: Using the concept of flow in the classroom

Flow is an important concept for young people at school as strong feelings of being in flow are vital for motivation. What is more, it can be useful to introduce the concept to young people to get them thinking about the types of activities where they are most likely to experience flow. It can also be helpful for the quality of young people's future lives if they are aware that satisfaction in life is more dependent on engagement in work and hobbies than it is on consumption and easy pleasures.

Mihaly Csikszentmihalyi lists the following eight ingredients of flow:

1. The experience occurs usually when we are involved in tasks that we have a good chance of completing.
2. We are able to concentrate fully on the activity.
3. The task has clear goals.
4. The task is such that it gives us immediate feedback on how well we are doing.
5. Our involvement is 'deep but effortless' and this 'removes from awareness the worries and frustrations of everyday life'.
6. There is a sense of exercising a sense of control over our actions.
7. 'Concern for the self disappears' but paradoxically our 'sense of self emerges stronger after the flow experience is over'.
8. We lose our normal sense of time – we can feel either that is has speeded up (and passed quickly) or slowed down.

Teachers could easily introduce these ideas to older primary school students or those at secondary school. Following a general introduction to the concept students could be asked to keep a 'flow' diary for a few weeks where they reflected on when they were in flow and the conditions which helped to create this feeling. The students could be encouraged to compare how they feel as a result of watching TV or other passive activities and activities where they are more engaged – eg, playing computer games. The teacher could facilitate a discussion between students who identified very different activities (eg, sports or reading) to look at how the feelings engendered were similar although the activities were very different.

Some students may be aware that they get into flow easily through computer games or surfing the net and it might be helpful for them to think through the benefits they get from this. Could they get the same feeling from participating in activities which are better at building more useful skills? What might these more useful activities be?

Many young people, particularly those who are switched off from academic activities, often only experience flow in leisure pursuits such as computer games. These games provide the ideal circumstances for flow in that they are usually challenging, but manageable with effort, under the individual user's control and give immediate feedback on performance. No wonder so many young people spend hours on the computer.

The importance of flow

Csikszentmihalyi believes that it is very easy for the human brain to be negative and chaotic and for us to turn this negativity on ourselves. Through the imposition of goals, the deliberate focusing of consciousness and the loss of a sense of self, flow allows us to establish order and grow and develop as individuals. So flow is important because it:

- gives us the opportunity to 'achieve mastery over consciousness'
- allows us to become much more complex, developed individuals
- builds 'psychological capital'
- allows us to have 'optimal experience'.

The problems with leisure

Csikszentmihalyi and colleagues conducted empirical research to find out how often people experienced flow and in what activities. What they discovered is that people are much more likely to report flow from work activities than in their leisure time. But this results in 'a paradoxical situation':

> *On the job people feel skilful and challenged, and therefore feel more happy, strong, creative and satisfied. In their free time people feel that there is generally not much to do and their skills are not being used, and therefore they tend to feel more sad, weak, dull, and dissatisfied. Yet they would like to work less and spend more time in leisure.*

For Csikszentmihalyi the problem with leisure is that many people spend their time in 'passive entertainment which leads nowhere'. Watching TV, for example, requires no skill and provides little challenge. This is why when watching TV most people's mood could be classified as 'apathetic'. So in Csikszentmihalyi's view:

> *Mass leisure, mass culture, and even high culture when only attended to passively and for extrinsic reasons – such as a wish to flaunt one's status – are parasites of the mind. They absorb psychic energy without providing substantive strength in return. They leave us more exhausted, more disheartened than we were before.*

Flow and meaning

Seligman's concept of the engaged life is basically Csikszentmihalyi's concept of flow and optimal experience. Seligman thinks it a less important type of happiness than that gained from meaningful activities. And here Csikszentmihalyi agrees. He points out that flow is basically value-free. One could be in flow when committing a terrorist act, for example, or playing computer games which do not necessarily contribute much to the social good. Csikszentmihalyi argues that for a life to be meaningful, it must involve some sense of purpose or what he calls 'vital engagement'.

Level 3 Happiness: The meaningful life

Seligman attributes many of the problems of modern society to the rise of individualism and what he calls 'the big I and the small we'. At the turn of the twentieth century, even in an individualistic culture like that of America, people were focused on serving institutions such as the church, the family and the nation. In modern society these have been eclipsed by what he often describes as 'the bloated self': a self overly obsessed with its own interests and vulnerable to depression, since it exaggerates the significance of life's inevitable adversities. Seligman does not attribute full responsibility for this to the self-esteem movement but he does think that they have intensified this effect. This is why he argues that the obsession with self-esteem, and how you feel, is contributing to an epidemic of depression for young people in America.

For Seligman the antidote to depression is for people to live more meaningful lives and meaning, he argues, is by definition serving a goal bigger than yourself. For example, this can be about having a clear idea of the mission and purpose of your life, contributing to charity, putting others' needs before your own and so forth. But, according to Seligman, the best way we can do this is to know what our 'signature strengths' are and then to be in a role – either at work or through volunteering – where every day we can use these strengths 'in the service of other people'. One of the most useful aspects of Seligman's formulation of the meaningful life is that it unites the individual and the collective. It recognises the importance of individuality and the fact that individuals will be most motivated to undertake activities where they have a particular contribution to make. But it suggests the best way to direct these strengths and interests is in the service of other people – not the aggrandisement of the self.

So what activities lead to most happiness?

According to Seligman's recent research, the pursuit of pleasure is the least important for happiness. This rather turns normal thinking on its head, given that we so often equate happiness with money, leisure, good looks and so on. It is in the pursuit of engagement and meaning that we find contentment, long-term satisfaction and happiness. Speaking at the Centre for Confidence and Well-being's Vanguard Programme in Glasgow (September 2005) Seligman summed up the results of his latest research on how to live the happy life:

> *What should we pursue if we want the most life satisfaction? The results are quite surprising. Basically, you can ask people the extent to which they pursue positive emotion in life, the extent to which they pursue engagement in life and the extent to which they pursue meaning in life. And we found that pleasure doesn't matter very much. If you'd asked me in advance, I would have said that pleasure was the big one – but it is the small one. So it's the pursuit of engagement and the pursuit of meaning that have the substantial effects on life satisfaction. It turns out pleasure matters but it seems to matter only if you have the other two. So if you have engagement and meaning in your life then pleasure adds significantly. The whole is greater than the sum of the parts if you have all three.*

TTT 22: Introducing students to ideas about happiness

There is now substantial research illustrating what contributes to a fulfilling and happy life. As we have seen in this chapter, this material plays up the importance of relationships, meaning and engagement and plays down the importance of money, pleasure and consumer goods. This research, and its implications for life, could be communicated to young people at school in Personal and Social Education or incorporated elsewhere into the curriculum. Since the *Curriculum for Excellence* expressly talks about 'social and mental well-being' such a focus on happiness would be appropriate. This material could also help counteract Scotland's growing problem of binge drinking and obesity and help teach young people a different route to satisfaction in life.

Word of warning

If schools are using external companies or trainers for this work they should look carefully at the messages they may be giving young people about happiness. Many of these companies are more interested in fairly conventional approaches to self-esteem building or the types of emotional literacy approaches which we critique in the next chapter. We recommend a more cognitive than emotional approach to anything that looks like happiness lessons for young people. The reasons for this will become clearer in the next chapter.

More on signature strengths

> *I do not believe that you should devote overly much effort to correcting your weaknesses. Rather, I believe that the highest success in living and the deepest emotional satisfaction comes from building and using your signature strengths.*
>
> Martin Seligman

Traditional, disease focused psychology has revolved round the Diagnostic and Statistical Manual of the American Psychiatric Association (DSM). It is here that we can find everything that can go wrong with the human brain and personality. Positive Psychology's answer to the DSM is the VIA (Values in Action) Classification of Strengths. This is work undertaken by Chris Peterson and Martin Seligman that lists 'character strengths' and 'virtues'. Seligman sometimes refers to this as the 'classification of the sanities'. Peterson argues that the point of the VIA is to focus on 'what is right about people and, specifically, about the strengths of character that make the good life possible'.

Seligman and Peterson argue that these character strengths and virtues consistently emerge from historical and international surveys of what people have always valued about one another.

Seligman and Peterson admit that many other thinkers have articulated what makes good character, but what is different about their work is their attempt to define and measure these strengths. Their VIA Inventory of Strengths is a self-report questionnaire of 240 items which can be completed free on-line at www.viastrengths.org. An individual gets immediate feedback on his/her top five strengths.

Seligman's research shows that when individuals find out their signature strengths and re-craft their work so they can use them more, their happiness levels increase. He cites the example of a woman who found her job packing groceries in a supermarket boring. She discovered that two of her signature strengths were kindness and social intelligence and resolved to use them in her job. She decided to try and make her interaction with customers one of the highlights of their day. This made her job much more meaningful and rewarding for her.

Young people and signature strengths

A youth version of the VIA, suitable for young people from ten to seventeen, is also available on line at the same website address as for the main inventory. Seligman devotes some attention in *Authentic Happiness* to explaining to parents how they can identify and build their children's signature strengths. Speaking at the Centre's Vanguard event on education, he said that he was very much in favour of taking a strengths-based approach in the classroom, which allows children to delve deeply into subjects of interest to them.

There are various techniques that teachers can use in the classroom to communicate the idea of signature strengths and to help young people work out what these may mean for them. Some of these ideas are outlined in Tools, Tips and Techniques 23.

Limitations of a strengths-based approach

Professor Martin Seligman's arguments on the merits of a strengths-based approach are somewhat antithetical to the basic tenets of Scottish education. Scotland has always valued breadth in the curriculum, rather than depth. What is more, Seligman is a home-schooler and so it is much easier for a parent at home to devise learning plans based on individual children's strengths. Given class sizes, it is not so easy to see how teachers can pursue such an approach in the classroom. This is particularly true given that 'signature strengths', Seligman's preferred system for identifying strengths, are not so obviously relevant to a conventional curriculum. Of course, there is a place for kindness, self-control, justice and so forth in the classroom but to appreciate how they could form the basis of children's educational development would, understandably, be beyond the wit of most teachers.

Another potential difficulty with emphasising a strengths-based approach is that it can easily fuel and encourage the 'fixed mindset' outlined in Chapter 7. In other words, a strengths-based approach could encourage young people to decide what are their strengths and then to try to ignore areas where they are weak. However, as Professor Carol Dweck argues, if these young people were encouraged to develop a growth mindset, then they would be more open to the idea that they could improve if they work hard, persevere and pay attention to correcting their weaknesses.

BOX 17: Character strengths and virtues

The following are the 24 strengths and virtues outlined by the VIA (Values in Action). These character strengths have been identified by Christopher Petersen and Martin Seligman:

Strengths of wisdom and knowledge

Creativity (originality, ingenuity)
Curiosity (interest, novelty-seeking, openness to experience)
Open-mindedness (judgement, critical thinking)
Love of learning
Perspective (wisdom)

Strengths of courage

Bravery (valour)
Persistence (perseverance, industriousness)
Integrity (authenticity, honesty)
Vitality (zest, enthusiasm, vigour, energy)

Strengths of humanity

Love
Kindness (generosity, nurturance, care, compassion, altruistic love, 'niceness')
Social intelligence (emotional intelligence, personal intelligence)

Strengths of justice

Citizenship (social responsibility, loyalty, teamwork)
Fairness
Leadership

Strengths of temperance

Forgiveness and mercy
Humility and modesty
Prudence
Self-regulation (self-control)

Strengths of transcendence

Appreciation of beauty and excellence (awe, wonder, elevation)
Gratitude
Hope (optimism, future-mindedness, future-orientation)
Humour (playfulness)
Spirituality (religiousness, faith, purpose)

TTT 23: 'Signature strengths' in the classroom

Here are a variety of suggestions for how the concept of signature strengths might be used with young people.

1. You could introduce the concept of signature strengths to the class and then ask them to write essays about some of the strengths. This could be on the basis of the strengths they find most important, or they could choose to write about a particular strength where they have a clear picture of what that strength is, as they know a character or a real person who exhibits this strength.
2. You could use various characters in history to teach the strengths. For example, you could use Robert the Bruce and the spider to teach about persistence, William Wallace to teach about bravery, Robert Burns or Mother Theresa about love, Ghandi about modesty and humility, and so forth.
3. If you are teaching young people aged from ten to seventeen and they can complete the VIA on line then they could complete the questionnaire and obtain feedback on their top five strengths. You could then devise various activities where they could use this information. This could be done privately by asking them to write an essay about their strengths and how they use them. This knowledge could even form the basis of artwork where students have to design a banner or poster of the strengths they use in everyday life. It could also be used for group work where people with similar strengths are grouped and then have to tell the rest of the class about the strengths.
4. Another way to get young people to think about strengths without going into the background of signature strengths is to ask them to write or tell a story about them 'at their best'. This exercise rarely elicits talents and is more likely to encourage people to say something about their strengths of character – the kind of strengths that VIA covers

Teacher enjoyment

Appreciative Inquiry is a methodology for working positively with organisations that was developed by Professor David Cooper-Ryder. This helps us to see how if we ask negative questions, and focus on problems and what is wrong, we find it more difficult to give enough weight to the positive and what is currently working well. As a counter to much of the coverage we are constantly treated to in the press about the problems of discipline and teacher stress in contemporary schools, I want to finish this chapter by reporting the findings of Dr Stephanie J. Morgan. She is a psychologist working in England, who published a report in 2006 on 'what makes teaching enjoyable'. Dr Morgan's research involved surveying the views of more than 1,000 teachers in England and 800 people in comparative careers. She also conducted in-depth interviews, observed teachers at work in the classroom and used 'the experience sampling method' with some teachers whereby they were prompted to record how they were feeling at several points in the school day.

Morgan's research shows that teaching is:

Fulfilling – giving a sense of meaning and purpose to work.

Exciting – offering variety, enjoyment, and a broad range of interactions.

Satisfying – enabling self-development as well as the pleasure from helping young people to develop.

Enjoyable – interaction with young people and with colleagues was found to be a source of immediate as well as long-term pleasure.

In this research many teachers said how much they loved the buzz of school, the variety and cyclical nature of the school year and the sense of enjoyment they get from interacting, in a meaningful way, with young people. Indeed, 94 per cent agreed, or agreed strongly, that helping young people was fulfilling. A large number (81 per cent) also reported that working with young people often made them laugh with pleasure.

One of the most striking aspects of Morgan's report is how much teachers' enjoyment of their job is about 'flow'. It was experienced regularly (between 'very often' and 'every day') by 44 per cent of teachers compared to 34 per cent of people in other careers.

Morgan's research echoes other studies which have shown that teachers report higher levels of satisfaction at work than the general population. However, Morgan's study goes further by attempting to tease out the nature of this job satisfaction by using Csikszentmihalyi's notion of 'optimal flow experience'.

Having a satisfied and fulfilled teacher workforce is important not only for teachers but also for students. Positive emotion is catching. Professor Barbara Frederickson's research on positive emotions shows how they are contagious and can lead to 'upward spirals'. For groups of people working or learning together this can mean more energy, motivation and learning. Given the importance of teacher enjoyment, it would be good if we could carry out Morgan's type of research on Scottish teachers.

Key points

1. Rather than focus attention on children's levels of confidence, optimism or happiness, it may be better to focus instead on what research shows are the circumstances to encourage young people to live good, flourishing lives.
2. Unlike 'psychology as usual', Positive Psychology is interested in studying success and strengths rather than weaknesses and failure.
3. Positive Psychology is not interested just in the individual but also in institutions such as families and organisations.
4. Positive Psychology should not be confused with positive thinking.
5. The brain is hard-wired to focus attention on what is negative, as this has survival value.
6. Extensive research shows how experiencing positive emotion is important for learning, creativity, relationships and health.
7. It is useful to teach people how to learn to amplify positive emotion and how to keep negativity in check.
8. Teachers should pay attention to ways in which they can ensure a positive climate for learning.
9. Happiness, as defined by Martin Seligman, is not just about pleasure but also engagement (experiencing flow) and meaning – serving a goal larger than yourself.
10. Research shows that people report greater happiness if they have engagement and meaning in their lives. Pleasure is not so important.
11. An important way for people to increase happiness is for them to find out what their signature strengths are and to be in a role where they can use these every day in the service of other people.
12. Using signature strengths in the classroom as a basis for education may be difficult to achieve, given classroom numbers, and may also contradict the generalism favoured by Scottish education. However, there are other ways in which young people can be encouraged to understand their strengths and be given credit for them.
13. Research on teachers shows how much teachers enjoy working with young people and have many opportunities to experience 'flow'.

The Potential Dangers of Teaching Emotional Literacy

15

> *There is no robust, independent evidence that making children and young people express their feelings in formal rituals at school will develop lifelong emotional literacy and well-being. Inserting a vocabulary of emotional vulnerability into education is likely to encourage the very feeling of depression and hopelessness it is supposed to deal with.*
>
> Kathryn Ecclestone

Education, like other walks of life, is influenced by fashion. One of the currently fashionable themes in education is emotional literacy, or social and emotional well-being. The Department for Education and Skills has now sent out guidance to all schools in England and Wales recommending they undertake this type of work in the classroom. Various local authorities in Scotland are also interested in pursuing these themes.

As this work is ostensibly about paying attention to young people's well-being, people assume that the Centre is promoting this type of approach; however, it is not. Following considerable research and deliberation on the topic I believe that much of the work carried out under this banner could easily backfire and unwittingly undermine young people's well-being and confidence in the longer term.

In this chapter I set out the intellectual background to emotional intelligence/literacy work and my various concerns. These concerns echo those of Kathryn Ecclestone, a professor of education at Oxford Brookes University.

Emotional Intelligence: Overview

> *The relationship between intellect and emotion has traditionally been viewed as involving a conflict between two different psychological forces.*
>
> Matthews, Zeidner and Roberts

A short history of emotional intelligence

During the Scottish Enlightenment some leading figures, such as David Hume, Adam Smith and Thomas Reid, were fascinated by emotions. They did not see reason and emotion as being at odds with each other. Smith, for example, believed that emotions such as sympathy were fundamental to human relationships and provided the foundation for morality and social cohesion. Hume argued famously 'reason is, and ought to be, the slave of the passions'.

Thoughts such as these stirred the great European philosopher Emanuel Kant 'from his slumbers'. He argued that moral behaviour could only arise from cool, unemotional reason. Kant's belief that human beings should be rational, logical thinkers – untainted by emotion – had an enormous influence on the subsequent development of western thought and it is commonplace in our culture for us to see emotion and rationality as enemies.

In the 1980s, however, this was challenged by the Harvard educationalist Howard Gardner. Gardner argued that we needed to broaden our view of intelligence and he included interpersonal and intrapersonal intelligence as two of his now-famous 'multiple intelligences'. Gardner's work had considerable impact on two academic psychologists – John Mayer and Peter Salovey. In 1990 they published a paper called 'Emotional Intelligence'. Their basic thesis was that emotions can 'serve rationality rather than interfere with it' and they supported Gardner's claim that we need to broaden our notion of intelligence.

But undoubtedly the main person responsible for bringing the importance of emotions to popular consciousness is the psychologist and journalist, Daniel Goleman, in his internationally bestselling book *Emotional Intelligence*, first published in 1995. Within a few years of publication the idea of emotional intelligence (EI) had entered public discourse and a small industry grew up to teach people the skills of emotional intelligence, or literacy as it is often called in education.

What is emotional intelligence?

Emotional ability

The originators of the term, Mayer and Salovey, specifically define emotional intelligence as 'the capacity to reason with emotion in four areas: to perceive emotion, to integrate it into thought, to understand it and to manage it'. What is important about the Mayer–Salovey model is that it is based on emotional ability and intelligence. Their work is about standard, objective ways to define emotions and their uses.

Even though Mayer and Salovey's work is at the intellectually respectable end of emotional intelligence, it has many critics. For example, there is still a major debate on definition (for example, are we really talking about emotional or social skills?) and measurement is still an issue. Indeed, almost everything about EI, particularly relating to teaching these skills and what the benefits may be, still has to be adequately researched. As the famous intelligence researcher Seymour Epstein put it: 'The jury is still out as to whether there is a scientifically meaningful concept of EI'.

Goleman's definition of EI

Most of the criticisms of EI from psychologists are, however, mainly directed at Goleman's work. For example, the famous intelligence researcher Robert J. Sternberg cannot contain his hostility to Goleman and his followers arguing that the movement they have spawned is often 'crass, profit-driven and socially and scientifically irresponsible'.

The main criticism of Goleman's work is that he has not restricted emotional intelligence to the idea of emotional ability but uses what is called a 'mixed model'. What this means is that alongside the notion of emotional ability he adds in a large number of characteristics such as: warmth, empathy, zeal, persistence, optimism, motivation, self-control and social skills. To confuse things further he adds into this melange the idea that part of emotional intelligence is about being able to get into 'flow' (being absorbed and engaged in tasks) and then for good measure argues that 'there is an old-fashioned word for the body of skills that emotional intelligence represents: character'. In short, Goleman's work is a rich soup of positive personality characteristics which he has then labelled 'emotional intelligence'.

This may not seem to be a problem but it is. Effectively, Goleman, and other popularisers, imply that these psychological variables are connected or packaged in some way, when they are not. In other words, much of Goleman's work simply points out the importance of optimism or flow, for example. He has not found a new characteristic called 'emotional intelligence' that brings all these different characteristics together. The danger of Goleman *et al's* broad approach is that it just morphs into anything they want it to be and cannot adequately be described or measured.

Goleman's shaky evidence base

> *Rather than old wine in a new bottle EI might more appropriately be considered a psychological form of snake oil.*
>
> Matthews, Zeidner and Roberts

On the surface Goleman's work appears 'scientific' partly because he is talking about 'intelligence' and partly because he uses, with much aplomb, the then little-known research of a neuroscientist Joseph LeDoux. The latter's work, published as *The Emotional Brain*, aims to show, for the first time, the real architecture of the brain and how it is the amygdala, in the old reptilian part of the brain, which sends messages to the cortex. In other words it is emotion that is often in the driving seat. This then leads Goleman to talk about how, through fear, the amygdala can 'hijack' reason. From there Goleman extrapolates that some people are better at controlling this than others – the emotionally intelligent – and how, given the rising tide of violence, we need to teach young people these skills.

However, if you read The *Emotional Brain* you get a different picture. LeDoux does not think it is possible to generalise about emotions. He thinks the brain has a number of systems for different emotions. 'We shouldn't mix findings about different emotions all together independent of the emotion that they are finding out about'. He also argues that 'We have little direct control over our emotional reactions'. Little of this is conveyed in *Emotional Intelligence*, where we are repeatedly told that we can learn how to control what Goleman calls ' emotional hijacks'. In a recent email correspondence with the Centre Joseph LeDoux told us that Goleman had used his work as a 'metaphor' – that is a polite way of saying that it has more to do with literature and story telling than science. This is important, as part of the attraction of Goleman's work for people in education is that it is supposedly 'scientific'.

Professor Howard Gardner, whose work is seen as pivotal to the development of the concept of emotional intelligence, has made some positive comments about Goleman's book but basically undermines the whole idea. For example, he disagrees with trying to 'expand' the concept of intelligence to include 'personality', 'motivation' and 'character' claiming that 'such stretching is likely to snap the band'; this is exactly what Goleman does with his 'mixed model'. More importantly, Gardner questions the entire notion of 'emotional intelligence', as 'Emotions are part and parcel of cognition'. In short, Gardner believes all intelligence can be described as emotional.

The dangers of labelling

Other prominent psychologists like Jerome Kagan have also warned of the dangers of labelling people 'emotionally intelligent', as this process can easily become as judgemental, and potentially damaging to those deemed deficient, as are measurements of IQ. Remember, the man seen as the creator of intelligence tests, Alfred Binet, argued against them being used as a crude indicator of IQ, but this is exactly what happened. If measurements of this type are carried out, then being low on EI is likely to carry exactly the same stigma as not being clever at school. Some people will be deemed deficient in both IQ and EI.

Indeed, it is concern over this development that particularly irks Professor Robert Sternberg. He writes:

> *The same people who criticize the conventional psychometric testers for potentially making a mess out of the lives of people who have potential but do not score well on conventional tests do much worse in promoting what, for the most part, are largely invalidated or poorly validated tests of emotional intelligence.*

Goleman's claims for the importance of emotional intelligence

Goleman estimates that about 20 per cent of life's success is attributable to IQ. This is not the controversial part of the equation: what is controversial is his implication that the remaining 80 per cent is due to factors related to emotional intelligence. Critics like Mayer and Salovey point out that people's success in life can be attributed to a range of variables – social class, contacts, regional area, market opportunities and luck, as well as a myriad of personality characteristics. In a later book Goleman argued that EI accounts for 67 per cent of success at work. However, Mayer *et al* write 'Such claims suggest that EI predicts major life outcomes at levels virtually unheard of in psychological science'. They report a meta-analysis of workplace studies which show that some personality characteristics that overlap with Goleman's definition of EI did not predict job performance.

A major weakness of Goleman's work is well set out in a critical piece written by Annie Murphy Paul entitled 'Promotional Intelligence':

> *Goleman often focused [in* Emotional Intelligence*] on a particular group of people – in one case, scientists at Bell Laboratories; in another "Harvard graduates in the fields of law, medicine, teaching and business." Tests of their intellectual ability, Goleman triumphantly informs us, bear no relationship to their later career performance. Yes, but: Harvard students and top-flight scientists have already been painstakingy selected for their braininess. In order to give the proposition a fair test, says Salovey, you'd have to follow the careers of a group that included "people who are severely mentally retarded and people who are average and people who are geniuses, Albert Einsteins." IQ, Goleman tells us, is merely a 'threshold competence' – just a foot in the door – but at such penthouse heights it's a threshold very few will have the opportunity to cross.*

Goleman himself now tacitly accepts that there are many 'hard' domains in life where cognitive abilities are more important to success than EI.

Does emotional intelligence exist and does it matter?

> *Anyone can become angry – that is easy. But to be angry with the right person, to the right degree, at the right time, for the right purpose, and in the right way – that is not easy.*
>
> Aristotle

To say that Goleman completely overstates the importance of what he calls emotional intelligence does not mean that it does not matter at all. It is evident from this book that I accept the importance in life of some of the positive characteristics Goleman emphasises, such as optimism, or the ability to get into flow. But I also accept the critique which says they do not come together as a package. However, this still leaves the question of emotional regulation, recognition or management. I have little doubt that some people are naturally better at this than others and that for some people, such as leaders, it may contribute to their success.

But while I think there may be some people who are naturally better at managing their own emotions and reading others this immediately raises the question – what are the potential benefits of allocating valuable education time to formally teaching young people emotional ability? Mayer, Salovey and Caruso give a fascinating insight into this in a 2004 article:

> **A composite picture**. *The high EI individual, most centrally, can better perceive emotions, use them in thought, understand their meanings, and manage emotions better than others. Solving emotional problems likely requires less cognitive effort for this individual. The person also tends to be somewhat higher in verbal, social, and other intelligencies, particularly if the individual scored higher in the understanding emotions portion of EI. The individual tends to be more open and agreeable than others. The high EI person is drawn to occupations involving social interactions such as teaching and counselling more so than other occupations involving clerical or administrative tasks. ... Such individuals may also be more adept at describing motivational goals, aims and missions.*

In short, emotional protégés look very like the people who are the strongest advocates, and facilitators, of emotional intelligence work: teachers, counsellors, coaches, trainers and leaders. Mayer *et al* write that emotionally intelligent people are less likely to be involved in clerical or administrative tasks (activities which tend to be dismissed) but this raises the question: could this also include professionals that society does tend to value more, such as scientists, engineers and artists? If so do we want to gear our education system more to the production of teachers, counsellors and marketing people? Do we have a problem getting enough people of this type? Of course, we should value these professions, but if emotional intelligence skills are particularly relevant to these occupational groups then this training could, and should, be carried out more appropriately as part of occupational training – not at nursery, primary or even secondary schools.

The downside of emotional intelligence

It is also useful to note before passing on that like all things in life EI can be over done – that someone can be too emotionally intelligent in one or more of the branches. Mayer *et al* quote research which shows that people high in EI tend not to be 'artistic'. Being artistic requires an individual to express themselves creatively and this can be inhibited, rather than facilitated, by too much attention to what other people think or feel. This may also apply to enterprising activity if what an individual wants to do is not necessarily supported by other people in their circle.

Secondly, the dark side of emotional intelligence is manipulation. This is in part about someone understanding other people's motivations and feelings and then using this knowledge, often discreetly, to achieve their goals. These are the skills of conmen, fast-talking salespeople or the 'hidden persuaders' of the political or marketing world. Encouraging people who are already skilled in emotional intelligence to be more like this may exaggerate this tendency. We also have to remember that emotional intelligence is neutral and can be used for moral or immoral purposes.

Emotional intelligence as a panacea

The belief that EI is a way to reduce social problems drives much of Goleman's work. Indeed, if you read *Emotional Intelligence*, it is apparent that Goleman thinks it imperative that we 'school the emotions' because of the rising tide of social problems, particularly violence and gun crime. Goleman makes much of the rise in shootings but interestingly never even raises the subject of gun control.

Throughout the book Goleman tells us that emotional intelligence will reduce violence, depression and stress, improve health, family life, remove prejudice and make organisations better. In short, Goleman presents emotional intelligence as a panacea in exactly the same way that the self-esteem movement did a decade or so earlier.

Goleman dislikes the concept of self-esteem and never once mentions it in his book, yet the parallels with the movement behind emotional intelligence and self-esteem are striking. Both see their favoured topic as a panacea and both find it difficult to support their inflated claims with sound empirical studies.

Emotional intelligence/literacy in the UK

> *Work on what in the UK at least is often called 'emotional literacy' is developing at an extraordinary pace in education, both under this particular banner, and under related themes such as emotional intelligence, emotional and social competence, mental health, and emotional and social well-being.*
>
> Katherine Weare

The controversy surrounding the concept of emotional intelligence has not prevented the development of an industry in the UK around these ideas. A number of practitioners have been selling programmes, particularly to schools in the UK, for some time now; a few local authorities, most notably Southampton, have spearheaded this type of work. One UK based academic, Professor Katherine Weare from the University of Southampton, has also written extensively on the topic and acted as one of the main advisers to the Department for Education and Skills. DfES have now put out guidance to all schools in England and Wales suggesting that they undertake this type of work in classrooms with children from three to eighteen. They have also created a huge library of resources on the topic.

The reliance on Goleman

Even a cursory inspection of the DfES or academic literature shows how heavily reliant this work is on Goleman. Indeed Professor Katherine Weare, and colleague Gay Gray, write that it was clear from their research that 'Goleman's book *Emotional Intelligence* is considered a seminal work in this area, and is much cited as an inspiration for developments in the recent past'.

However, Professor Weare, the leading UK academic in this field, simply glosses over the fact that psychologists have attacked Goleman's claims. In a 2004 book on the topic she notes that 'it has been suggested that Goleman overstated the case' and that conventional intelligence is still very influential. But she then goes on to say 'However, it appears to be true' that emotional intelligence gives people an edge over others who are equally intelligent. She then finishes the paragraph with the statement: 'So to this extent there is no doubt about how influential emotional intelligence is'. This is at odds with the evidence presented in the previous section.

The use of other research

However, Goleman's work is not the whole rationale for the current fascination with emotional literacy in the UK. Ostensibly there are a variety of US studies that give support to the importance of developing young people's emotional and social competences. Professor Katherine Weare and her colleague Gay Gray were commissioned by the DfES to write a report called *What Works in Developing Children's Emotional and Social Competence and Wellbeing*? published in 2003. As in her other work, Weare is candid about how difficult it is to learn from some of this research. She cites numerous problems including the fact that few of these studies have control groups and have been conducted in such different ways that it is very difficult to compare them or assess the benefit of the intervention.

The recommendations to the DfES

> *... in spite of current theorizing about EI programs, we really do not know that much about how they work, for whom they work, under what conditions they work, or indeed, whether or not they work at all.*
>
> Matthews, Zeidner and Roberts

Given the lack of convincing evidence, Weare and Gray should have called for large-scale, well-funded pilots in this area of work so that we could really see, in a UK context, what might work. They do recommend in their report that the DfES and LEAs require baseline data to be collected on all new initiatives; that DfES develops a research strategy; and that more money should be made available for evaluation and some other steps.

However, with very little hard supporting evidence they then recommend that schools '*prioritise* work on emotional and social competence and wellbeing' (my emphasis) and then go on to recommend to the DfES that they ensure a whole school approach is taken and that schools:

> *develop and adopt programmes designed to promote emotional and social competence and wellbeing that include the taught curriculum, and which teach emotional and social competences in a comprehensive, organised, explicit and developmental way.*

In short, Weare and Gray recommend that all children in schools in England and Wales are given explicit teaching in social and emotional skills on a year-on-year basis. This means they prescribe a course of treatment which will be as intense as possible in its effect. Nothing like this has ever been carried out by an education system so this prescription takes emotional literacy into the realm of large-scale psychological experimentation. We think that Robert J Sternberg is right when he points out:

> *We would not want drugs to go to market that are essentially untested and that have only their promoters' claims to back them up. Yet we routinely rely on such claims to buy educational and organizational products and services. People's lives may be affected in much the same way as their lives can be affected by drugs ...*

Blinded by faith

Professor Weare is good at pointing out the limitations of the research base, and in her books equally good at warning us of some of the potential downsides of this type of work, but she is too committed to emotional literacy to rein in her obvious enthusiasm and commitment to get this work off the ground in schools. I have little doubt that Professor Weare, and the other people who are enthusiastic about emotional literacy, are genuinely committed to the improvement of young people's well-being. However, I believe their desire to see large-scale, intensive work across schools on emotional literacy is based on a prior commitment to this type of work rather than the evidence.

Weare and Gray are adamant that for benefits to accrue children must be formally taught these skills. However, this is not a necessary part of introducing these ideas into schools. On their own admission 'there is evidence that the school environment is the largest determinant of the level of emotional and social competence and wellbeing in pupils'. This means that much could be achieved through school reform which attends to ethos, behaviour, leadership and so forth.

In writing their prescription, Weare and Gray also make a huge, unsubstantiated assumption – because some work of this type may be helpful then more will be better. But this makes no sense. One vitamin pill might help our health but taking the whole bottle may not just be a waste of money but could be dangerous. Psychology is an even more complicated area than physical health, and we cannot make the assumption that more is better.

The Social and Emotional Aspects of Learning (SEAL) Guidance

The recommendations made by Weare and Gray essentially form the basis of the Guidance documents issued to schools by the DfES in 2005 for pre-school and primary and in 2007 for secondary schools. This Guidance recommends that schools take a whole school, taught approach to social and emotional skills. The Guidance gives checklists of competences against which pupils should be evaluated. For pre-school and primary there are 42 skills and for secondary 50 skills.

The Guidance outlines a range of different themes for this work. There is some variation between primary and secondary but essentially what is covered ranges from emotional awareness and expression, social skills and good to me/self-esteem building activities common in American classrooms.

It is important to point out that between 2003 and 2005 the DfES conducted a 'Primary Behaviour and Attendance Strategy' pilot which involved 25 local authorities. The pilot aimed to test the effectiveness of DfES strategies to improve behaviour and attendance in primary schools and to embed the 'whole school policy and practice and work on teaching and learning', including SEAL.

The report on this work appeared in 2006 – after the Guidance document on SEAL for three to eleven-year-olds had been issued. The research was carried out for DfES by the Institute of Education at the University of London.

A superficial reading of the report on the SEAL pilot gives the impression that it was a success. This positive impression is formed because the bulk of the report comprises interview material with teachers and head teachers who were specially selected to comment on the basis of their interest and other unspecified criteria. However, further analysis reveals a different picture. The pilot did not evidence improvement in attendance or academic work. More significantly the survey data on young people's attitudes and skills (eg, attitudes to emotions) showed little or no improvement. In fact across the SEAL pilot the scores, particularly for boys, declined for most of the measures.

In the following section I highlight some of the main reasons why I firmly believe that the Weare/DfES approach to the development of young people's social and emotional skills might backfire and unwittingly undermine their well-being, and their confidence.

The potential dangers of this approach

A deficit model

Emotional intelligence/literacy experts make great play of the fact that, until recently, some children at school were singled out for being deficient in social and emotional skills problems and were given remedial work to help them develop these skills. They tell us their approach is much better as it will eliminate this deficit by giving all children explicit teaching. However, this approach does not in fact eliminate the deficit: all it does is extend the deficit to all children. The implication behind Weare *et al's* whole approach is that all young people need to be taught a range of skills – managing their feelings, making friendships, keeping calm. These are skills that previous generations acquired without express help. Weare *et al's* approach is exactly what Professor Frank Furedi and others claim is leading to the 'professionalisation' of our emotional lives and to the idea that we are fragile, vulnerable people who need to depend on professionals to be taught how to feel, control ourselves and relate to other people. In short, express teaching of these skills in the classroom is turning children's emotional lives and their friendships into a problem which needs to be solved with the help of professionals. We need at least to ask whether this way of viewing life is one of the reasons why we have a rise in people seeking help for mental health problems.

What is more, as Weare and other exponents of emotional literacy acknowledge, there will still have to be a 'tiered approach' to developing social and emotional skills. They accept that there will always be a group of children and young people at school who are particularly deficient in these skills and who will require additional help. The SEAL report even shows in diagrammatic form an inverted triangle illustrating three levels: the whole school approach for 'all children'; 'small-group intervention for children who need additional help in developing skills'; and then 'individual intervention' of an unspecified nature. In other words, it is in essence a deficit model operating on three levels.

The problem with self-expression

Another key aspect of Weare's recommendations and the SEAL guidance is the emphasis they place on young people not just recognising and managing their feelings but 'expressing' them as well. One of the major planks in this work is encouragement for young people to talk about their feelings. Indeed Professor Weare believes 'we all need to learn to express our emotions, because expressing an emotion is an integral part of experiencing it'. However, this view is not universally accepted in psychology. Expression of emotion varies enormously according to personality and cultural norms.

In recent years in western cultures the 'hydraulic' view of emotion has come to dominate. The hydraulic view of emotion is the idea that if people 'bottle up feelings', to use the everyday term, then the pressure will build up and they will either 'blow their top' in anger or have an explosive bout of crying. If this does not happen, the hydraulic theory suggests, the person may become ill. It is worth pointing out in passing that many eastern cultures do not believe it is essential for people to express emotions and yet this does not undermine their mental health.

Modern western culture, however, has been very influenced by the views of Sigmund Freud. In his great little book *Emotion* Dylan Evan writes:

> *We look back at the stiff-necked Victorians with a smug sense of superiority. 'Emotional literacy' is held in high esteem. People who cannot talk openly about their feelings are regarded as psychologically immature, relics of a bygone age when repression reigned supreme. However, psychologists are increasingly realising that the hydraulic theory of emotion is too simplistic. It may well be good on some occasions to indulge in the spontaneous expression of emotion. On other occasions, however it can be positively harmful.*

The potential harm of emotional expression has become evident partly as a result of research into post-traumatic stress/critical incident debriefing – something which has become the norm in contemporary society. Following any disaster – rail crash, pile up on the motorway or shooting incident – counsellors are brought in to help along with emergency staff. The idea here is that the 'victims' need help with their psychological injuries as well as any physical ones. However, research shows that this type of debriefing/counselling after such events can make people worse, not better. People have natural healing mechanisms which make them resilient. Our minds, just like our bodies, are designed to repair themselves. Counselling, or other psychological interventions, can get in the way of this spontaneous healing. This is one of the reasons why we have to be very careful about introducing a focus on emotions in the classroom.

Authors of *One Nation under Therapy* Christina Hoff Sommers and Sally Satel (a practising psychiatrist) argue that

> *... recent findings suggest that reticence and suppression of feelings, far from compromising one's psychological well-being, can be healthy and adaptive. For many temperaments, an excessive focus on introspection and self-disclosure is depressing.*

This is partly the effect of what some psychologists refer to as 'the negativity bias'. The brain is hard wired to prioritise negative information and has a tendency to become negative through introspection. So it is not difficult to see why it may often be 'adaptive' to deal with negative emotions not by recognising and paying attention to them but by suppressing or distracting from them. Mayer – one of the originators of the term 'emotional intelligence' – has the good grace to admit that it may sometimes be the best course of action not to pay attention to one's feelings. This may be particularly the case for young people from abusive backgrounds. Dissociating from their feelings may not be healthy but it may be better (more adaptive) than experiencing the bad feelings that neglect and abuse engender. In other words, encouraging them to focus on their feelings could make them feel worse.

Why instructions to 'calm down' may backfire

In Professor Weare's work, and in the SEAL Guidance, there is a heavy emphasis on the importance of young people learning how to 'calm themselves'. Professionals working with very young children have always had to devote considerable time to helping children calm themselves and recover from upset feelings so that they can concentrate on other activities. Few professionals would survive working with young children if they were not able to do this.

However, as a result of the advice of emotional literacy experts, children have to be taught more direct ways of calming themselves through, for example, breathing techniques, taking their pulse or telling themselves 'be calm ... be calm ... be calm'.

What this new approach is doing is to make 'calming down' into a problem for all children. Gone is the expectation of calmness – this is now something children have to learn. As soon as we put it in these terms we see that it introduces the idea of failure – of not being able to induce a calm state. It is very easy to see how by going on about how important it is to be calm, rather than providing a context where calm is expected, teachers could unwittingly increase children's feelings of nervousness around not being calm.

There is another psychological mechanism at work which suggests that an emphasis on calming down in the classroom is likely to backfire. A social psychologist, Dan Wegner, has published many articles on what he calls 'ironic processes of mental control'. This means that often by trying to control our mind in some way we often, ironically, induce the opposite. The mechanism at work is this: if we try not to think about a white bear (one of the experiments Werner recounts) then the mind sets up a goal (don't think of the bear) and will automatically set up a monitoring process for this goal so that it knows if success has been achieved. When the goal is a mental process the mind then automatically keeps checking to see if it is being successful – am I thinking about a white bear? – and so the very thing we are trying not to think about keeps coming into our thoughts.

Ironic effects are particularly common around sleep and relaxation – the more we try to relax the more aware we become of being tense. Werner *et al* write: '... too often our efforts to cool down, withdraw, or calm ourselves seem to backfire – producing greater agitation than we had suffered before we even tried to relax'. They even report that people suffering from anxiety 'who are given a paradoxical instruction to become anxious sometimes fare as well in relaxation as those who are instructed to relax'. Werner and colleagues suggest that it may be better for professionals to take much more indirect approaches and 'disguise the overall aim of relaxation procedures in some way'.

In short, all that emphasis on being calm in the classroom could well make young people's excitability and lack of control worse – not better.

The dangers of political control and social conformity

Before the emphasis on emotional literacy/intelligence, schools were mainly concerned about behaviour – it was how you behaved or what you said that mattered. What you felt was your own business. But this new approach to social and emotional skills means that feelings, the most intimate part of our lives – are going to be managed ostensibly by children but in reality by the people drawing up the lists of emotional and social competences. As Professor Weare herself points out, deciding what goes into such a list 'cannot be value-free, culture-free or an apolitical exercise'. She is acutely aware that there is a particular problem for children in this. She writes: 'The associated competences that are thought to be appropriate for children tend to focus on conformity, "good behaviour", co-operation and positive thinking, usually adult defined'.

Even more sophisticated programmes based on objective emotional ability (ie, based on right and wrong answers) have this potential downside – a downside acknowledged by Mayer and Salovey. In this case it is not subjective views of list makers that will predominate but the emotional norm. It is not too difficult to see why encouraging children to read others' feelings, and develop empathy, could at least for some children lead them to be overly concerned with other people's views and feelings. This could inhibit them from taking any action which others may not like. Remember, Mayer *et al* report research which shows that artists often do not score very highly on emotional intelligence, since they pay attention more to their creative impulses – something which is often out of sync with others' emotions and views.

The problem of control goes much further than who draws up the lists of competences on which children are to be judged and trained. Who decides, for example, what level of self-expression is appropriate for a child or which feelings 'suit' particular situations or people? The obvious difficulty posed by this question is one of the reasons why some psychologists and psychiatrists have dismissed the whole idea of teaching young people emotional intelligence or drawing up checklists. As soon as Goleman's book appeared, Dr Paul McHugh, one of America's most distinguished psychiatrists, was critical of some of its basic assumptions about teaching emotional intelligence. He particularly criticised the idea that children can be taught the right emotions to have in different situations. 'We don't even know the right emotions to be taught to adults', McHugh stated forcefully.

Encouraging rebelliousness

As soon as we start to talk about the dangers of social control and conformity the prospect of rebellion rears its head. Professor Weare is aware of this difficulty with behaviour approaches as she tells us:

> *There is some evidence that using behavioural approaches with younger children to engage them in practising healthy behaviour achieves compliance in the short term, but can backfire as children get older and more knowledgeable, and lose trust in the truthfulness of their teachers as a result of being coerced.*

She uses this to argue that, rather than trying to change children's behaviour, we have to attend to their emotions. But why should this be different? Children are likely to react to attempts at emotional management in exactly the same way.

This is exactly what emerges from the pilot undertaken on SEAL. The authors state that some head teachers reported a rise in 'fixed term exclusions' since the SEAL programme had been introduced. One head teacher reported that it had had little impact on the children who normally behaved well but for those who were already 'lacking in emotional literacy it probably has not made much of a difference and ... I think in some cases has made children worse'.

Another head teacher reported that some children 'have rebelled against the SEAL programme'. The authors say: 'It seemed that the SEAL programme impacted positively on the behaviour of the majority'. However, this majority was unlikely to present much of a problem in schools. The ones who were already a problem in many cases seemed to worsen and this is why there was a rise in exclusions.

Evaluation and stigmatization

Imagine for a moment the prospect of going into your boss's office so that he or she can discuss with you whether you express your feelings adequately or appropriately; whether you recognise other people's feelings enough; whether you pay enough compliments or how you are doing on dozens of 'skills' of these kinds. This discussion will then result in your boss making some kind of evaluation of your skills and setting you goals for improvement. No doubt, like most people, you balk at the prospect.

Professor Weare in her 2004 book and in the report to the DfES, does not raise the spectre of profiling staff for their social and emotional skills. Weare and Gray write:

> *It would not be helpful if emotional and social competence were to become a factor which teachers and carers are expected to take on and be assessed against. They need to have their own emotional needs to be taken into account, and to be valued and respected, be given resources and help.*

But if such assessment is a no-go area for staff then why is it acceptable for students? Why should we think it is all right to formally rate young people on lists of social and emotional competences? Weare as usual raises some of the possible problems and objections to this type of assessment and evaluation with young people, but then tells us it is not only desirable but essential to do so. Indeed she even draws our attention, without one word of criticism, to a 'Record of Assessment for Emotional Literacy Checklist' drawn up by the Southampton Emotional Literacy Interest Group. This 'checklist invites the teacher to grade each child A – D' on a range of social and emotional competences.

The SEAL Guidance for three to eleven-year-olds, makes clear that children's ability and performance on the 42 skills outlined should be evaluated. The document then indicates how 'judgements teachers make about children's progress' will be linked to various key stages. It also says that teachers are 'encouraged' to use formative, rather than summative assessment. In other words, children will be expected to discuss their skills in this area against a predetermined checklist of skills, take feedback from the teacher and set goals for improvement. Other children may also be involved in the assessment. This is exactly the process that most adults would object to.

But what happens if the child has not managed to evolve the right kind of self-expression, for example? In brutal language, what if they do not evaluate well on a good number of the 42 skills? Children are not easily deceived: they will know that in the social and emotional game of life they have been judged and found deficient. For those who are not performing well academically this is going to be yet another blow. The designers of these materials can talk about self-esteem and confidence, but unwittingly the approach they are trying to bring into schools will lead many children to feel negative about themselves, as they will know they are failing to meet standard expectations.

Not a child-centred agenda

This leads on to one of the deceptive aspects of this agenda. So many people nowadays have been put off by the target-driven, management-by-objectives approach which dominates public sector organisations including schools. To many it seems far too impersonal and cold to turn people's lives into such data. So at a superficial level the emotional literacy agenda can seem a welcome diversion from this. After all the cold logic and strategies is it not great to hear people talking about emotions and feelings? This is further enhanced by the fact that advocates continue to talk about the importance of a 'holistic' approach. It also seems to be trying to put all those government-driven targets on numeracy and literacy in their place and to be more child-centred.

But government departments and inspectors of schools do not operate like this. They will find it difficult to resist making this type of work in schools conform to what has become their standard way of operating. All young people's emotional lives (not just the few who have obvious difficulties) will become the focus for checklists, assessments and evaluations. Who knows, the next step might even be targets! Professor Weare is aware of the difficulties with this agenda and the potential for bias and labelling but she cannot resist advocating this type of assessment because she fears that this work will never get off the ground unless it can be grafted onto familiar approaches to assessment.

Feelings, emotions and relationships are the core of our personal lives. They are an intimate part of us. For me, the prospect of all children's emotional lives being managed by professionals working for government departments is a good enough reason on its own to object to this type of approach in schools.

All about me – the dangers of 'the bloated self'

There is another major difficulty with Weare *et al's* approach to social and emotional competences and it is the fact that it is very similar to the type of activities in the American classroom that have undermined children's well-being and academic standards. Weare and Gray's list of emotional and social competences, for example, puts self-esteem at the top of the list: 'having self-esteem, a competence which includes valuing and respecting yourself as an unique individual and seeing yourself as separate from others'. Self-esteem is not one of the headline themes in SEAL but there is in the materials a major emphasis on the 'good to me', 'I'm special' approach which appears to have fostered narcissism and undermined well-being in the US by encouraging too much focus on the self.

Parents' responsibility

Professor Weare argues that 'there is considerable evidence that effective work on emotional and social education is more effective if it involves parents'. However, the pilot project on SEAL showed that 'parents were reluctant partners with the programme'. Very few wanted to get involved.

In reality much of the rationale for SEAL, at least from the DfES's point of view is that they believe parents are failing in their duties. The Guidance document states:

> *Research is bringing home the wide extent of various types of neglect and abuse. This is being exacerbated by the breakdown of extended families and communities which reduces support for the nuclear family, and the higher rates of divorce and subsequent one-parent families. This has led to a shake-up in the belief that we can leave children's emotional and social development entirely to parents: other agencies have to get involved as well.*

It was the inclusion of this paragraph, with no empirical research to support it that led one newspaper when the Guidance was made public to state in their headline: 'Government tells schools to focus on emotional development as parents cannot be trusted'.

At the Centre we have little doubt that the rising tide of alcohol and drug abuse means that there are more and more children suffering from neglect and abuse. We are also aware that primary schools report a growing number of children in deprived areas who do not have the skills required to be in a primary one classroom. But they are certainly not the majority and if schools now take on the responsibility of all children's emotional, social and behavioural skills whose fault is it going to be if children don't do well in them? Will schools and teachers get the blame? We agree with the concern expressed by the NUT on the SEAL document that requiring schools to concentrate on this type of activity 'adds to some parents' assumptions that their children are someone else's responsibility'. Will some parents increasingly leave the job of regulating children's emotions and teaching them basic social skills to schools? Will they think, erroneously, that professionals will do it better than they can?

We must always bear in mind with this agenda that the percentage of children's time spent at school is small – only 15 per cent of their lives. Schools will never be able to devote the necessary time to it and taking this responsibility on will create more problems for them in the longer term. We think that schools should only directly teach these skills to young children on a 'needs must' basis. If children need this help because they are not getting it at home, then devote time to it. If some schools have a particular problem then they should devote time to it. But blanket coverage is sending out the wrong signals to parents and to children themselves. No doubt the argument against this is that it will stigmatise some children but this is already provided for in the document, with its three tiers of intervention. We still see targeted intervention as preferable to making emotions and social skills a problem for all children.

The Centre believes that it is a mistake to think that there is one solution or panacea. We certainly do not think that schools and teachers can, or should, shoulder the burden of trying to plug the gaps in children's lives. We believe this is what Professor Weare *et al* are attempting to do. We have set out various reasons for our opposition to this approach in preceding sections and why we think that this solution, far from making this better, may make matters worse for young people in the longer term.

In the remainder of this chapter I set out what the Centre for Confidence and Well-being sees as preferred courses of action.

Alternative ways to enhance young people's well-being

Early engagement

The Centre has been influenced by the work of Alan Sinclair on what he calls 'early engagement'. As Alan explains in his report *0–5: How Small Children can Make a Big Difference*, 'The most important six years in a person's life are up to the age of five'. He summarises research which shows how important the early years of life are to the development of the child's cognitive, social and emotional skills. It is not just the first few years of life that are particularly important but also the months preceding birth when the developing foetus can be adversely affected by the mother's stress. Research indicates that prenatal stress can increase the chance of behavioural and social problems as well as impair language and cognitive development.

Alan argues passionately for the need for 'early years enrichment' and engagement. The models he advances for this type of work mainly come from Scandinavia where considerable sums are invested in good quality day care and parenting support. This ensures that parents, who may fail their children by not providing enough attention and stimulation, are supported by what the Scandinavians call 'pedagogues'. When this involves supporting parents in the home, this does not have a punitive feel to it such as it can in the UK.

Why early engagement is needed

If we examine the data on the rise of alcohol and drug use and the number of children being brought up with parents with these problems, it is impossible to deny that there are growing numbers of children who are neglected and abused. This is further compounded by the decline in the extended family and the rise in single parents, many of them teenage mothers who have themselves been inadequately parented. Many schools report that a growing number of children are attending P1 without the necessary skills to be in a classroom and some are setting up 'nurture units'.

Facilitating children's social and emotional development has to be done through sensitive provision for pregnant women who are at risk of stress and through various schemes which provide high quality day care and parental support in the first five years of life – particularly the first three.

In order to ensure that the children who need most support with their cognitive, emotional and social development resources get good provision, we need to target the groups most at risk. Alan Sinclair argues that the 'logic' of addressing the problem means that –

> *To get the most out of our public spending, expenditure on parenting and enriched day care should be skewed to households most likely to struggle. That means targeting the*

children of workless households, single parents, and the working poor and, in an age creating more alcohol and drug casualties, elderly carers of infants.

Support for individual children in schools

More is now being done to give vulnerable young children additional support but more help is needed. Where the numbers warrant it, schools should set up nurture units to give additional help with social and emotional skill development to the children most in need. If the difficulty remains beyond P1 then these children should be given additional support and be explicitly taught social and emotional skills if necessary. The Centre has no difficulty with the idea that teachers should give one-to-one help for individual children, or small groups, with social and emotional skills on a 'needs must' basis.

The obvious objection to such targeted help is that it is too much of a deficit, problem-focused approach. But even Weare *et al* recognise that there will always be children who need help in social and emotional skill development beyond the curriculum activities they envisage for the whole class.

Other steps schools can take to enhance well-being

The Centre recognises that the issue of child well-being is probably a much wider one than might be inferred from the numbers of children displaying obvious difficulties. We also think that schools can play a part in ensuring a more supportive environment for children. Here are a few of the Centre's ideas on how this can be done.

i. Creating positive classrooms and positive schools

We believe that the best teachers and the best schools are those that instinctively manage to create a positive, supportive environment for learning in the classroom or the whole school. They do this through high expectations, clear rules and sophisticated methods to build relationships and respect. Such a positive atmosphere is not only good for learning but also for young people's well-being. This means that we wholeheartedly support training and development initiatives which are designed to equip school staff with the knowledge and skills required to create positive relationships, positive classrooms and a positive school ethos. Some of the specific techniques which the Centre particularly favours for doing this have been included in this *Handbook*.

The Centre also believes that teachers and others working with young people need to have a much better than average understanding of themselves and others and be skilled in managing their own moods and emotions. This means that we agree that teachers and others may benefit from high quality training on emotional literacy or intelligence and that these insights have some part to play in creating a more positive learning environment.

ii. Teaching by example

The Centre also believes that teachers and other professionals have some role to play in teaching young people social and emotional skills. However, we believe that these skills are best learned in specific life situations and teachers and other professionals should ideally teach these skills by example rather than via a year-on-year, explicit teaching approach. The Centre believes that some of the more robust emotional intelligence training (ie, Mayer and Salovey's concept of emotional ability) could have a role to play here.

iii. Tackling bullying

The evidence suggests that there is a growing problem with bullying at school. We think that this is an important agenda item for schools but believe this can be addressed via whole school approaches on behaviour. This may require some specific teaching on what bullying is and what it is not, as well as encouragement for students to tell school staff about incidents. We do not think it necessary to introduce a social and emotional competences approach as part of an anti-bullying strategy.

iv. Reducing anxiety about school work and the emphasis on academic tests

In the SEAL pilot the biggest problem for the young people surveyed was 'anxiety about school work'. The UK as a whole has become obsessed with tests, measurement and academic performance and some recent research shows that this is putting undue strain on young people. Educational policy makers should pay more attention to the experience of some of our European neighbours where children attend formal school when they are seven and spend the first few years of life more in play and social learning than in academic learning. This practice is consistent with higher academic results in the longer term. We also think it important to keep an emphasis on the importance of children achieving academic skills while at the same time broadening the curriculum at secondary level to cater for those students who simply do not have an interest in pursuing a very academic range of subjects. We also think that more attention should be paid to harnessing children's intrinsic motivation.

Explicit teaching

When it comes to improving children's emotional and social skills the Centre prefers an approach where the skills are caught from the teacher rather than formally taught in lessons. However, we are not dogmatic about this and believe that there may be some occasions when explicit teaching may be advantageous. Earlier in this *Handbook* I suggested that it may be useful to explicitly teach resiliency skills, optimism and a growth mindset to young people.

Differences between the Centre's recommendations and Weare *et al's* social and emotional competences

Following our critique of the social and emotional competences approach, it may seem like special pleading to say now that some of the approaches we favour should be permissible in schools. However, while our approach may seem at first glance to overlap with some of Weare's views or the SEAL materials, what we envisage has a very different ethos.

The most fundamental difference between the Centre's approach to lessons on personal development themes and the SEAL curriculum is that we are absolutely opposed to the idea of a checklist of social and emotional competences and to evaluating or profiling students. We would never recommend evaluating children's optimism or assertiveness in a way that would lead an individual student to feel that they had now to make changes to reach an acceptable level. The Centre is of the view that schools should simply offer training to students on the basis that they might find it useful and helpful. The Centre is keen on the idea of pre- and post-intervention measurements to see if there are any tangible benefits as a result of the training, but we would always want this to be undertaken on a group, not an individual, basis.

Another difference between the Centre's preferred approach and the one I have critiqued here is that we are primarily interested in focusing on giving young people information on cognitive/problem solving skills. The type of information which we think would be useful for young people includes some of the latest psychological research on what helps people lead happy and fulfilling lives. The skills involved in raising optimism or building resilience in young people are primarily cognitive. This means that our approach is consistent with school's role in developing young people's cognitive and intellectual skills.

So where we differ from Weare and colleagues is that we do not think it helpful to encourage schools to focus explicitly on young people's emotional development unless there is a specific difficulty which needs to be addressed. Nor do we think it useful to encourage young people to focus on their feelings or emotions too much as this can easily lead to self-obsession. We do not think it helpful to convey to young people that we all need help from professionals with the development of our emotional and social lives. This approach is likely to fuel mental health problems for many young people rather than contain them. What is more, we do not think that most teachers will ever be trained well enough to deal with the subtleties of this agenda or the problems which are likely to arise.

Finally, the Centre is keen to see schools develop young people with the skills and motivation to act in the world. Rather than focus on feelings and dwell on 'all about me' activities, reminiscent of American classrooms, we want teachers to help young people to acquire skills and confidence. The precise ways we think schools can help raise confidence, and improve well-being, is the subject of the next chapter.

Key Points

1. Emotional literacy and approaches to develop young people's social and emotional skills, or emotional well-being, have become fashionable in schools in the UK.
2. Much of this work derives its intellectual rationale, and evidence base, from Daniel Goleman's international best-seller *Emotional Intelligence.*
3. Goleman's work has attracted considerable critical attention from psychologists. They particularly critique the fact he uses the term to include a range of positive characteristics which are completely unrelated, and sometimes at odds with one another.
4. Another major criticism of Goleman's work is that he massively overestimates the importance of what he terms 'emotional intelligence'. Goleman now tacitly accepts this criticism and that IQ is often more important.
5. Critics also warn that using emotional intelligence to label people's abilities will eventually have exactly the same stigma and negative effect as IQ testing.
6. Emotional intelligence is seen as a panacea. This is an echo of the self-esteem movement that also believed that all society's ills could be cured by influencing young people's psychology at school.
7. In the UK, work on emotional literacy in schools is gathering momentum. The DfES in England and Wales has now issued guidance to all schools recommending that they formally teach all young people social and emotional skills on a year-on-year basis. This initiative is called SEAL (Social and Emotional Aspects of Learning).
8. The Centre is sceptical of the underlying intellectual rationale of SEAL as it is heavily reliant on Goleman, on US projects and on the DfES's own pilots, which were inadequately constructed and which actually produced few or negative results.
9. SEAL is based on the idea that all children formally need to be taught about their feelings and about relationships from professionals. We take the view that this is not a positive message to give young people.
10. The SEAL/emotional literacy approach recommends that young people learn to express their feelings as this is good for them. But this is not a view widely accepted in psychology. Talking about feelings can cause problems under some circumstances.
11. Other techniques advanced by SEAL and emotional literacy experts likewise could undermine young people's well-being. For example, research suggests that teaching young people techniques to calm down could result in making them feel more anxious.
12. The Centre is also opposed to the idea of evaluating young people against a checklist of social and emotional competences. This is what is recommended in the SEAL document. We believe this will lead to social conformity and stigmatisation and ultimately reduce children's confidence. We also think this approach could encourage rebelliousness.

13. Emotional literacy/emotional well-being approaches sound as though they are child-friendly as they talk about the whole person and appear to be at odds with a tick box, target-driven culture. But this is not the case. Indeed, SEAL is extending the tick box approach to young people's emotional lives.
14. Much of the SEAL approach is very similar to the practices of the American self-esteem movement as it is very focused on 'all about me' activities. This can lead to an obsession with the self and undermine well-being.
15. The Centre also believes that if schools formally take on the responsibility for children's social and emotional skills this may encourage parents to abdicate responsibility.
16. The Centre believes that there are better ways to improve young people's well-being. This includes early engagement strategies and the types of interventions and techniques outlined in this *Handbook*.

PART VI
conclusion

16 Integrating Confidence and Well-Being

I claim to be an average man of less than average ability. I have not the shadow of a doubt that any man or woman can achieve what I have, if he or she would make the same effort and cultivate the same hope and faith.

Mahatma Gandhi

The Centre for Confidence and Well-being has now devised a working model of confidence. This is made up of four elements: **two core elements** – *self-efficacy and optimism* – and **two elements which sustain and foster confidence** – *support from others and learning from others*. The core elements reflect the definition we gave of confidence in Chapter 2 and the sustaining/fostering elements summarise the approach taken throughout this *Handbook*.

Our model reflects the fact that people are different and not everyone will be born with the same level of confidence. Professor Martin Seligman and others estimate that about 50 per cent of optimism is heritable – ie, it is part of an individual's genetic make up. Albert Bandura too believes that some children are naturally more 'efficacious' than others.

However, while levels of optimism and efficacy are influenced by innate factors, of much greater significance are external factors which can help, or hinder, the development of core confidence. In our model, we have called these 'sustaining/fostering elements' to convey the idea that they help to nurture or support a person's self-efficacy or optimism. These external factors often boil down to the influence of significant people in our lives – particularly parents and teachers as well as other adults and members of our peer group. The prevailing culture too plays a significant part here as it helps to shape the type of support and encouragement we get as individuals from these crucially important people. As we saw in Chapter 6 there are good reasons to believe that Scottish culture has not been particularly good at fostering, or sustaining, individuals' confidence.

Confidence and action

Things won are done; joy's soul lies in the doing.

William Shakespeare

Our concept of confidence is related to doing and making things happen. Robert White was a Harvard psychologist and at the end of the 1950s, after extensive studies of animals and humans, he argued that people and many mammalian species have a desire for what he called 'effectance'. Psychologists often talk about this as the need for competence or mastery. Essentially, White's concept of effectance involves humans' desire to interact with, and control, the outer environment in some way. In his inspirational book *The Happiness Hypothesis*, the psychologist Johnathan Haidt says of effectance:

> *You can see it in the joy infants take with 'busy boxes', the activity centres that allow them to convert flailing arm movements into ringing bells and spinning wheels. ... And you can see it in the lethargy that often overtakes people who stop working, whether from retirement, being fired, or winning a lottery.*

Haidt also reminds us of Aristotle's notion that people are like archers who need a clear target at which to aim. Without such a target we are left with what Haidt calls 'the animal default' where we just graze idly, following the herd. However, as Haidt points out, much of the enjoyment humans derive from their goals is not so much in their achievement but in our progress towards them.

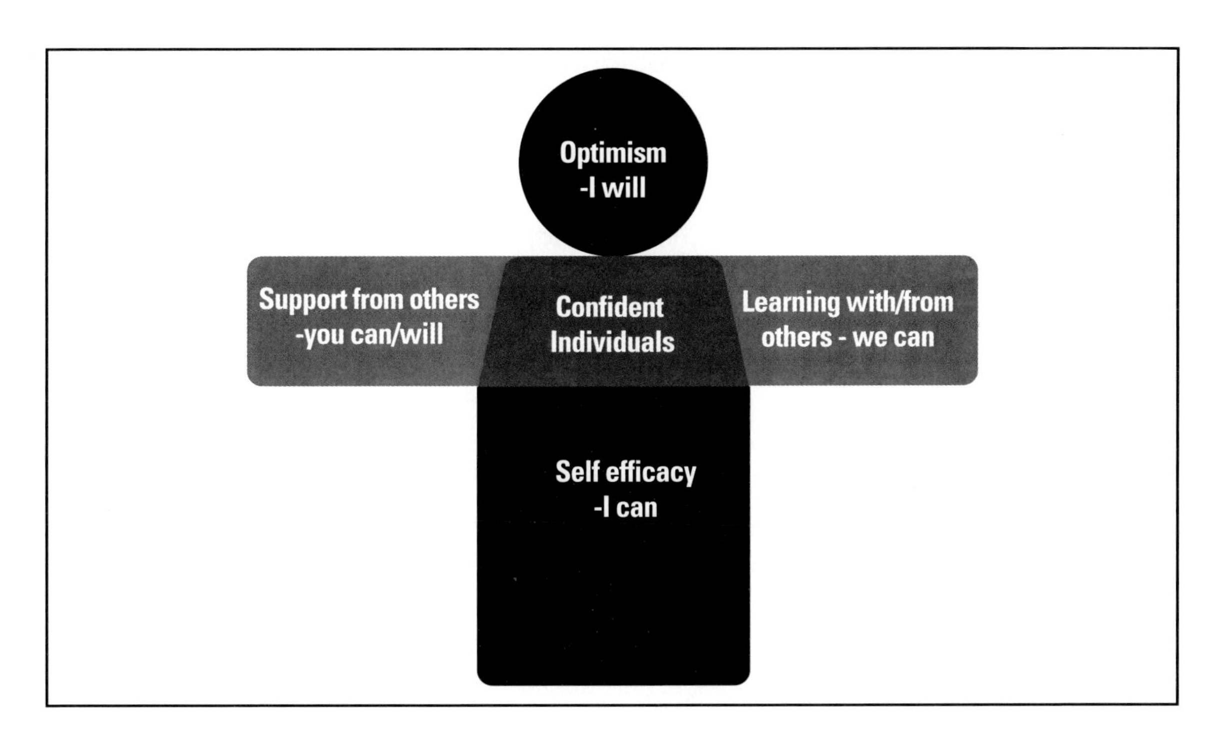

The Centre's Confidence Model – Core elements

1. Self-efficacy

Watchword:	I can.
Essential requirement:	Belief in our ability to meet specific, challenging goals.
Helped by:	'Growth mindset', hard-work, good strategies for learning or performance, optimism (see below).
Outcome:	Success, mastery, sense of achievement and self-worth. Achieving the goal boosts confidence to tackle harder goals.
Hindered by:	Interacting with people with a fixed mindset; growing up in a culture/family/school environment which is pessimistic or discouraging.
If overdone:	We can become too isolated from others and too competitive, ego-driven or task-focused. We may become workaholics and lose sight of everything but our goals.

2. Optimism

Watchword:	I will.
Essential requirement:	Optimistic 'explanatory style'.
Helped by:	Positive mental strategies (eg, positive self-talk, hope) which keeps us energised and focused on our goals.
Outcome:	Resilient thinking style which allows us to bounce back after difficult times and keep believing we can achieve our goals.
Hindered by:	Growing up in a culture/family/school environment, which encourages a pessimistic explanatory style.
If overdone:	Mental strategies (eg, unrealistic positive thinking) may be preferred over hard work. This could result in becoming an impractical Pollyanna.

The Centre's Confidence Model – Fostering/sustaining elements

3. Support from others

Watchword:	You will.
Essential requirement:	Others who are prepared to invest time, energy or resources in our goal or our self-belief. People who believe we have potential – ie, who adopt a 'growth' rather than a 'fixed' mindset.
Forms the support can take:	i. *Verbal:* Encouragement (eg, people taking time to discuss our goal, telling us they believe we can achieve it). Other people keeping us motivated and energised through appropriate, well-judged praise, appreciation and other positive conversational strategies. *ii. Practical*: Other people investing time, money or other useful resources to support us or our goals.
Outcome:	This type of social and practical support not only helps to encourage and sustain our self-belief but also helps boost our resilience in difficult times. This support can help us to maintain confidence and a positive outlook during times when life is hard or stressful.
If overdone:	We can become overly dependent on what people think. We could become praise junkies who constantly need positive affirmation from others. This would then undermine confidence in the longer term – not sustain it.

4. Learning from others

Watchword:	You can.
Essential requirement:	Others who can help us get better at the specific tasks we need to accomplish and achieve our goals.
Forms this learning can take:	*i. Modelling/mentoring*: Human beings are hard-wired to learn from others. Working alongside/under supervision of others who can do what we want to do can maintain our confidence that we too can learn these skills if we apply ourselves in similar ways. ii. *Feedback*: Someone skilled at what we want to do can accelerate our learning by giving us feedback on what we are doing well (praise) or what we need to do better or differently (criticism). iii. *Co-operation/team-working*: Learning that support of our efficacy need not happen in a top-down fashion (eg, master/apprentice; teacher/student). We can learn from peers when we work collaboratively in pairs, work groups and teams. Our peers can also give us useful feedback on how well we are doing.
Outcome:	Role-models and mentors can help us increase our skills and ensure that we learn from our experience. They also help us by showing that the challenging goal is achievable. Being exposed to people who are working at a higher level can help us become more ambitious.
If overdone:	We become too dependent on others and their achievements, feedback and skills.

Confidence for what?

Confidence is a word which tells us very little when used on its own. 'Confident individuals' helps us to know whose confidence we are talking about but it still begs the question, confident for what? Many see me as a confident individual as I can stand up in front of large audiences and give talks. I also repeatedly put myself in situations where I have to be confident about my ideas, my capacity to communicate them and to interact with people who disagree. I also consider myself confident about handling lots of life's challenges. However, I am very unconfident about whole areas of life – singing, playing musical instruments, drawing, changing the tyre on my car, putting up shelves. The list is enormous. However, I have a 'growth mindset' and I have come to see that I could learn to do all of these things, and my confidence would rise, if I put in enough hard work and had a good teacher. So even if an individual is confident in the areas of life they care about, the model I have elaborated here could be helpful for them in working out what they needed to do to raise their confidence to reach different types of goals.

There are some very confident, entrepreneurial types who would argue that they are always confident, since they are confident about learning and face life's challenges head on. While I would not question the breadth of their skills I still contend that they would not be confident about everything. For example, doing a job – such as caring – where there would be less scope to use their irrepressible entrepreneurial ideas and which could be too repetitive.

There is a more important point to be made about the fact that confidence has to relate to something and does not exist in a vacuum. Confidence may or may not be a good thing, depending on what it is related to. A thief could be confident that he could rob a bank; Hitler was confident that Germany could conquer Europe. In short, confidence may be good in as much as it helps individuals to accomplish goals in life but these goals can be judged as good or bad, worthless or worthwhile, depending on what they seek to achieve.

This leads to the important question: what do we think young people will ultimately achieve in life from being confident? Asking this question immediately poses a dilemma for us at the Centre for Confidence and Well-being. We fear that the two parts of our agenda may not only be misaligned but actually at odds with one another.

Confidence and well-being

> *Ever more people today have the means to live, but no meaning to live for.*
>
> Viktor E. Frankl

Psychologists from the Self-Determination school argue that a sense of competence, the ability to take action for ourselves, and strong relationships with others are all vitally important for a sense of well-being. They support their claims with findings from international, empirical research. So confidence, as defined in this book, can easily be seen as a keystone in the creation of a flourishing, satisfying life in as much as confidence helps and encourages people to interact with the world, acquire skills, hone strengths and achieve self-determining goals.

However, people do not live in a social vacuum, either as children or adults. In western societies – particularly in the US and the UK – there is a strong, pervasive achievement and materialistic ethic that helps to shape people's individual ambitions and motivations. This is an ethic that encourages us to believe that the main aim in life is to become a successful individual. What is more, as a result of the rise of the mass media, the notion of success in contemporary culture is increasingly couched in terms of power, fame, money and looks. This media agenda also encourages us to believe that becoming successful in this way will give us access to all the trimmings that we hope will bring us happiness – a nice house, holidays, clothes, cars and countless consumer goods.

So the Centre's confidence agenda could easily become part of this endless, individualistic quest for achievement and success. If so we may simply be encouraging, and equipping, young people to go down a very materialistic path – a journey which may well undermine their well-being.

'The Goods Life' v. The Good Life

As we saw in Chapter 14, the problem with consumer goods and a successful life style is that it rarely brings us the satisfaction we seek. Within a year of their windfall, lottery winners are back to their original level of happiness or even below it. Research shows that money is related to happiness but the relationship is much more complicated than people think. People who are materially insecure – ie, have no roof over their heads or wonder where the next meal is coming from – do often feel unhappy. But once these basic needs are met, more money does not necessarily bring more happiness. This is why happiness research shows that as the western world becomes wealthier happiness levels hardly rise.

Research also shows that relationships are of vital importance to people's happiness. Self-Determination theorists maintain that our need for affiliation is as important as our need for competence and autonomy. Our need for relationships is hard-wired. An influential theory advanced by Robin Dunbar maintains that human beings have large brains so that they can process the huge amounts of information needed to relate to others and live successfully in a large group.

Research shows that married people are happier than those who are single (or even co-habiting). It also shows that the happiest people are those who spend lots of time with other people. Socialising is not simply good for our happiness but also our physical and mental health. What is more, social support systems are not just good for people because they provide a safety net: research also shows that giving support or caring is often more beneficial to the person giving than to the person receiving.

All of this accords with the research carried out by Professor Jennifer Crocker, reported in Chapter 3, which shows that people's well-being is undermined by pursuing egotistical goals and enhanced by what she calls 'eco goals', which are based more on other people or the environment.

So one of the problems with the confidence agenda is this: it could encourage people to put their personal development before their relationships and if they do, this may undermine their well-being rather than build it up. Jonathan Haidt posits this problem, not with reference to achievement and confidence, but to personal freedom; it is essentially the same point:

> *An ideology of extreme personal freedom can be dangerous because it encourages people to leave homes, jobs, cities, and marriages in search of personal and professional fulfilment, thereby breaking the relationships that were probably their best hope for fulfilment.*

Meaning

The problem with pursuing an individual achievement agenda is that it may also undermine, not just our relationships with others, but a sense of meaning. Like other thinkers, Professor Martin Seligman argues that meaning is, by definition, about serving a goal bigger than yourself. For him one of the main problems with the values of contemporary society and individualism is that they encourage people to focus too much on themselves, their desires and their feelings. This is why he talks about 'the bloated self'.

Following his extensive research on happiness, Professor Martin Seligman maintains that one of the most important pieces of advice he can give on how to increase happiness and well-being is this: find out what your signature strengths are and then be in a role – a job or voluntary work – where every day you can use some of these strengths in the service of other people.

Johnathan Haidt too talks about the need to restrict the self to find meaning, and therefore happiness and fulfilment in life. In his attempt to explain why spiritual feelings often accompany exposure to nature – particularly when we contemplate the stars or are in places which are vast or grand, Haidt writes: 'Something about the vastness and beauty of nature makes the self feel small and insignificant, and anything that *shrinks* the self creates an opportunity for spiritual development'. (My emphasis.)

Haidt argues that individuals find particular fulfilment if they can experience through their work what Csikszentmihalyi and colleagues call 'vital engagement'. This happens when an individual simultaneously experiences what Csikszentmihalyi refers to as flow (total involvement in challenging, absorbing work) with a sense of meaning. Committed teachers no doubt experience some of their best teaching moments as 'vital engagement'.

The Centre's Well-being Compass

> *He who has a why to live for can bear almost any how.*
>
> Victor E. Frankl

Keeping these ideas in mind, let us go back to our model of confidence and now situate it within what the Centre is calling its Well-being Compass – something to guide individuals' confidence towards a meaningful, flourishing and fulfilling life.

Confidence can help people to achieve goals in life and become competent. This means that confident individuals are people who have strengths and skills. If they then link these attributes, not just to the pursuit of their own personal interest, but to others' interests as well, this can take them in a much more positive direction. There are two different ways to do this.

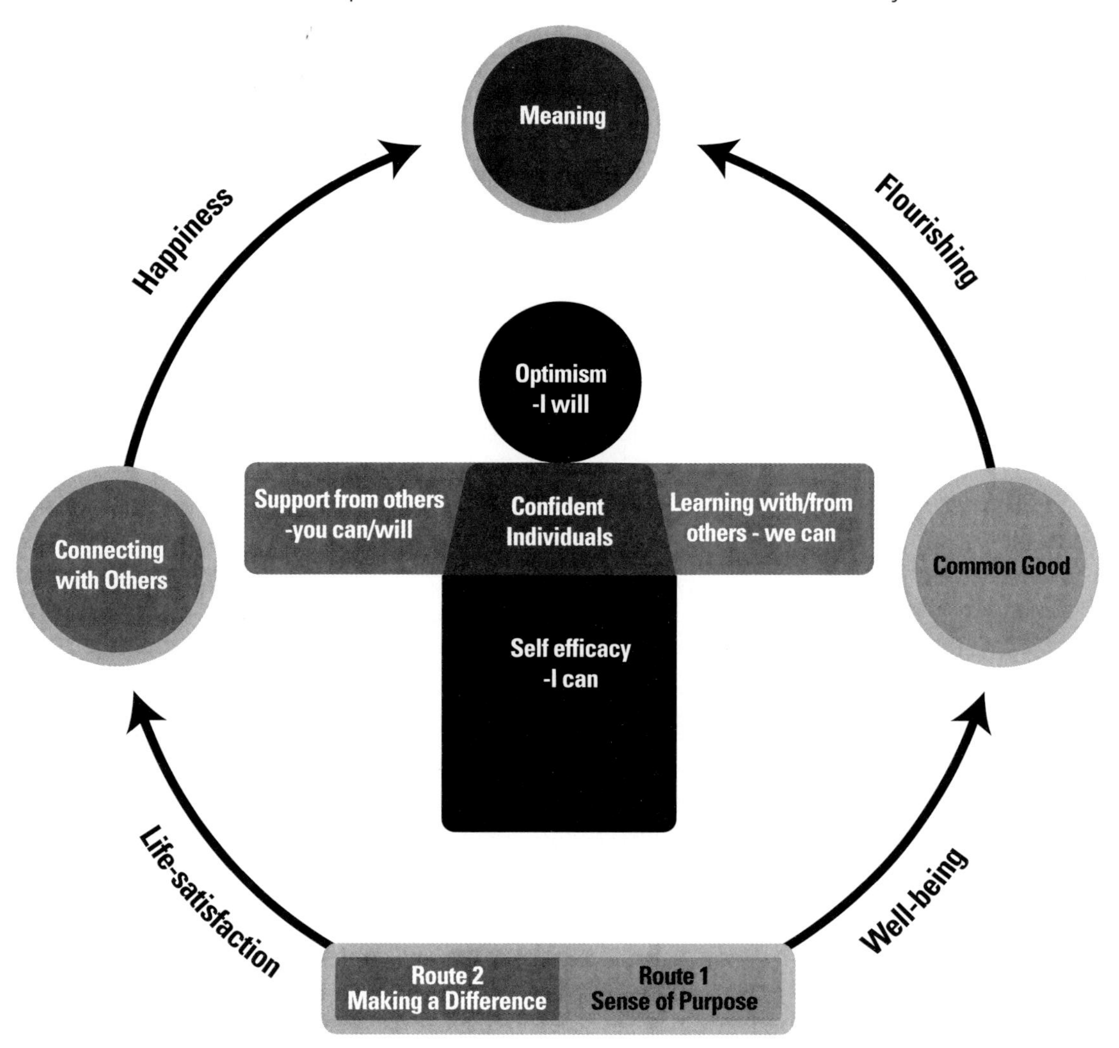

Route 1

Vocation is the spine of life.

Friedrich Nietzsche

i. Sense of purpose

The first way is to link our confidence in achieving something to a sense of vocation or calling. This means wanting to immerse ourselves in a particular type of work or activity that is not only motivating and satisfying but gives a strong sense of direction to our lives. Research shows that people in all occupations, no matter how lowly or poorly paid, can have the sense of their job as a vocation.

ii. Common good

This sense of purpose can be directed towards the idea of the common good or the notion of social improvement. This is likely to be about human beings but it could be about animals or environmental issues. These values could lead us as individuals into charitable work. They could also involve an individual dedicating him/herself to sport or another activity which they believe dignifies human existence in some way. This could cover athletes whose motivation is less about personal aggrandisement and more about Olympian ideals or the belief in the importance that sport can have in helping to structure and transform individuals' lives. It could also include academics, or writers, who are committed to research or writing believing that such activities are an important facet of human life or of a civilised society. Of course, this does not mean that everyone will agree on what the common good is – in fact there can, and should be, hugely different interpretations. Without this plurality the importance attached to the common good can easily give rise to totalitarianism.

iii. Meaning

Grounding achievements and confidence in values such as 'the common good' or social improvement then gives individuals a sense of meaning in their lives. If people have meaning they are likely to experience happiness, life-satisfaction and well-being and lead flourishing lives.

Route 2

To know even one life has breathed easier because you have lived. This is the meaning of success.

Ralph Waldo Emerson

We recognise, however, that individuals are not always motivated by the sense of purpose or common good outlined above; that for many people such ideas will be much too abstract and 'airy fairy'. So there is another route to harness confidence and achievement so that we can get more meaning in our lives.

i. Making a difference

If well-being is undermined by too much fixation on the self, and its own gratification and motivation, then what can improve our lives is the idea that by using our strengths and skills we can make a difference. This is about becoming more conscious of how our lives and actions can have a positive effect on the lives of others round about us.

ii. Connecting with others

If we encourage this idea of making a difference to grow it can lead us to make even more of an effort to connect with other people. Managers, for example, realise that they can use their strengths and skills to develop and influence other people and give more time to this task. Knowing they can make a difference to others' lives, people volunteer their time, energy and skills to help others. This has links with the idea of the common good but it is of more immediate relevance and directed towards specific individuals.

iii. Meaning

This sense of giving and being connected to others reinforces the idea of being a small part of a bigger whole and so lends meaning to life.

Uniting the individual and the collective

The advantage of Seligman's prescription of using your signature strengths in the service of other people, and the Centre's notion of directing individual confidence towards something bigger than yourself, is that these formulations unite the individual with the collective. Both conceptual frameworks recognise that as individuals we are different from one another and so have different strengths and personal motivations. But they then suggest that this individuality is best directed to the pursuit of a collective, rather than an individualistic, end.

The Well-being Compass and real life

These ideas may seem 'pie in the sky' and overly idealistic yet they accord with real life. It is almost impossible nowadays to avoid knowing something of celebrities' lives and to see that amidst all the glamour, riches, fame they acquire they often lack a sense of meaning or connection. Some get caught up in self-destructive hedonism while others try to find meaning in charitable works or good causes.

Mick Jackson, a young Scottish entrepreneur, reports that he knows many successful business people who, once the 'initial elation of success' wears off, say very similar things: 'It's not what I thought it would be. I feel empty; what has my life been about? What was all that work for? I'm bored'.

The desire to find meaning in life is indeed often apparent in people who have made fortunes through business. One of the earliest self-made men turned philanthropist was Andrew Carnegie, who emigrated from Dunfermline as a small boy. Carnegie worked his way up in business and eventually became a multi-billionaire who, during his life, gave away his fortune for human betterment. He once wrote that 'the man who … dies rich dies disgraced'. Carnegie did not believe in giving money simply to relieve suffering but to create opportunities to provide 'ladders upon which the aspiring can rise'. His money funded the creation of 2800 free public libraries in America and the UK. On his insistence, each library bears the inscription 'let there be light'.

Contemporary Scotland too has a clutch of prominent wealthy entrepreneurs who believe in investing much of the money they have amassed as a result of business in ventures which may benefit the public. For example, Sir Tom Hunter is keen to encourage more entrepreneurial spirit, philanthropy and financial support for the third world and uses his Hunter Foundation for this purpose. Sir Tom Farmer is another Scottish entrepreneur with strong philanthropic values.

Mick Jackson's own solution to the problem of 'empty success' is to invest the money he makes commercially in a stationery business called Wildhearts in Action. All the profits from this stationery company (and Jackson picks up staff costs) are given to feeding children in the third world. As you can see in the profile of Jackson and his views on success, they endorse our model of confidence and our notion of a well-being compass

Scottish values

These ideas are also very in tune with Scottish values. The Scots have always had a very strong notion of society and social progress – this is why the origins of social science as we know them can be traced back to the Scottish Enlightenment. The belief that we are all 'Jock Tamson's bairns' still appears to be strong in modern Scotland, as is the desire to strengthen these ties. The great Scottish Enlightenment thinker, Adam Smith, the founder of modern economics, is often portrayed as a stalwart defender of the free market. But Smith considered himself a moral philosopher. There is little doubt he was a thinker who believed in strong social ties, facilitated by human beings' capacity for sympathy. Smith writes:

> *How selfish soever man may be supposed, there are evidently some principles in his nature, which interest him in the fortune of others, and render their happiness necessary to him, though he derives nothing from it except the pleasure of seeing it.*

So, given our Enlightenment past, it seems appropriate that in Scotland we should adopt a model of confidence which stresses human strengths, action and agency and directs such confident action towards social improvement, compassion and meaning in life.

BOX 18: Local Hero

Michael Anthony Jackson is a Scottish entrepreneur who set up a successful company selling outdoor and sports products on line. This business in part reflects his own passion for the outdoor life as he is a mountaineer and sky-diver. In 2001 he went on an expedition to climb K2. On the ascent one of the Sherpas suffered a collapsed lung and only had three days to live. The hospital would not send a helicopter because the man was too poor so Mick Jackson decided to take the Sherpa to the hospital himself. This meant carrying the man on his back for over four days. Given the weather and the mountainous terrain, this journey was likely to kill not just the Sherpa but Jackson as well. Despite the odds both of them lived.

Jackson has now written a book called *Life Lessons from History's Heroes* in which he records some details of this incident and then reflects on his own philosophy of life. Even before this incident, Jackson records that he felt humbled by his experience of living alongside people who had little food and who were routinely dying because of the lack of medicine. He writes in his diary: 'Spoke to my dad on the satellite phone; wanted to tell him that I am so ashamed of the man I had been: of all the days that I squandered in apathy, complacency, the vanities, the egotism'.

In the course of the book Jackson reflects on achievement, success and what gives life meaning:

... When we read that someone whose achievements we really admire struggled with a drink problem, had their heart broken or suffered from depression, we realise that we can succeed despite our failings and setbacks. It teaches us compassion and helps us to forgive ourselves, to be philosophical and not take it personally when life kicks us in the teeth. Anyone can be confident and serene when things are going well; greatness and heroism are displayed in adversity.

We are all part of the fabric of each other's lives and our beliefs and behaviours have a profound affect on those around us. Every time you succeed you give another person hope.

As we begin to succeed in life, it is essential that we endeavour to increase our compassion, humility and wisdom and not just our bank balance.

I don't think it is necessary for us all to go and work in the Third World in order to find meaning. It's much more practical for most of us to find a way of seeing how much of what we do on a day-to-day basis contributes to what we value in a deeper sense.

Key Points

1. The Centre has devised a model of confidence. It comprises two core elements (self-efficacy and optimism) and two sustaining/fostering elements (support from others and learning with/from others).
2. The word confidence on its own is not very meaningful. It begs the question 'confidence for what?' Confidence is about the confidence to do something.
3. Confidence is value free. It could mean being confident to undertake an evil or anti-social act.
4. Confidence as defined by the Centre could be used as encouragement to achieve and gain success in life in ways that are part of the materialist ethos of the contemporary world.

5. Research shows that such materialism, by undermining meaning, can detract from people's well-being. This means that the two aspects of the Centre's agenda – confidence and well-being – may be in conflict with one another.
6. To solve this problem the Centre wants to situate its model of confidence within a compass of well-being. This helps to direct confidence in ways that will enhance, not undermine, an individual's well-being.
7. There are two possible routes to take to link confidence with well-being. One is for a person to direct his/her confidence founded on skills and strengths towards the common good. The other is to direct this confidence to making a difference in the lives of individuals. Both routes help individuals acquire meaning and so both lead to happiness, life-satisfaction, well-being and flourishing.
8. This emphasis on meaning may seem 'pie in the sky' but there are many examples of people who are successful but who feel this success is empty unless they can serve a goal bigger than themselves.
9. These ideas are very much in harmony with traditional Scottish values.

17 Confidence in Scotland's Schools

> *One of the prime purposes of education is to make our young people aware of the values on which Scottish society is based and so help them to establish their own stances on matters of social justice and personal and collective responsibility. Young people therefore need to learn about and develop these values. The curriculum is an important means through which this personal development should be encouraged.*
>
> Curriculum Review Group

The *Curriculum for Excellence* sets out the four values or purposes of education as aspiring to create: successful learners, effective contributors, responsible citizens and confident individuals. At the Centre for Confidence and Well-being, we believe that our definition and model of confidence, within the context of our compass of well-being, very much accords with the ethos and four purposes outlined in the *CfE*.

i. Successful learners

An earlier section of this *Handbook*, 'Learning From America's Mistakes', warns of the dangers of following in its footsteps by emphasising the importance of self-esteem, as this can too easily lead to grade inflation and the weakening of academic standards. By contrast, our definition of confidence as the fusion of self-efficacy ('I can') plus optimism is designed to lead to a much more successful learner than the 'I feel' approach. Throughout this *Handbook* I have sought to reinforce the importance of a challenging, engaging yet supportive environment for learning, as well as basic communication, literacy and numeracy skills. In emphasising the importance of Assessment for Learning, 'the growth mindset' and optimistic attributions, I believe that learning would increase rather than be diminished by the confidence-building techniques advanced in this *Handbook*.

ii. Effective contributors

Here too the Centre's model of confidence, which is more about action and doing rather than feeling, is critically important to the notion of contribution. Encouraging people to take action and contribute requires them, as the *CfE* acknowledges, to be resilient and enterprising. Again, resilience and acquiring a 'can do' attitude go hand in hand with the view of confidence advanced here.

iii. Responsible citizens

Yet again the Centre's model of confidence, set within its well-being compass, encourages individuals to direct their confidence, derived from their strengths and skills, towards a goal larger than themselves. This is another way to think about responsibility to one another and to society at large.

iv. Confident individuals

The *CfE's* own outline of this capacity is completely in tune with what we have promoted here – individuals who are active, skilled, self-reliant and empowered. We have suggested ways in which this can be achieved so that relationships with others are enhanced, rather than compromised. We also believe that we have put forward a view of confidence which ultimately promotes rather than undermines emotional well-being.

The Centre is particularly attracted to the *CfE's* four purposes for education as this formulation is designed to produce a robust, empowered individuality (not individualism) where the skilled individual co-operates with others in pursuit of common goals. This is also reflected in our own definition and model.

The individual teacher

> *... few people, in any walk of life, make dramatic changes to the way in which they operate – very rarely are practices suddenly transformed. Teaching is no different. If teachers are going to make changes, they are more likely to make small changes – tweaks – to their current practice.*
>
> Mike Hughes

My work in education over fifteen years taught me that there is a tendency for many groups in schools – students, teachers, head teachers – to suggest that they are powerless to act differently and so they argue that change can happen only at a higher level. I disagree with this view. People generally have more power to do things differently than they think. In writing this book I have chosen topics where the individual teacher has scope to make changes within the confines of the current system. For example, with some study and perseverance the individual teacher can change from a fixed to a growth mindset; use more optimistic language; and speak to or interact with students in a way that may enhance, rather than undermine, their resilience. Given that there are many other influences on young people's lives, this might not be enough to make a radical transformation, but it could make a difference to some of them. This would be a worthwhile achievement.

BOX 19: The starfish story

An old man is walking along a beach after a storm when he sees a little boy in the distance. As he approaches him he sees that the storm has washed hundreds of starfish on to the sand. The little boy is running up and down, picking up starfish one at a time, and throwing them back into the sea. The old man cynically smiles to himself at the futility of the child's actions, and as he approaches he says 'Heh, why don't you go and enjoy yourself? You can't save them all, so what difference will it make throwing one or two back?' The little boy picks up another starfish, and as he sends it flying back to its home, he looks at the old man and says 'Well, it made a big difference to that one'.

Taken from Michael Anthony Jackson's *Life Lessons from History's Heroes*

We're already doing it

I have little doubt that many teachers who read this *Handbook* may conclude that they are doing much of it anyway. I would be surprised if this was not the case. Few children leave school shivering wrecks. Most leave with a good modicum of confidence. But no doubt, for some at least, there is scope for improvement. Helping teachers and other practitioners to reflect on their current practice, and why it may be working, is a useful exercise. More importantly this *Handbook* should encourage teachers and others in Scotland to be more questioning of some of the current fads in education around self-esteem and emotional literacy that may unwittingly undermine, rather than build, young people's confidence.

Another reason why it would be helpful for teachers and others to think that what I am saying is not a million miles from their current practice is that most people do not embrace radical change – it is too challenging and uncomfortable and so virtually not feasible at a practical level. What is useful is for readers to see the possibility of a refinement, or improvement, on their current practice. This might mean, for example, no longer praising students for talent, and concentrating instead on praising for genuine effort and good strategies.

If the *Handbook* makes teachers more confident about practice which is in line with what I am outlining then this also would be worthwhile. Many commentators note that teachers as a profession often appear underconfident. So if this *Handbook* helps them to model confidence to their students, this too would be a useful step.

Confident schools

Various education reviews have shown that CPD in education is much more effective when it takes place at a whole school level. Other research shows that the ethos of a school has a bearing on the quality of learning. I have little doubt about this and I am aware that students' confidence is more likely to increase if the type of approach outlined here is not just used by one or two of the teachers whom they meet in the course of their education, but is normalised within the life of the schools they attend.

One of the most interesting books to appear indicating that confidence is important to the achievement of collective entities such as teams and organisations, has been written by an American professor of business at Harvard University, Professor Elizabeth Moss Kanter. Her work is based on empirical research with a variety of teams and her conclusions echo some of the work of Positive Psychologists such as Professor Barbara Fredrickson. Readers interested in knowing more about Kanter's ideas can find a summary on the Centre's website.

It is worth pointing out here that confidence can be encouraged at a whole school level if the school's ethos, leadership and working practices support:

- optimistic explanations of progress and views of the future
- priming young people with a growth rather than a fixed mindset
- opportunities for the involvement of students in the running of the school
- opportunities for students to be involved in a wide range of activities that provide good vehicles for growth and confidence-building
- staff modelling the type of behaviour which helps to foster confidence and taking responsibility for creating a positive learning environment.

Please note that this does not mean that all staff would be expected to be confident in the same way – for example, confident about speaking in public or at meetings. What it does mean is that all staff would have an understanding of the conditions for creating confidence in young people and would be making a positive contribution to creating these conditions.

System changes

Much can be done by teachers and schools within the confines of the present system to foster confidence. However there are some other helpful changes which are already in the pipeline and which need the continued, and growing, support of policy-makers. For example:

- Making the curriculum more relevant for secondary school students who are not currently motivated by abstract academic learning.
- Providing more opportunities for young people to participate in activities which engage them (eg, different types of sports or martial arts).
- Investment of money for early engagement with babies and infants (and their parents) who are not receiving enough support for the development of their intellectual or social/emotional skills. The problems presented by children who are inadequately supported in the first five years of their lives are currently being addressed by schools that are setting up nurture units, but more should be done to support these children before they come to school.
- More emphasis placed on teacher development and empowerment. We cannot educate young people to be confident if teachers themselves are not confident.

The opportunities and pitfalls of aiming to foster young people's confidence in schools

At various points in this *Handbook* I have argued that confidence matters increasingly in the modern world and that it would be advantageous for schools to foster confidence in young people. I have also given information on how this might be achieved. However, I have also argued that this is a complicated agenda and that the actions of teachers or the decisions of policy makers could easily cause young people's confidence to decline, not rise. The following is a list of the most likely pitfalls for teachers and policy makers involved in this agenda, the potential unintended consequences and what we need to do to prevent these.

Pitfall 1: Defining confidence as a specific set of skills or activities

Recently I have run a number of workshops with teachers on confidence and they have demonstrated that teachers see confidence primarily as social confidence or the ability to communicate well. Such skills are most likely to be demonstrated by certain personality types – most notably extraverts. What is more, some students may not be sufficiently motivated to excel in these types of activities. Many people with a preference for introversion, for example, do not have a particular need to communicate their thoughts and feelings to others. Some of these students may even have more confidence in their ability to communicate in writing than in their ability to speak formally in class. The preference for introversion may appear to go against the grain of western culture but is considered the norm in many eastern cultures. Defining confidence as social confidence or confident oral communication may, therefore, lead many students to feel they do not measure up to teachers' expectations of how they should be. This judgement is unlikely to foster the student's confidence; in fact, it is more likely to undermine it.

To make sure this does not happen teachers should focus on encouraging self-efficacy or self-belief. This is about students believing that they can reach very particular goals. By all means evaluate students' ability to communicate verbally in English, as this is an important skill, but do not define this type of communication as the essence of confidence.

Pitfall 2: Adopting too direct an approach

The belief that confidence can, and should, be taught directly could easily lead some teachers to run classes in confidence for students. We believe this is too direct an approach and could backfire. In Chapter 15 we came across the research on what are termed 'ironic effects'. This means that when people deliberately try to do something, such as relax or fall asleep, the brain sets up a monitoring process to see if the goal is being reached. For example, if we are deliberately trying to relax we become conscious of any tension we feel and this can then lead us to feel more tense, thus making relaxation less likely. Exactly the same process could happen with confidence. The more that teachers, or the education system as a whole, tell young people that they must feel confident and the more they try consciously to do this the more likely it is that some young people will become aware of their lack of confidence. Telling young people that being confident is a prerequisite for achieving things in life could then lead these young people to see their lack of confidence as a barrier to their development, which it need not be.

What teachers need to do is to create the conditions for young people's confidence to rise. This is about young people learning skills, seeing teachers modelling confident behaviour, having supportive relationships with school staff and being exposed in a school environment to beliefs that encourage optimistic attributions and a growth mindset. There is certainly scope for teaching specific skills which may help young people develop confidence, such as optimism, coping skills or assertiveness. There are also useful activities to be undertaken in priming young people for a growth mindset. But any such lessons have to be set up in ways which do not lead young people to feel forced into this type of behaviour or judged as inadequate if they do not want to use these skills. Our preference is for teachers to understand these skills for themselves, to model them for students and to teach them directly in response to specific situations or where there is a demonstrated need.

Pitfall 3: Evaluating young people on confidence

Nowadays it is commonplace for governments to set up systems to evaluate performance and to set targets for improvements. The justification for this is that it is the best way to ensure value for money and enhanced performance. In education this approach has come to mean an obsession with examination performance and a sense that the system is designed, not to educate children for life, but to teach them to pass exams. There is increasing concern that the fixation with test results is putting undue strain on young people and undermining their well-being.

At present these tests are mainly confined to traditional academic skills. However, as we saw in Chapter 15, in England the SEAL curriculum proposes evaluating young people against a set of social and emotional competences. Critics of emotional intelligence warn that EI, and presumably off-shoots such as SEAL, will simply repeat the same mistakes as were made about IQ, in that young people will be evaluated on various types of skills/abilities and then labelled. Just as has happened with IQ there will be an elite who are considered gifted or talented in demonstrating these skills, and a further group who will be judged as inadequate in some way. Even if this evaluation is done in a formative way, it is impossible to see how some children will escape feeling that they have been labelled as inadequate when judged against a set of pre-determined competences.

Social and emotional skills are not being put at the heart of the new *Curriculum for Excellence* but confidence is, and it is not difficult to see how a similar exercise could be carried out in Scottish schools with regard to evaluating children on a range of confidence measures. In the Centre's opinion this would be a huge mistake and could easily undermine many young people's confidence as they will be labelled and judged in ways that would not be helpful. Of course, policy makers may need to have some measures in place to see if confidence is generally rising across education or in specific schools. The need for such information would lead to various instruments being used to get base-line measures and then used intermittently to chart progress. However, this is entirely different from profiling and assessing individual students against a range of competences or pre-determined ideals of appropriate levels of confidence.

Even with a system that is only collecting data on a global basis, we shall have to take care that it is not being used in a judgemental, heavy-handed way in schools.

Pitfall 4: Generation Me

As we saw in Part 1 of this *Handbook* in the US there has been an increase in narcissism in young people. This may well be the result of rising individualism and messages of consumer culture, but no doubt attempts to build young people's self-esteem have contributed as well. Critics like Professor Frank Furedi in the UK also argue that the emphasis on feelings and emotions is creating the notion of a 'fragile self' and encouraging a rise in mental health problems. The distinguished psychologist, Professor Martin Seligman agrees that too much of a focus on the self can encourage young people to feel depressed. This means that in making confidence one of the main purposes of education we must be careful that it does not lead to excessive individualism and an obsession with feelings and emotions. The Centre's model of confidence, within a compass of well-being, attempts to get round this problem by emphasising the importance of agency and taking action, and encourages this activity towards making a difference in the world.

TTT 24: Be careful about talking to young people about confidence issues

Since the adoption of the *Curriculum for Excellence* enthusiastic teachers and head teachers are repeatedly telling young people about the importance of confidence. They are doing this by talking about it to young people in assemblies and classes or by pinning up posters listing the four capacities. We believe this is a mistake and could encourage young people to feel unduly anxious about whether they lack confidence. This could then backfire giving young people more of a problem with confidence than they might have had. Instead we think it is the job of teachers and schools to create the conditions for confidence to rise. Of course, it may be relevant from time to time to talk about confidence issues. but we think this should happen naturally rather than be part of a planned approach. The specific ways in which this can be done have been covered throughout this *Handbook*.

Wisdom

The opening quote in this chapter from the *Curriculum Review* stresses the importance of young people in Scotland developing themselves in ways which are consistent with strong Scottish values. Everything which I have advanced in this *Handbook* is consistent with these, as the Centre's Model of Confidence is encouraging an emphasis on engagement, hard work, mastery, social connections and meaning and purpose. All of this goes with the grain of Scottish culture. Since these values have dimmed in recent years with the advent of individualism and the mass media we can reconnect with them without the danger of exaggerating their importance.

The mace which lies in the Scottish Parliament building has four words inscribed on it: compassion, integrity, justice and wisdom. If we are to be successful in creating more confidence for students and teachers involved in Scottish education what we need above all else is more wisdom.

Wisdom is difficult to write about as it is involves balancing different perspectives. For example, it is about being simultaneously logical and emotional and giving due weight to what is and what might be. The wise know that more can often be learned from failure in life than from easy success. Wisdom also helps us to understand that there are few hard and fast rules in life – that what might be suitable and appropriate in one context might be useless in another. Wisdom also helps us to see that because something is good, more is not always better, or that sometimes we can achieve goals if we do not pursue them directly. In short, wisdom is about understanding that people's minds and their lives are complex.

If this *Handbook* helps teachers and other professionals to understand the complexity of confidence, if it gives rise to more questions than answers, then this will indeed be a very positive achievement.

Final word

Creating Confidence is the title of this book and its most important message is this: it is counterproductive to lecture young people about confidence or try to force them to be more confident. All we can do is create the conditions for confidence to rise.

Key Points

1. The Centre's model of confidence, within its well-being compass, is consistent with the four values, or purposes, of education set out in the *Curriculum for Excellence*.
2. Most of the suggestions in this *Handbook* can be carried out by the individual teacher in the classroom without any changes to the current system.
3. Much of the *Handbook* is already in tune with current practices in Scottish education. This is an asset rather than a liability because most people do not embrace radical change. If teachers make small changes to their practice this may have beneficial effects on some of their students.
4. Undoubtedly it is better if schools, rather than single teachers, embrace some of the practices outlined here as this will help to reinforce some important messages.
5. There are some system changes which could also help to create the conditions for confidence. For example, making the curriculum more relevant for certain groups or investing more in early engagement.
6. In pursuing a confidence agenda in schools those working with young people may make certain, yet avoidable, mistakes. In my view the most likely candidates are: defining confidence as a specific set of skills or activities – most notably public speaking or social skills; too much direct teaching about confidence; measuring confidence in ways which may lead young people to feel judged; and encouraging too much fixation with the self and feelings.
7. To help us avoid these problems we should cultivate wisdom – one of the four core values enshrined in the Scottish Parliament. Wisdom will help us to see the complexity of the issue and that there are no hard and fast rules.

Information on supporting resources

Special Handbook section on the Centre's website

The Centre has now created a special section on its website for resources to support this *Handbook*. This can be accessed at:
www. centreforconfidence.co.uk/confidencehandbook .
The following is a list of material that can be accessed there:

1. Notes and references

Extensive notes and references for this book can be accessed on line. The notes are given on a page-by-page basis and list precise references for all the main quotes used in the book.

2. Assertiveness material

This includes a large overview essay on assertiveness – the four behaviours, body language, assertiveness skills, etc.

3. Questionnaires

A number of questionnaires in use by the Centre, along with scoring instructions, can be viewed on line. We also have the facility for these questionnaires to be completed on line by secondary school students and others. Please contact the Centre for further information.

4. Centre's Model of Confidence and Well-being Compass

If you would like to use the Centre's Model, please email;
contact@centreforconfidence.co.uk

Discussion forum on this *Handbook*

We hope that readers who have comments and questions about the material included in this *Handbook* will use the Centre's discussion forum. This can be accessed from the dedicated section of the site (URL given above).

Other useful information

The Centre has a wealth of supporting information already on the website. The material most relevant to this *Handbook* is mainly in Resources for Positive Psychology or in a (forthcoming) section on young people and well-being. These sections can be accessed from the home page – www.centreforconfidence.co.uk. Here is a list of some material that is particularly relevant and useful for readers of this *Handbook*:

Optimism/disputation

Further information on this can be found in the Optimism section of PP Resources on the Centre's website. The material that is most relevant is the overview essay and the information contained in the tools, tips and techniques section. Also click on audio and listen to the second section of sound material from Dr Karen Reivich. You can also listen to Professor Martin Seligman discuss optimism.

Eco/Ego system goals

In the Confidence section of PP Resources you can listen to Professor Jennifer Crocker talk about her work. Click on audio to access.

Generation Me

You can also listen to Dr Jean Twenge talk about her work and view her data. Go to the Confidence section of PP Resources and click on audio.

Self-esteem

You can listen to Professor Nicholas Emler talk about his work on self-esteem by going to the Confidence section of PP Resources and clicking on audio.

Resilience

You can listen to Professor Brigid Daniel talk about vulnerable children by going to the Resilience section of PP Resources and clicking on audio.

Mindsets

From November 2007 onwards you will be able to listen to Professor Carol Dweck talk about her work on a new section in PP Resources. There will also be access to other material relevant to mindsets by that date.

Acknowledgements

I could not have written this book without the help and support of a range of people. I would like to thank Patricia Watt for her contribution to the self-efficacy chapter; Eric Young for his input into the section on formative assessment; and Isobel MacNaughtan for helping me with the section on Co-operative Learning. In the past fifteen years, I have discussed issues related to confidence with countless teachers and head teachers in the various courses I have run. Many of these discussions have also had an impact on the argument I present here and so I would like to express my gratitude to these nameless contributors.

Staff and associates at the Centre also made invaluable contributions to this book. So thanks are due to Hazel Black, Emily Durrant, Barry Fitzpatrick, Angus Skinner and Alan Sinclair. I would like specifically to thank Debbie McIntyre from the Centre for project managing the final stages of editing and production. Without her dedicated effort the book would have taken much longer to produce. Thanks too are due to Pete Fletcher for designing and producing this *Handbook* to such a high standard. Thanks too to Patricia Baxter for copy-editing and to Fred Shedden for help with proof reading.

I would like to express the Centre's indebtedness to a far-sighted Scottish business – Morris and Spottiswood. Without their generous moral and financial support the Centre would have been unable to embark on such a time-consuming project. Thanks are also due to George Morris for writing the foreword.

My final thanks go to the Board of Directors for the Centre for Confidence and Well-being who, like me, are passionately committed to the creation of a confident Scotland.

Many people have supported me in the writing of this book but I alone am responsible for the content and for any errors of fact or judgement.

Permissions

Where possible we sought permission to use other writers' material in this book. Sometimes we were unsuccessful. We would like to thank Professor Carol Dweck for permission to reproduce some material from *Mindset*; Drs Helen McGrath and Toni Noble for permission to use various sections from *Bounce Back* and Professor Brigid Daniel for use of the diagram on resilience.

Further Reading

The following is a list of the main text that has been consulted in the compilation of this Handbook. Information on articles and reports used can be found on line at www.centreforconfidence.co.uk.

Bandura, A., 1997, *Self-efficacy: The Exercise of Control,* Worth Publishers, New York

Branden, N., 1994, *The Six Pillars of Self-esteem,* Bantam, New York

Bryce, T.G.K. & Humes, W.M., 1999, *Scottish Education,* Edinburgh University Press, Edinburgh

Csikszentmihalyi, M., 1990, *Flow: The Psychology of Optimal Experience,* HarperCollins Publishers, New York

Csikszentmihalyi, M. & Csikszentmihalyi, I.S., 2006, *A Life Worth Living: Contributions to Positive Psychology,* Oxford University Press, New York

Daniel, B. & Wassell, S., 2002, *The School Years,* Jessica Kingsley Publishers Ltd, London

Ellis, A.., 2005, *The Myth of Self-esteem,* Prometheus Books, New York

Emler, N., 2001, *Self Esteem: The Costs and Causes of Low Self Worth.* York Publishing Services, York

Evans, D., 2001, *Emotion: The Science of Sentiment,* Oxford University Press, New York

Furedi, F., 2004, *Therapy Culture: Cultivating Vulnerability in an Uncertain Age,* Routledge, London

Gladwell, M., 2005, *Blink,* Allen Lane, London

Goleman, D., 1996, *Emotional Intelligence: Why it can Matter More than IQ,* Bloomsbury Publishing, London

Goleman, D., 2003, *Destructive Emotions: A Dialogue with the Dalai Lama,* Bloomsberry, London

Goleman, D., Boyatzis, R. & McKee, A., 2003, *The New Leaders: Transforming the Art of Leadership into the Science of Results,* Time Warner Paperbacks, London

Haidt, J., 2006, *The Happiness Hypothesis,* William Heinemann, London

Salerno, S., 2005, *SHAM: How the Gurus of the Self-help Movement Make us Helpless,* Nicholas Brealey Publishing, 2005

James, O., 1998, *Britain on the Couch,* Arrow Books, London

LeDoux, J., 1999, *The Emotional Brain,* Phoenix, London

Linley, P.A. & Joseph, S., 2004, *Positive Psychology in Practice,* John Wiley and Sons Inc, New Jersey

Lopez, S.J. & Snyder, C.R., 2003, *Positive Psychological Assessment: A Handbook of Models and Measures,* American Psychological Association, Washington

Mackenzie, R.F., 1991, *A Search for Scotland,* Fontana

Martin, P., 2006, *Making Happy People,* Harper Perennial, London

Matthews, G., Zeidner, M. & Roberts, R.D., 2004, *Emotional Intelligence: Science and Myth,* MIT Press, Cambridge US

McGrath, H. & Noble, T., 2003, *Bounce Back! Teacher's Handbook,* Pearson Education, Australia

McLean, A., 2003, *The Motivated School,* Sage, London

Morris, E. & Casey, J., 2006, *Developing Emotionally Literate Staff: A Practical Guide,* Paul Chapman Publishing, London

Mos Kanter, R., 2004, *Confidence,* Random House, London

Peterson, C. & Seligman, M.E.P., 2004, *Character Strengths and Virtues,* Oxford University Press, New York

Noren, J.K., 2002, *The Positive Power of Negative Thinking,* Basic Books, Cambridge USA

Seligman, M.E.P., Reivich, K., Jaycox, L. & Gillham, J., 1995, *The Optimistic Child,* Harper Perennial, New York

Seligman, M.E.P, 2002, *Authentic Happiness,* Free Press, New York

Stout, M., 2000, *The Feel-Good Curriculum: The Dumbing Down of America's Kids in the Name of Self-Esteem,* Da Capo Press, Cambridge

Weare, K., 2004, *Developing the Emotionally Literate School,* Paul Chapman Publishing, London

Index

A

B

C

D

E

F

G

H

N

O

P

Q

R

S

T

U

V

W